D1594128

THE SEPHARDIC FRONTIER

A VOLUME IN THE SERIES

Conjunctions of Religion and Power in the Medieval Past

Edited by Barbara H. Rosenwein

A list of all the books in the series may be found on the last page of the book.

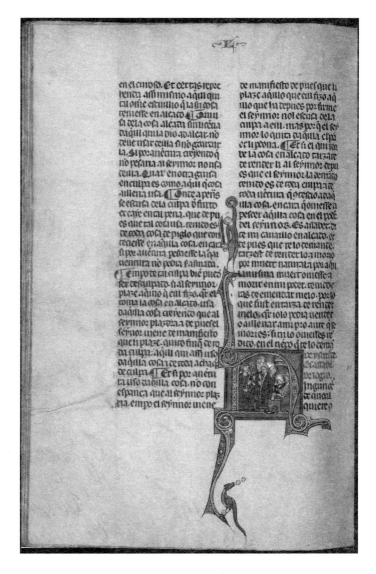

Michael Lupi de Çandiu. *Initial N: Two Men Speaking before a King and Another Man Exchanging a Goblet for a Purse of Money with a Jew. Vidal Mayor.* The J. Paul Getty Museum, Los Angeles. 83.MQ.165 (Ms. Ludwig XV 6), folio 175v. Copyright © The J. Paul Getty Museum. Reproduced with permission.

THE SEPHARDIC FRONTIER

THE *RECONQUISTA*
AND THE JEWISH
COMMUNITY IN
MEDIEVAL IBERIA

JONATHAN RAY

Cornell University Press

Ithaca and London

This book is published with the aid of a grant from the Program for Cultural Cooperation between Spain's Ministry of Education, Culture and Sports and United States Universities.

First published 2006 by Cornell University Press

Printed in the United States of America

Library of Congress Cataloging-in-Publication Data

Ray, Jonathan (Jonathan Stewart)
    The Sephardic frontier : the reconquista and the Jewish community in medieval Iberia / Jonathan Ray.
        p. cm.— (Conjunctions of religion and power in the medieval past)
    Includes bibliographical references and index.
    ISBN-13: 978-0-8014-4401-2 (cloth : alk. paper)
    ISBN-10: 0-8014-4401-2 (cloth : alk. paper)
        1. Jews—Spain—History—To 1500. 2. Jews—Portugal—History—To 1500. 3. Spain—Ethnic relations—History. 4. Portugal—Ethnic relations —History. 5. Spain—History—711-1516. 6. Portugal—History—To 1385. I. Title. II. Series: Conjunctions of religion & power in the medieval past. DS135.S7R38 2006
946'.0004924—dc22

2005025040

Cornell University Press strives to use environmentally responsible suppliers and materials to the fullest extent possible in the publishing of its books. Such materials include vegetable-based, low-VOC inks and acid-free papers that are recycled, totally chlorine-free, or partly composed of nonwood fibers. For further information, visit our website at www.cornellpress.cornell.edu.

Cloth printing   10 9 8 7 6 5 4 3 2 1

CONTENTS

Acknowledgments   vii
List of Abbreviations   ix

Introduction   1

Part I. The Jewish Settler and the Frontier   11

1. The Migration of Jewish Settlers to
    the Frontier   15

2. Jewish Landownership   36

3. Moneylending and Beyond: The Jews in
    the Economic Life of the Frontier   55

Part II. The Jewish Community and the Frontier   73

4. Royal Authority and the Legal Status of
    Iberian Jewry   75

5. Jewish Communal Organization
    and Authority   98

6. Communal Tensions and the Question of
    Jewish Autonomy   131

7. Maintenance of Social Boundaries on
    the Iberian Frontier   145

    Conclusion   176
    Glossary   181
    Bibliography   185
    Index   195

[v]

070549⁴

ACKNOWLEDGMENTS

The completion of this book could not have been achieved without the generous assistance and support of a number of people. It was inspired by my studies at the Graduate School of the Jewish Theological Seminary and Columbia University, and bears the intellectual imprint of my teachers and colleagues. A principal goal of this book, to locate the development of Sephardic history within the broader narrative of medieval Iberia, is a direct result of the disparate yet often complementary approaches of the history departments of these two institutions.

My initial research was made possible by a fellowship program sponsored by the Charles H. Revson Foundation, as well as a grant from the Memorial Foundation for Jewish Culture, both of which supported my collection of archival data. Among the archives I visited, I owe special recognition to Spain's Bibilioteca Nacional and the Archivo Histórico Nacional, Portugal's Arquivo Nacional/Instituto Torre do Tumbo, the Archivo de la Catedral de Sevilla, and the Archivo de la Corona de Aragón/Arxiu de la Corona d'Aragó in Barcelona. The necessary research for this study would not have been possible without the patience, attentiveness, and consideration of their respective staffs. In particular, I thank the ACA's Jaume Riera, archivist and scholar, for sharing his intellectual energy and vast knowledge of both the archive and medieval Catalan Jewry. Throughout the research and writing of this book, I have also relied on the unflagging help and support of the library staffs at the Jewish Theological Seminary, Butler Library of Columbia University and Sterling Memorial Library of Yale University.

I owe a debt of gratitude to David Wachtel of the Rare Book and Manuscript Collection at JTS and my friend and colleague Maud Kozodoy for help in guiding my reading of the Hebrew sources. I also thank Adam Kosto, Seth Schwartz, and Raymond Scheindlin for their willingness to read early drafts of the manuscript and for their insightful and cogent comments. Most important, I owe thanks to my teacher and friend, Benjamin Gampel, who continued to provide invaluable advice and support throughout the process of composition and revision.

A generous grant awarded to me by the Jacob and Hilda Blaustein post-doctoral fellowship, under the auspice of the Program in Judaic Studies at Yale University, enabled me to complete this book. The arguments set forth here were also greatly shaped by the intellectual climate at Yale, in particular, the many provocative conversations I enjoyed with Ivan Marcus, Paul Freedman, Rebecca Kobrin, and Paula Hyman. I am also deeply indebted to Barbara Rosenwein and John Ackerman at Cornell University Press for their detailed and helpful editorial advice and guidance. Finally, I thank my friends and family for their seemingly boundless energy, support, and goodwill. Thank you to all those who have helped along the way; I remain forever grateful.

J. R.

ABBREVIATIONS

ACA	Archivo de la Corona de Aragon
ACC	Archivo de la Catedral de Córdoba
ACJ	Archivo de la Catedral de Jaén
ACS	Archivo de la Catedral de Sevilla
ACM	Archivo de la Catedral de Murcia
AMC	Archivo Municipal de Sevilla
AME	Archivo Municipal de Elche
AMM	Archivo Municipal de Murcia
AHN	Archivo Histórico Nacional, Madrid
AHPC	Archivo Histórico de la Provincia de Córdoba
ANTT	Arquivo Nacional/Instituto Torre del Tombo
ARM	Archivo del Reino de Mallorca
AUC	Archivo de la Universidade de Coimbra
BCC	Biblioteca de la Catedral de Córdoba
BN	Biblioteca Nacional, Madrid
CML	Camara Municipal de Lisboa
Adret	Solomon ben Abraham ibn Adret. *Sheelot u-Teshuvot, (Responsa)*. Vol. 1 (Bologna, 1539); vols. 2 & 3 (Leghorn, 1657, 1778); vol. 4 (Vilna, 1881); vol. 5 (Leghorn, 1825); vols. 6 &

7 (Warsaw, 1868); vol. 8, Adret's responsa attributed to Nahmanides (Warsaw, 1883).

Ordenações Afonsinas	*Ordenações Afonsinas, Livro II.* 2nd ed. Lisbon, 1998 [1792].
PMH, Leges	*Portugaliae Monumento Historica a saeculo octavo post Christum usque ad quantumdecium, Leges et Consuetudines.* 2 vols. Lisbon, 1888.
Siete Partidas	*Las Siete Partidas del rey don Alfonso el Sabio,* 3 vols. Madrid, 1807.

THE SEPHARDIC FRONTIER

The Iberian Peninsula, 1212

The Iberian Peninsula, 1264–1492

INTRODUCTION

N
o subject looms larger over the historiographic landscape of medieval Spain than that of the reconquest.
During much of the nineteenth and twentieth centuries, in which the academic and popular narratives
of Spanish history were constructed, the contest between Islam and Christianity for mastery of the Iberian Peninsula served as a unifying symbol of
national identity. If, as many of these early scholars argued, the Spanish nation was born in the Visigothic era, its soul was forged through the epic
struggle to reclaim *Hispania* for Christianity.[1] Even those Hispanists who, in
following Américo Castro, championed a more inclusive view of medieval
Spain as the land of the three religions, did recognize the formative nature
of the reconquest. Though shorn of most its more xenophobic and tri-
umphalist sentiments, the current discourse on the reconquest continues to
acknowledge its centrality to the study of medieval Spanish and, to a lesser
extent, Portuguese civilization.[2]

Though the struggle for peninsular domination lasted from the Muslim

---

[1] The historiography on Spanish nationalism is discussed by Peter Linehan, "Religion, Nationalism and National Identity in Medieval Spain and Portugal," *Studies in
Church History* 18 (1982): 161–199; idem, *History and Historians of Medieval Spain* (Oxford,
1993); and Manuel González Jiménez, "¿Re-conquista? Un estado de la cuestión," in *Tópicos y realidades de la Edad Media*, ed. Eloy Benito Ruano (Madrid 2000), 1:155–178.

[2] See Castro's *The Spaniards: An Introduction to Their History*, trans. Willard F. King
and Selma Margaretten (Berkeley, 1971), 449–456. Derek Lomax and Peter Linehan both
place the genesis of the formative concept reconquest in the century following the Muslim conquest of the peninsula in 711. Lomax, *The Reconquest of Spain* (London, 1978), 1–2;
and Linehan, *History and Historians*, chap. 4.

invasions of the early eighth century to the fall of Granada in 1492, a permanent shift in the balance of power took place during the century following the combined Christian victory over the Almohads at Las Navas de Tolosa in 1212. Unlike earlier Christian advances such as the symbolically significant capture of Toledo in 1085, it was not only the vast amount of territory gained in the thirteenth century, but also the subsequent colonization, or *repoblación*, of these lands that signaled the ascendancy of the Christian kingdoms of the north.[3] The thirteenth century marks an important turning point in the development of the most essential values and attitudes of medieval Spanish society. Indeed, throughout the peninsula, the world of the thirteenth century was a world transformed, as the remarkable advances of the Christian *reconquista* and the following demands of the *repoblación* wrought sweeping changes in the organization and disposition of Iberian civilization.[4]

In light of this continued scholarly interest in the Christian conquest and colonization of Muslim territory and its social ramifications, it is therefore striking that there has yet to be a study of how these processes affected the third great religious group of medieval Iberia, the Jews. This omission reflects the prevailing opinion among medievalists that the Jews of Spain and Portugal played only a minor role in Christian territorial expansion. Even the most recent studies of the *reconquista* continue to view Jews in the most conventional medieval trope, as financiers who might have helped to contribute to the necessary funds to support the military campaigns. As a result, the most important social histories of the *reconquista* have failed to address its impact on the peninsula's Jewish communities, while studies of Jewish life during this period tend to focus on intellectual and cultural trends and fail to relate the Jewish experience to the dominant socio-political developments of the age.[5]

In this study, I fill this gap by exploring the early development of Jewish

[3] For the *reconquista*'s shift from border raids to broader wars fueled by a mix of avarice and ideology, see Ann Christys, "Crossing the Frontier in 9th c. Hispania," in *Medieval Frontiers: Concepts and Practices*, ed. David Abulafia and Nora Berend (Cambridge, 2002); Eduardo Manzano Moreno, "Christian-Muslim Frontier in al-Andalus: Idea and Reality," in *The Arab Influence in Medieval Europe*, ed. Dionisius A. Agius and Richard Hitchcock (Reading, 1994), 83–99; and Joseph O'Callaghan, *Reconquest and Crusade in Medieval Spain* (Philadelphia, 2002), 1–22, 25.

[4] For recent discussions of these developments, see Teofilo Ruiz, *From Heaven to Earth: The Reordering of Castilian Society, 1150–1350* (Princeton, 2004), and Marta Vanlandingham, *Transforming the State: King Court and Political Culture in the Realms of Aragon (1213–1387)* (Leiden, 2002).

[5] See O'Callaghan, *Reconquest and Crusade*, 155, 171, 173, and Reyna Pastor de Togneri, *Del Islam al Cristianismo: en las fronteras de dos formaciones económicos-sociales: Toledo, siglos XXIII* (Barcelona, 1975). For shifts in Jewish intellectual culture, see Bernard Septimus,

The Sephardic Frontier

settlements and communities in the various peninsular kingdoms during the transition from Muslim to Christian rule—its central period being the eleventh through the thirteenth centuries. The model I have chosen for this enterprise is that of the "frontier": that borderland between Christian and Muslim controlled territory stretching from southern Portugal in the west, across the territories of Andalusia, Murcia, and Valencia, to the Balearic islands in the east. The concept of the frontier and frontier societies as a theoretical model for understanding the nature and diversity of European civilization has proved to be one of enduring interest to medievalists, particularly those studying the Iberian Peninsula.[6] However, such studies have tended to concentrate on the model itself, analyzing the cultural interaction and exchange which make the society of the frontier distinct without examining the impact of these border regions on the development of their constituent social and ethnic groups. As a result, there has yet to be a study of Jewish life in the newly Christianized territories of the thirteenth century that ventures beyond the discussion of Christian attitudes or the Jews' function within this society. An exposition of the development of Jewish society in southern Iberia, this book argues that the contours of the Jewish community were principally defined by external forces. The regnant social, political, and economic factors of the frontier during the second half of the thirteenth century helped to create Jewish communities that were characterized by a high degree of fluidity and relatively little internal organization and stability. The absence of long-standing public institutions and political structures in this region, which might have promoted Jewish communal autonomy and authority, aided both the crown and individual Jewish settlers in pursuing their own agendas.

The Jewish settlements that were established throughout the newly Christianized territories of southern Iberia also shared many of the features found in the older centers of Toledo, Saragossa, and Barcelona. What distinguishes the former is our ability to follow their development from conquest through colonization. The unprecedented scale of the thirteenth-century conquests and the equally dramatic process of resettlement and reorganization of these territories under Christian rule provide a unique

---

Hispano-Jewish Culture in Transition: The Career and Controversies of the Ramah (Cambridge, 1982).

    6 For the concept of the frontier in Iberian historiography, see Peter Linehan, "At the Spanish Frontier," in *The Medieval World*, ed. idem and Janet Nelson (London, 2001), 37–59; Manzano Moreno, "Christian-Muslim Frontier"; Robert I. Burns, "The Significance of the Frontier in the Middle Ages," in *Medieval Frontier Societies*, ed. Robert Bartlett and Angus Mackay (Oxford, 1989), 307–330; and Nora Berend, *At the Gates of Christendom: Jews, Muslims and 'Pagans' in Medieval Hungary, c. 1000–c. 1300* (Cambridge, 2001).

setting in which to examine the central features of Sephardic civilization. In studying the reestablishment of a Jewish presence along this frontier, we are able to witness the birth and early development of an entire Jewish society, the size, scope, and rapid growth of which is unparalleled in the history of medieval Jewry.

SOURCES AND METHODOLOGICAL CONSIDERATIONS

The absence of Jewish social and political history from studies of Christian expansion into southern Iberia can be attributed, to some degree, to a lamentable dearth in sources. There is very little extant information regarding the social and political history of the Jews (and non-Jews) in Muslim Iberia during the final decades of the Almohad dynasty beyond a general sense of overt persecution and subsequent emigration. The resulting difficulty in tracing the journey of Jews from Muslim territories to the Christian kingdoms of the north has led most historians to limit their work to the fourteenth and fifteenth centuries, a period for which documentation is far more plentiful.[7] Those works that have focused on Hispano-Jewish history from the late twelfth through the early fourteenth centuries have also been shaped by the relative availability of sources and reflect a strong regional bias favoring the Jewish communities of the medieval Crown of Aragon.[8]

With respect to Jewish sources, we possess regrettably few collections of rabbinic responsa from the first half of the thirteenth century, and none at all from the kingdom of Portugal.[9] The extant compilations of the two

[7] A notable exception is the work of Robert I. Burns on the thirteenth-century kingdom of Valencia. Among his many studies on this subject, see *Medieval Colonialism: Post-crusade Exploitation of Islamic Valencia* (Princeton, 1975), and *Muslims, Christians, and Jews in the Crusader Kingdom of Valencia* (Cambridge, 1984).

[8] The royal charters, privileges, and other letters which refer to the Jews of this period preserved in Barcelona's Archivo de la Corona de Aragón (Arxiu de la Corona d'Aragó) greatly surpass those of any other royal, municipal, or ecclesiastical collection in the peninsula. Archival information for thirteenth-century Castile is considerably more scarce, due in large part to the migratory character of the medieval Castilian court. In Portugal, the relative paucity of material on the Jews of the twelfth and thirteenth centuries appears to reflect the size of the community at this time. However, the various royal and monastic collections housed at the Arquivo Nacional/Instituto Torre do Tumbo in Lisbon remain a largely untapped source for the study of Jewish history during this period.

[9] The collections of the eleventh-century Andalusian scholar Isaac Alfasi and his student Joseph ibn Migash (d. 1141) predate the great *reconquista* of the thirteenth century,

greatest rabbinic authorities of this period, Meir ha-Levi Abulafia (1180–1244) of Toledo, and the great Catalan scholar Moses ben Nahman (1194–1270), are relatively sparse, and it is not until the second half of the thirteenth century and the beginning of the fourteenth that we begin to possess a more extensive body of literature on which to draw.[10] Beyond the scarcity of material for certain periods, the use of the responsa literature as a historical source also presents the researcher with several methodological obstacles.[11] Rabbinic responsa were preserved for their discussions of legal issues and, in the inevitable truncation of the original queries and responses which took place as these letters were copied and recopied, valuable historical details were often lost. In addition to the names of the parties involved, common omissions also include references to the communities from which these questions were sent. The frequent absence of geographical designations in these collections thus greatly inhibits the value of the responsa literature as a source for studies focused on a specific region or community.[12]

Historical analysis of Iberian Jewry prior to the fourteenth century has also been hampered by the disparate historiographic attitudes that often separate historians of medieval Spain from those studying medieval Jewry. The approach favored by the majority of Spanish medievalists has been to limit the scope of their investigation to a particular city or region and then write about the Jewish communities therein. The result has been a series of microcosmic portraits of individual Jewries (the Jews of Seville, Mallorca, etc.), with no clear treatment of the commonalities and differences between

---

though I have made use of them whenever applicable. On the leading rabbinic respondents of medieval Iberia, see Avraham Grossman, "Legislation and Responsa Literature," in *The Sephardi Legacy*, ed. Haim Beinart (Jerusalem, 1992), 1:188–219.

[10] These include the collection of Solomon ibn Adret (1235–1310), by far the most prolific respondent of the Middle Ages, his student Yom Tov ben Abraham Ishbili (c. 1250–c. 1330); Asher ben Yehiel (d. 1327), who was active in Castile after immigrating there from Germany in 1304, and his son Judah ben Asher. See Meir ha-Levi Abulafia, *Responsa, Or Tzaddikim* (Warsaw, 1902); Moses ben Nahman, *Kitvei Rabenu Moses ben Nahman*, 2 vols., ed. Charles Chavel (Jerusalem, 1964). For these and other responsa collections, I have also used the various editions compiled by the Bar Ilan Responsa Project, CD ROM version 8.0, (Ramat Gan, 2000).

[11] See Bernard D. Weinryb, "Responsa as a Source for History (Methodological Problems)," in *Essays Presented to Chief Rabbi Israel Brodie on the Occasion of His Seventieth Birthday*, ed. H. J. Zimmels et al. (London, 1967), 399–417; Haim Soloveitchik, *The Use of Responsa as a Historical Source* [Hebrew] (Jerusalem, 1990); and Abraham I. Laredo, "Las 'Sheelot u-Teshubot' como fuente para la historia de los judíos españoles," *Sefarad* 5 (1945): 441–456.

[12] Luminaries such as Solomon ibn Adret and Asher ben Yehiel received missives from all over Europe and the Mediterranean world, undermining the possibility that the issues dealt with in these discussions represent an exclusively Iberian, or Sephardic, environment.

such communities. Furthermore, since the principal concern of these works is the broader history of medieval Spain, their treatment of Jews is all too often reduced to noting contributions made by Jews to their host culture. In many ways, Jewish historians of this period have often suffered from the opposite problem. They have tended to view their subject as "Sepharad," which is to say, the history and culture of those Jews living anywhere in the medieval Iberian milieu with very little attention to temporal or geographic context. Such studies imagine a Jewish world that possesses a natural and inherent unity centered on the Jewish individual's dedication to his religious community. Though this approach provides a greater focus on the internal structures of the Jewish community, it generally fails to address the debt owed by these structures to the broader social, political, and economic forces of non-Jewish society.[13] Another hurdle that confronts the historian of Iberian Jewry is the task of seeing their history on its own terms, rather than as measurement of Christian-Jewish relations. Much as the Holocaust invades all studies of modern European Jewry, so too do the twin subjects of Inquisition and expulsion cast a long shadow over the study of Jewish history in the peninsula in the high and late Middle Ages. It is thus necessary to make a concerted effort not to read their history as a prelude to expulsion, sorting events of the thirteenth and fourteenth centuries into categories of "Golden Age" and "Evidence of Decline."[14]

AN IBERIAN SOCIETY

In attempting to bridge this historiographic divide and to address some of these methodological concerns, I have endeavored to create an image of Jewish Iberia that transcends both standard royal tenures and national boundaries. The thirteenth-century Iberian frontier that I have delineated as the model for this investigation is my own construct. Like all such paradigms, whether they be spatial or temporal, it was developed in the hope that it might serve as a vehicle by which we can gain greater insight into the subject under investigation, in this case, the social, economic, and political experience of Iberian Jewry under Christian rule. In drawing upon medieval rabbinic sources, as well as a host of unpublished material from royal, eccle-

[13] Medieval Jewish historians have tended to be more sensitive to the cultural and intellectual influences which Muslim and Christian society have had on Iberian Jewry.
[14] The pioneering work of Yitzhak Baer remains the most influential source of this view. See his magnum opus, *A History of the Jews in Christian Spain*, 2 vols. (Philadelphia, 1961).

siastical, and municipal archives throughout Spain and Portugal, I am able to create an image of medieval Iberian society that highlights the common experience of settlers along this broad frontier, a viewpoint lost in most regional and national histories of medieval Spain or Portugal.

Rather than consider Jews solely in their communal context, as representatives of a particular ethno-religious minority, I present them as individuals whose relationship to the Jewish polity was but one of many aspects of their identity. Such an approach reveals that Jews consciously and frequently pursued lives that blurred the lines of religious and communal affiliation long before the age of the *Conversos*. The attractiveness and accessibility of many facets of Hispano-Christian society ensured that the Jews who came to settle the frontier were as much members of the broader Iberian milieu as they were of the Sephardic community. In many ways, the area I have identified as the thirteenth-century frontier can also be seen as a case study of Spanish or Portuguese society in the high Middle Ages. Thus, just as the study of the periphery can help deepen our understanding of the center, it is my hope that my analysis of the Jewish experience on the frontier will help to illuminate both the general history of medieval Hispano-Jewry and the broader developments of Iberian society during this period of demographic expansion, political reorganization, and social change.

The following study is divided into two parts. The first traces the reconstitution and early development of Jewish settlements in southern Iberia as the region passed from Muslim to Christian rule. Information regarding Jewish life in this initial period of transition is scarce, but becomes steadily richer throughout the century. Beginning with the earliest royal documents drawn up in the wake of conquest there is evidence of the reestablishment of a significant Jewish presence in the newly Christianized territories. Part 1 will focus on the process of Jewish immigration and settlement and will examine Jewish landownership and the nature and diversity of economic opportunities that drew Jews to the frontier. Close analysis of the context in which these new settlements developed also demonstrates that the Jews of these regions were an integral part of the landscape of the frontier from the very beginning of Christian rule.

Over the course of the late thirteenth and early fourteenth centuries, the early settlements established by these immigrants matured into more organized and elaborate communities, and the second half of this study will explore the social and political dynamics of Jewish society on the frontier. For Jewish settlers and their descendants, life in these new territories was greatly shaped by forces external to the Jewish community and chapters 4 through 7 will examine the impact which royal, ecclesiastical, and municipal authorities had on the development of their legal status, the organization and autonomy of their communities, and their relationships with their non-Jewish neighbors. The tenor of these chapters is more synchronic than those of part 1. Their depiction of the medieval Sephardic community and its intricate relationship to royal power both illuminate the experience of Jewish settlers on the frontier and transcend it. The challenges to Jewish communal autonomy and cohesion, though in many ways more pronounced in the new territories, were also typical of contemporary Jewish centers of the interior. In this respect the present work stands as a new model of the medieval Jewish community that underscores the complex and often contradictory nature of Jewish authority and solidarity.[15] It contests the widespread assumption that the community, with all its attendant institutions, was a permanent and inevitable feature of the medieval Jewish world. My emphasis on Jewish individuals and factions, rather than on the general outlook of Jewish or Christian society, is thus meant to reveal the complex texture of Sephardic identity and the volatile nature of their communities. Finally, part 2 will continue to trace the forces that led to the gradual constriction of Jewish society in southern Iberia and the degree to which the independent spirit of the Jewish settler was able to endure in spite of the eventual "closing" of this Hispano-Jewish frontier.[16]

In addition to revising the standard monolithic portrayal of medieval Jewish social and political structures, a primary objective of this study is to situate the narrative of Sephardic Jewry securely within the broader context of the history of medieval Iberia. The thirteenth century was more than just the period of greatest conquest and shift in peninsular domination. It was a critical stage in the social and institutional development of medieval Spain and Portugal, and a true appreciation of Jewish life in these realms can only be obtained in light of these historical processes. Despite a unique relationship with the crown as "servants of the royal chamber," a status that placed Jews outside the normal social framework of medieval society with its intricate web of feudal and local ties, the experience of Jewish settlers in southern Iberia closely resembled that of their Christian counterparts. We see that they owned rural land and even acted as landlords in the Christian fash-

---

[15] As such, this study forms part of a current re-evaluation of the basic narrative of Sephardic history. See the recent work of Mark Meyerson, *Jews in an Iberian Frontier Kingdom Society Economy and Politics in Morvedre. 1248–1391* (Leiden, 2004), and *Jewish Renaissance in Fifteenth-Century Spain* (Princeton, 2004). For new considerations of Jewish-Gentile relations in the thirteenth century, see David Nirenberg, *Communities of Violence: The Persecution of Minorities in the Middle Ages* (Princeton, 1996), and Lucy K. Pick, *Conflict and Coexistence: Archbishop Rodrigo and the Muslims and Jews of Medieval Spain* (Ann Arbor, 2004).

[16] See the pioneering study by Archibald Lewis, "The Closing of the Medieval Frontier," *Speculum* 33 (1958): 475–481.

The Sephardic Frontier

ion, living and working beyond the bounds of their designated Jewish quarters. Much to the chagrin of their own rabbis and communal officials, these Jews also undermined the stability of their own governing councils through their frequent patronage of Christian courts and blurred social and religious boundaries by taking non-Jewish concubines. In sum, not only did they take advantage of royal incentives and charters that granted them a protected legal status, but they also openly and successfully entered into economic and political relationships that conferred upon them a social status generally reserved for Christians.

It is thus my objective to abandon the well-known yet facile dichotomies of Golden Age and decline, persecution and tolerance, in favor of a more nuanced portrait that presents medieval Sephardic history in all its complexity. For these Jews, urban residence did not exclude involvement in rural life, legal prohibitions did not signal social reality, and the extension of royal authority could simultaneously help to protect Jewish settlers and to threaten the strength and autonomy of their communities. The seeds of social resistance inadvertently sown by the royal exemptions and safeguards that initially drew Jews to the frontier had a lasting effect on their communal development. This created a dynamic and open society that would endure for generations.

PART I

THE JEWISH SETTLER AND
THE FRONTIER

The transition of Jewish society from Muslim to Christian Iberia was already well underway by the thirteenth century. The great Jewish centers of al-Andalus that had survived the long political and cultural decline of Muslim rule were unable to endure the vicissitudes of the eleventh and twelth centuries. During this period, a series of Berber rulers from North Africa set out to restore Islamic dominance in the peninsula, and abruptly ended the long-standing tradition of tolerant policies toward the region's *dhimmi* (Jewish and Christian) populations. Beginning in the late eleventh century, the Almoravids and their successors, the Almohad dynasty, instituted a program of extortion and religious persecution of Andalusi Jews and Christians that drove waves of refugees across the northern borders into the lands of Castile, Aragon, and southern France. At the same time, the Christian kingdoms of northern Iberia were undergoing an unprecedented period of territorial expansion and institutional development. By 1228, the Christian armies had defeated the Almohad rulers and driven them from the peninsula. Thus, within a century of their mass departure from al-Andalus, the descendants of these Jewish exiles were able to follow the tide of Christian victory back to the cities of southern Iberia.

The dual phenomena of *reconquista y repoblación*, of conquest and resettlement of Muslim territory, had been a primary feature of Iberian society since the ninth century. However, it was the permanence and, more importantly, the size of the territories taken by the Christians in the late twelfth and early thirteenth centuries that set them apart from lands taken in early campaigns. Between their combined victory at Las Navas de Tolosa in 1212 and the fall of Seville in 1248, the crowns of Aragon and Castile reclaimed nearly half of the peninsula, including the regions of Andalusia, Murcia, Valencia, and the Balearic Islands, and established a boundary between Christian and Muslim Iberia that would stand for two and a half centuries. While historians have long since noted the prominent role that Jews played in the administration of these newly conquered territories, little attention has been given to the impact that Christian expansion had on the Jews themselves. In his twelfth-century chronicle, *Sefer ha-Qabbalah*, Abraham ibn Daud describes the dire situation of the Jews in Muslim Iberia on the eve of the Christian conquest.

The rebels against the Berber kingdom had crossed the sea to Spain after having wiped out every remnant of Jews from Tangiers to al-Mahdiya. "Turn again thy hand as a grape-gatherer upon the roots." They tried to do the same thing in all of the cities of the Ishmaelite kingdom in Spain, "if it had not been the Lord who was for us," let Israel now say.

The chronicle goes on to depict the arduous journey of the escaping refugees and the suffering of those who were unable to flee. Those who fled northward into Christian Castile were welcomed at the frontier castle of Calatrava by Alfonso VII through the person of his Jewish agent, Judah the Nasi.

Now when this great Nasi, R. Judah, was appointed over Calatrava, he supervised the passage of the refugees, released those bound in chains and let the oppressed go free by breaking their yoke and undoing their bonds. . . . When all the nation had finished passing over [the border] by means of his help, the King sent him and appointed him lord of all his household and ruler over all his possessions.[1]

The successes of the renewed Christian *reconquista* were swift and vast, and a half-century after the exodus described by ibn Daud, the Jews stood poised to return to the lands of the south. In the second half of the thirteenth century, the chaos and instability caused by war and the mass-migrations of whole populations gave way to a colonized frontier that was steadily incorporated into the political, cultural, and socioeconomic life of the various peninsular states. As the defeated Muslims fled the farms and

[1] *A Critical Edition and Translation of the Book of Tradition (Sefer ha-Qabbalah) by Abraham Ibn Daud*, ed. Gerson Cohen (Philadelphia, 1967), 96–99, English section.

Part I. The Jewish Settler and the Frontier

cities of southern Iberia, a succession of Christian kings granted lands, tax exemptions and other privileges in order to attract new settlers, Jews as well as Christians. These incentives attracted Jewish settlers from every corner of the peninsula and abroad to help populate and develop the new cities of the frontier. For the Jews of these territories, the success of the thirteenth-century conquests led to the proliferation of new Jewish settlements, and signaled the return to prominence of former Jewish centers such as Córdoba, Seville, and Valencia, which had been decimated by the Almohad persecutions.[2] If the Jews, as a group, did not play a major role in the *reconquista* and *repoblación* of the newly Christianized territories of southern Iberia in the thirteenth century, individual Jews did take advantage of the social and economic opportunities created by Christian expansion.

In the first half of this book I will endeavor to reconstruct the early stages of Jewish settlement in the newly Christianized territories of southern Iberia. In addition to a scarcity of sources, the effort to trace the development of Jewish communities from the ground up has been further frustrated by the long-standing historiographic tradition of viewing medieval Jewries in communal terms. The reasons behind this tendency are indeed many and complex, ranging from the impact of Christian and Jewish legislative sources and tax records that address Jews corporately, to the religious and philosophical agendas of historians who imagine Jews as a people. The centrality of the communal paradigm to the perception of Hispano-Jewish history is particularly striking. In contrast to northern Europe, Iberian Jewry boasted a seemingly unbroken presence in the peninsula since Roman times, a fact that has fostered the assumption of an eternal and inevitable Jewish community.[3] The establishment of Jewish settlements in Christian Iberia during the high Middle Ages has thus been understood less in terms institutional development than in terms of changing cultural context and political jurisdiction. The Jews are seen as already living in organized communal entities, merely exchanging one overlord for another.

---

[2] For the effects of the persecutions and forced conversions on Andalusi Jewry, see Abraham Halkin, "History of the Forced Conversion under the Alhmohads," in *The Joshua Starr Memorial Volume* (New York, 1953), 101–110 [Hebrew]. On the religious fundamentalism of the Almoravid and Almohad dynasties, see Richard Fletcher, *Moorish Spain* (New York, 1992), 105–130.

[3] The "communal approach" to medieval Jewish history is so prevalent that it is almost impossible to single out influential works. However, see Salo Baron, *The Jewish Community, Its History and Its Structure to the American Revolution* (Philadelphia, 1942); Yitzhak Baer, "The Foundations and Beginnings of the Jewish Community Structure in the Middle Ages," *Zion* 15 (1950) [Hebrew], 1–41; and Jacob Katz, *Exclusiveness and Tolerance: Studies in Jewish-Gentile Relations in Medieval and Modern Times* (New York, 1961).

This model of Jewish settlement is illustrated by the charters granted to the Jews of Tudela (c. 1115 and 1170) and Tortosa (c. 1145), which have come to be viewed as emblematic of the transition of Jewish society from Muslim to Christian rule over the course of the *reconquista*. The former were granted to a pre-existing Jewish community that had fled the city during its siege and was now being asked to return. At Tortosa, the charter given by Ramón Berenguer IV more closely equated settlement with community, stating that:

In that quarter you shall remain and live securely and peacefully with all your goods for all times. If more Jews come to settle, I shall give them homes to occupy and settle. [...] I grant you those good laws and all customs and usages which the Jews of Barcelona enjoy, as relates to sureties and arbitration and judgments and testimonies and all good customs which the Jews of Barcelona enjoy.[4]

Our first encounter with these Jews is thus as members of established communities. In contrast to this paradigm of Jewish transition during the *reconquista*, the creation of Jewish settlements in southern Iberia affords us the opportunity to chronicle the evolution of a Hispano-Jewish community as it takes form. Rather than begin with Jews already living in fully functioning corporate entities, this study takes as its point of departure the individual settlers from which these communities were formed. Moreover, by locating the process of Jewish settlement and economic development within the framework of Christian conquest and colonization we obtain a much stronger basis for understanding the nature of Jewish communal organization and the Jews' social and political relationships with Gentile society.

[4] The charters have achieved a relatively high level of circulation and influence in Jewish Studies through their translation and publication in Robert Chazan's sourcebook *Church, State, and Jew* (West Orange, N.J., 1980), 69–73. For Tortosa, see also Yizhak (Fritz) Baer, *Die Juden im christlichen Spanien* (Berlin, 1936), vol. 1, no. 28, pp. 16–17.

CHAPTER ONE
THE MIGRATION OF JEWISH SETTLERS
TO THE FRONTIER

I weep like an ostrich for Lucena.
Her remnant dwelt innocent and secure,
Unchanged for a thousand years;
Then came her day and her people were exiled and she a widow . . .

I will shave my head and cry bitterly over the exiles from Seville,
Over her noble men that were slain and their sons enslaved,
Over refined daughters converted to the foreign faith.

Alas, the city of Córdoba is forsaken, her ruin as vast as the sea!
Her sages and learned men perished from hunger and thirst.
Not a single Jew was left in Jaén or Almeria;
Mallorca and Malaga struggle to survive.

The Jews who remain are a beaten and bleeding wound.
For this I mourn and learn a dirge and wail with bitter lamentation;
I shout in my distress: They have vanished like water.
    —Abraham Ibn Ezra

The Berber invasions of the eleventh and twelfth centuries brought to a tragic halt one of the longest and
most glorious chapters in Jewish history. The Jews of
Muslim Spain had been the successors to the great rab-
binic centers of Baghdad and Jerusalem, and their diverse cultural achieve-
ments and general prosperity were unrivaled by any contemporary Jewish
center. Moses ibn Ezra, an older relative of the poet cited above, summed
up the attitude of superiority that Andalusi Jews possessed with regard to
their intellectual tradition:

There is no doubt at all that the inhabitants of Jerusalem from whom we, members of the Spanish exile, are descended, were more knowledgeable in rhetorical eloquence and in rabbinic tradition than the residents of other cities and towns.[1]

For such aesthetes as the Ibn Ezras, the delicate flower of Andalusi Jewish culture could not easily be transplanted in the soil of Christian Spain. In contrast to the cosmopolitan cities and glittering courts of the Andalusi princes, the Christian castles of the north seemed crude and uninviting, and provided little to assuage the Jews' bitterness over the fall of their illustrious communities. Such poignant lamentations over the ruin of Andalusi Jewry and the subsequent removal of its surviving members to Christian lands are, to this day, a powerful image of the precarious nature of medieval Jewish life. Yet the despair echoed by these poets represent but one aspect of the transfer of Jewish society from Muslim to Christian Spain.[2]

By the eleventh century, Jewish communities had already become well established in the burgeoning Christian towns of northern Iberia, and Jewish advisors, physicians, and civil servants had become fixtures at royal and baronial courts across the peninsula. Indeed, when the Christian knight Rodrigo de Vivar—the famed "*El Cid*"—briefly conquered Valencia at the end of the eleventh century, he appointed a Jewish vizir to govern the city.[3] With the great advances of Christian arms in the late twelfth and early thirteenth centuries came a chance for Jews to extend their roles as royal administrators and interpreters. They saw new prospects for Jewish settlement and an attendant influx of new goods to the Jewish markets of the north. Thus whatever the point of view of the intellectual elite, the average Jew saw the newly Christianized territories as lands of social, political and economic opportunity.

The most immediate and significant impact of the *reconquista* for Iberian Jewry was the creation of substantial Jewish settlements, if not yet full communities, in the cities throughout the central and southern portion of the peninsula. Some of the *libros de repartimiento* (Catalan *llibres de repartiment*), or land registers, record the persistence of small Jewish populations that had existed prior to Christian conquest. Jews who had remained dur-

<hr/>

[1] *Sefer ha-'iyunim veha-diyunim: 'al ha-shirah ha-'ivrit*, ed. Abraham S. Halkin (Jerusalem, 1975), 54. The association of Sephardic Jews with the elite of the Jewish Diaspora has its roots in the Biblical passage from Obadiah: 1:20.

[2] For the response of Andalusi Jewish intellectuals to the harsh policies of the Almoravid and Almohad regimes see Baer, *History*, 1:59–77.

[3] See the translation of Ibn 'Alqama's contemporary account published by Evariste Lévi Provençal, "Le prise de Valence par le Cid," in *Islam d'Occident*, ed. idem (Paris, 1948).

Part I. The Jewish Settler and the Frontier

ing the final years of Muslim rule were quickly joined by those in the service of the Christian kings, as new Jewish settlements were established and older ones broadened. The Jews present during conquest and the initial land partitions would only be the beginning. As Jewish settlement followed the arc of Christian conquest, which moved roughly east to west, the newly incorporated cities of the frontier attracted Jews from every corner of the peninsula and many from abroad. The grants and privileges received by Jews during the initial land partitions thus represent the beginning of a new era of Jewish life in southern Iberia, and provide a prism through which we can view the development of Sephardic communities from their inception.[4]

THE COURT JEW AS SETTLER

The most enduring image of the Christian reconquest is that of the crusading knight, a symbol of a martial and triumphant Christianity whose supremacy was proven through force of arms. By adopting the nickname "the conqueror," Iberian monarchs connected themselves to this imagery, recalling the legendary exploits of figures such as Saint James "The Moor-Slayer" and "The Cid."[5] Yet the great crusading kings of the thirteenth century were also state-builders in a much broader sense. Their goal was not merely the subjugation of Muslim territory, but ultimately, the political and economic integration of these regions into their realms. To that end, the Christian armies were always accompanied or closely followed by a cadre of royal administrators, and the reestablishment of a Jewish presence in the towns and cities of southern Iberia was spearheaded by Jewish civil servants with ties to the royal court.

These Jewish courtiers played a significant role in the process of capitulation and partition of several Muslim cities and were rewarded for their services with extensive properties in these regions. Chief among them were the royal scribes, or *alfaquims*, whose knowledge of Arabic made them indispensable to the formal negotiations that brought about the transition to Chris-

---

[4] Thomas Glick, "Reading the *Repartimientos:* Modeling Settlement in the Wake of Conquest," in *Christians, Muslims, and Jews in Medieval and Early Modern Spain,* ed. Mark Meyerson and Edward English (Notre Dame, 2000), 20–39.
[5] The appellation "conqueror" was given to Afonso Henriques of Portugal and Jaime I of Aragon. On the image of Santiago Matamoros and the *reconquista,* see the epilogue to Richard A. Fletcher, *Saint James's Catapult: The Life and Times of Diego Gelmírez of Santiago de Compostela* (Oxford, 1984).

tian rule. In the territories conquered by the forces of Jaime I of Aragon, the brothers Bahiel and Salomon Alconstantini drew up the official letters of surrender of Mallorca and Menorca, and the Barcelonan Jewish notable, Astruc Bonsenyor helped to oversee the capitulation and subsequent partition of the frontier town of Elche.[6] In the regions annexed by Castile, the fiscal management of the frontier was granted to a series of Jewish tax farmers (*almoxarifes*). These royal administrators represent the largest and, in terms of their land holdings, the most significant group of Jews in southern Iberia in the first years following its conquest.

Several other Jews who appear in the earliest land registers have no official title, but were obviously of prominent social standing judging by the large grants of property they received. At Murcia, Çag Alconqui was classified by the official *partidores* as a *caballero mayor*, that is to say, of the highest social rank. Alconqui, whose name may derive from his participation in the conquest, was given a large parcel of land in the rural district of Benetúcer that was augmented twice in subsequent partitions. Interestingly, the grants were made with the understanding that he maintain a horse and arms as required by the local *fuero*, or charter.[7] The use of this sort of aristocratic imagery is worth noting since, even as standard rhetoric, such language reflects a certain elevated status that would put wealthy Jews on a par with Christian nobles.[8]

Jewish courtiers further simulated the stature of the Christian landed nobility in their general relationship to the frontier. As in the case of the great Christian magnates of the period, the acquisition of property in the new territories did not necessitate settlement for Jews with ties to the royal administration. Rather, these Jews were allowed to act as absentee landlords in much the same fashion as their wealthy Christian counterparts. That is, as long as they saw to it that their holdings were actively settled and cultivated,

    [6] See the 1975 facsimile reprint of *Repartimientos de los reinos de Mallorca, Valencia y Cerdeña*, originally edited in 1856 by Próspero de Bofarull y Mascaró; and the more recent edition by Ricard Soto i Company, *Còdex català del Llibre del Repartiment de Mallorca* (Barcelona, 1984). On the Alconstantini, see *Jaume I, Crónica o Llibre dels Feits*, ed. Ferran Soldevila (Barcelona, 1982), nos. 44, 118, and for Bonsenyor, nos. 422, 436, 437, 439.

    [7] Juan Torres Fontes, *Repartimiento de Murcia*, (Madrid, 1960): 242. For a discussion of municipal charters and their impact on Jewish status, see below, chap. 4.

    [8] See my comments on Jewish dress below, chap. 7. Another of the principal Jewish recipients of property at Murcia, Çag Cohen, received a number of houses in the Jewish quarter in addition to rural land. The value of these houses, which can be gauged by the fifty *tahullas* of land that were paid in recompense to their former, Christian, owner testifies to Cohen's importance, and would seem to indicate ties to powerful Christian officials. Ibid., 241, 221, 225.

Part I. The Jewish Settler and the Frontier

they were allowed to collect the profits from these lands just as they did from the mills, vineyards, and urban houses or stores they possessed elsewhere.[9] While many Jews needed little encouragement to help settle the crown's newly acquired territories, those who belonged to the old, powerful families of the northern cities were less eager to uproot themselves in search of greener pastures. Rather, they seem to have been interested in extending their economic and, in some cases, political influence into these new regions. For these wealthy Jews, the acquisition of land in the south generally represented an opportunity to expand their holdings by obtaining a valuable commodity that they could then sell or borrow against.

In contrast to the majority of Jewish settlers who would migrated to the frontier in order to take advantage of its social and economic opportunities, Jewish courtiers showed little interest in leaving their seats of power in the north. Yet their skills as urban administrators were in high demand in the developing towns of the south, and the crown often convinced them to move there, even if only temporarily, in order to help develop the economic and political infrastructure of the new territories. An illustration of this practice can be seen in a case involving Judah de la Cavalleria. One of the wealthiest and most powerful Jewish courtiers of his era and future bailiff of Saragossa, Judah maintained a long connection to the territory of Valencia from the earliest years of Christian rule. He played an active administrative role at the Aragonese court in the decades following Aragonese expansion, a service for which he received continual augmentation of his holdings in the south. An addendum to one of these later grants states that, in order for Judah to receive the land, he would have to settle one of his sons in the kingdom of Valencia. It is worth noting that the king did not require the son to settle this particular plot of land, nor for that matter did he stipulate any particular function to be fulfilled by the younger de la Cavalleria.[10] Don Judah was not the only member of a great northern Jewish clan to expand his power into the Valencian frontier. Members of another rich and powerful Saragossan family, the Alconstantinis, also received extensive land grants

[9] Listed among the highest-ranking nobility, several Jewish notables were granted large groves of fig and olive trees in San Lucar, Valencia del Río, as well as extensive tracts at Jérez, Carmona, and throughout Andalusia. Julio González, *Repartimiento de Sevilla* (Madrid, 1951), 2:30–31, 176–77, 232–33, 263–265. For wealthy Christians receiving land on the frontier without the responsibilities of settlement, see Ricard Soto i Copmany, "Repartiment I 'repartiments': L'ordenació d'un espai de colonització feudal a la Mallorca del segle XIII," in *De Al-Andalus a la sociedad feudal: los repartimientos bajomedievales* (Barcelona, 1990): 20–21.

[10] ACA, reg. 11, fol. 186v; and Robert I. Burns, *Diplomatarium Regni Valentiae 1257–1263* (Princeton, 1991), vol. 2, no. 323a.

in the region, and carried their old rivalry with the de la Cavallerias into the Crown of Aragon's new territories.[11]

The preeminence of Jewish courtiers among those listed in the various *repartimientos* thus effectively marks the extension of the established Jewish oligarchies of both Castile and Crown of Aragon into the newly conquered lands of southern Iberia. Nowhere is the process clearer than at the Andalusian city of Seville where the primacy of Toledan Jews reflects their prominent position at the court of Alfonso X. The entire village of Paterna Harah, located in a fertile area just southwest of Seville along the river Guadalquivir, was granted to a group of royal tax collectors and advisors. This settlement quickly became known as "The Village of the King's Jews," and was clearly marked as separate and distinct from the communal property set aside for the local Jewish *aljama*. In the official *repartimiento*, the Jews of Paternah are listed among other members of the royal entourage rather than with other Jewish settlers.[12]

In addition to the Jewish notables listed at Paterna, Seville's land register also cites the courtier Don Juçef Barchilon as receiving land with other members of the royal household. The total of his grant there, "200 arrançadas and 6 yugadas and one barrio, the smallest," was among the largest grants on the Castilian frontier. Juçef's inclusion with Christian royal officials rather than with fellow Jews further highlights the fact that position at court was at least as important a factor as religion.[13] In a situation analogous to that of the de la Cavallerias in Valencia, the Jewish courtiers of Toledo remained a significant, if temporary, presence throughout Andalusia, and rabbinic sources from the period reflect the frequency and ease with which they moved between the royal seat at Toledo and the growing Jewish center at Seville. This ambivalent relationship between courts and the nascent communities of the frontier would become increasingly problematic over the course of the century. Just as Christian magistrates were often seen by municipal officials as agents of royal intrusion on local rights, so too would the

[11] María de los Desemparados Cabanes Pecourt and Ramón Ferrer Navarro, *Libre del Repartiment del Regne de Valencia* (Saragossa, 1979), nos. 162, 289, 314, 592, and 1153. For the rivalries among the leading Jewish families of Valencia see below, chap. 6.

[12] González, *Repartimiento de Sevilla*, 2:65–66, and 1:280–281. The partition of Paterna comes between the lands given to the "*alcaldes* of the king Don Alfonso" at Vesvachit, and the royal *ballesteros* at Machar Chacosa.

[13] González, *Repartimiento de Sevilla*, 2:71, 1:280. Similarly, at Jérez, a Jew named Velloid who is listed as a "mounted *ballestero* [bowman], of the king," inherited land both as a member of the Jewish community and as a member of the royal *ballesteros*. See Manuel González Jiménez and Antonio González Gómez, *El Libro del Repartimiento de Jérez de la Frontera, estudio y edición* (Cádiz, 1980), lxiv and part. no. 1921.

Part I. The Jewish Settler and the Frontier

Jewish communal leaders of the frontier develop a tense relationship with the courtiers of Toledo, Lisbon and Saragossa.[14]

There is evidence that a few of the wealthier and more influential Jews who received land during the initial partitions did come to the frontier to stay. The first mention of a Jew in the southern Valencian outpost of Ori- huela is the courtier Jacob Avendino, who was among the twenty-six citizens (*vecinos*) who successfully repelled an attack by Muslim rebels in 1264.[15] Avendino's influence can be gauged by the fact that, despite having grants revoked several times for his failure to settle them or have them settled, he always was compensated during the following revision of the official land registers, and usually given extra donations as well. One such improvement notes that he was given new land to replace the plots he had received earlier but which, he seems to have complained, "were not in a good locale, being enclosed in the castle."[16] Notable is the receptiveness of the royal *partidores* to Avendino's requests. Though the exact process by which lands were allot- ted to specific individuals remains unclear, it stands to reason that the loca- tion of grants given to Jews during these partitions must have come in re- sponse to specific requests, just as the various monarchs and their representatives would later respond to a number of complaints and requests originating with certain Jewish individuals or communities.

Cases like that of Avendino notwithstanding, the majority of Jews who came to settle the frontier were men of lesser rank. Like their more promi- nent brethren, the experience of these Jewish colonists also closely paral- leled that of their Christian counterparts. In the kingdom of Valencia, the first Jewish settlers seem to have come from many of the same towns in Old Aragon and Catalonia from where most of Christian colonists came. Among the names that appear in the initial land divisions of the region are Salamon of Gerona, Crescas of Belcayre, Simeon Abenpasat from the Aragonese town of Alagón, Salomon from Villafranca, in Catalonia, Alaçar, son of Açe-

---

[14] On the continued relationship between the Jewish elite of Toledo and Seville, see Baer, *Juden*, vol. 2, no. 241, pp. 228–229; Yehudah ben Asher, *Zikhron Yehudah* (Jerusalem, 1967), no. 82; and the responsum from Rabbi Solomon ibn Adret, *Responsa*, section 5, no. 240 (hereafter referred to as Adret, followed by the vol. and no. of the responsum). The tensions between courtiers and local Jewish officials is discussed below, chap. 5.

[15] Justo García Soriano, "La Reconquista de Orihuela, Su leyenda y su historia," *Bo- letín de la Real Academia de la Historia* 104 (1934): 217. Though listed among the 'defenders' of the castle, there is no evidence that Avendino was anything more than a royal func- tionary who found himself besieged along with the rest of the castle's inhabitants. Thus, *contra* Salo Baron's comments in *A Social and Religious History of the Jews* (hereafter *SRHJ*) (New York, 1965), 10:355 n. 4.

[16] Juan Torres Fontes, *Repartimiento de Orihuela* (Murcia, 1988), 4a part., p. 67.

cri Abiniuçef of Huesca, and Baruch son of Bonet Abenbaruch, from Lérida.[17] Similarly, the first Jewish settlers to Mallorca included merchants from Barcelona and Tortosa, as well as a butcher from Lérida. These and other Jewish settlers to the Balearics were fully integrated into the economic life of the islands within a few years of their conquest, becoming active in banking, international trade, and the local agricultural economy.[18]

CHAOS AND CONTINUITY

The arrival of settlers from the north also created a measure of disorder within the pre-conquest Jewish communities. Despite royal policies that generally sought to maintain the status quo with regard to the location and property rights of any older Jewish settlements, Christian expansion during the thirteenth century, and the ensuing partition of land resulted in the temporary displacement of many Jews. Throughout southern Iberia, the remnants of native Jewish communities eagerly welcomed the end of Almohad sovereignty. Yet in the process of transition to Christian rule, these Jews often suffered the same fate as those Muslims who remained behind, enduring dislocation and loss of property at the hands of Jewish and Christian settlers alike.

Though some of the Jewish newcomers to Valencia are listed as forfeiting their grants for failure to occupy them, more common were instances of native Jews whose lands were confiscated and redistributed to Christian settlers throughout the various partitions of city.[19] In addition to these instances of former Jewish property being reallocated for Christian settlers, the native Jewries of these frontier settlements also lost land to other Jews who arrived with the Christian conquerors, or soon thereafter. In the first partition of Valencia, in 1238, the Jewish colonist Cresches of Belcyare was granted the houses formerly belonging to a local Jew, Farayx Abunçeyd.

[17] Cabanes Pecourt and Ferrer Navarro, *Libre del Repartiment*, nos. 1153–1154, 1207, 1333–1334, 1449. The register also lists a Castilian named Sampson who received a granary in the *partida* given to the men from Lérida, and who was most likely a Jew, no. 1521.

[18] Soto i Company, *Còdex català*, fols. 6, 8v, 11, 18, 34, 35, and Prospero de Bofarull, *Repartimientos*, 16, 35. See also the record of Jews processing olive oil for a local monastery in Pau Mora and Lorenzo Andrinal, *Diplomatari del monestir de Santa Maria de la Real de Mallorca* (Palma, 1982), no. 23.

[19] Cabanes Pecourt and Ferrer Navarro, *Libre del Repartiment*, p. 124, no. 1102; p. 125, no. 1112; p. 126, no. 1122; p. 130, nos. 1163–1164; p. 135, no. 1221; p. 129, no. 1154; and p. 133, no. 1191. There is evidence of sizable Jewish communities already in existence upon the arrival of the Christian forces at both Valencia and Jérez de la Frontera.

Part I. The Jewish Settler and the Frontier

Such instances were less indicative of royal favoritism to the Jews of Christian lands than of the general disorder and confusion caused by the wars of conquest, and the subsequent displacement of large numbers of local inhabitants through voluntary emigration and the royal redistribution of land. Indeed, we also see a certain Ibraym, whose Arabized name and designation as a *iudeus valentinus* mark him as a member of the pre-conquest community, who received a royal grant at the expense of another native Jew.[20] What seems most noteworthy here is the degree to which Iberian Jews were fully integrated into the process of resettlement from its earliest stages. In their rush to take advantage of the various opportunities opened up by the successful advance of the *reconquista*, Jews viewed the new lands of the frontier much as Christian settlers did. That is to say, the disruption and chaos caused by the transition to Christian rule created a climate in which religious affiliation and a sense of communal solidarity mattered little to settlers as they petitioned the rights to lands and sought to expand their commercial and residential properties.

A similar panorama of partial continuity amid general dislocation and disorder can be seen with respect to the Andalusian city of Jérez de la Frontera. The Muslim population of the city had accepted Castilian sovereignty after the fall of neighboring Seville in 1248, but attempted to reassert their independence upon the death of Fernando III. His son and successor, Alfonso X, was thus forced to besiege and retake Jérez shortly after his accession to the throne in 1252. Occupied with his plans to invade North Africa and short on Christian settlers, Alfonso allowed the city's inhabitants to retain their houses and lands in exchange for their recognition of his dominion. The early years of Castilian rule at Jérez were thus characterized by a small Christian presence and a general state of political instability.

This disorder persisted through the city's partition in 1266, leading the local Jewish population to establish a temporary *casa de merced*, or "house of mercy," which aided in the repatriation of Jewish captives and refugees. This building, formerly a storehouse for the pre-conquest Jewish community, was not a permanent structure, as has been suggested, but was created in response to the upheaval of the reconquest.[21] The land register from Jérez mentions that one Jew died during the battle for the city, and another lost property solely on the grounds that he had resided in the town under Muslim rule. Other native Jews appear to have deserted their houses during the

---

[20] For Jews losing land to Jews from outside city, see ibid., part 1, nos. 1153–1154 and 1207; and to Christians, part 1, nos. 1102, 1164; part 3, nos. 541, 1085, 1590, 1604–1611.
[21] For the *casa de merced*, see González Jiménez and González Gómez, *Repartimiento de Jérez*, part nos. 1852, 1922.

chaos of the Muslim rebellion prior to the city's partition. Upon the abandonment of their property, the houses of local Jews were generally given to those members of the community who remained in Jérez.[22] However this sensible policy was often undermined by the crown's arbitrary interference on behalf of particular Jews. The case of Yuçaf Alcaçabi is illustrative. The text of the *repartimiento* states:

> We gave these in partition to Yuçaf Alcaçabi; and afterwards there arrived a letter from the King that we should give them to Çac Quixaros. And Alcaçabi had renovated them a great deal, and he lived in the town in the time of the Moors, and he lost that which he had, and for this reason he was not given the grant.[23]

Yuçaf, a resident of the city prior to the conquest, appears to have gone to the royal *partidores* and obtained new rights to his old property. However, the king had already considered all the old property of Jérez to be effectively ownerless, and thus granted these houses to Çac. Thus, Yuçaf was not denied ownership because he left his land unoccupied, but rather because he had lived in Jérez under Muslim rule and lost his property rights in the course of the conquest of the city.[24]

Despite the disruption caused by properties being gained and lost by native and newcomer alike, there are also examples of continuity on the frontier. At Jérez, the royal *partidores* declared that houses belonging to a native Jew who had died, possibly as a result of the conquest itself, were to remain in the possession of his wife and children. Thus, in some instances, efforts were made to try and maintain the same ownership of land. The presence of family groups among the Jewish recipients at Jérez also points to the continuation of a native Jewish population. The Alcuxco, Axucury, and Aben Açot clans, most likely the leading families of the pre-conquest community, all had several members who were granted houses and land.[25]

The central institutions of these Jewish communities also seem to have continued much the same under Christian rule. At Mallorca and Valencia, as

---

[22] Ibid., nos. 1863, 1865, 1867.

[23] Ibid., no. 1863.

[24] Other members of the Alcaçabi clan seem to have retained ownership of their houses, see ibid., part. nos. 1870–1873. For a similar case of conflict of ownership among the Jews at Jérez, see nos. 1884 and 997.

[25] Ibid., part. nos. 1851 and 1928. For the Alcuxco family, see part. nos. 1887 and 1890; for the Axucury family, part. nos. 1860, 1869, 1916; and for the Aben Açot family, part. nos. 1845, 1848, 1856, and 1867.

at the Castilian towns of Seville, Córdoba, and Jérez, efforts were made to maintain the existence of the former Jewish quarter (*judería*), while expanding and altering their dimensions. These *juderías* lay within the city walls, often near the seat of royal power, and were usually separated from the rest of the town by another, interior wall.[26] When first established, Seville's *judería* stood outside of the residential and commercial center of the city, but the burgeoning community soon expanded, and became encircled by a new protective wall. This wall, with its two gates, at once connected the Jewish settlement with the rest of the city while at the same time maintaining its boundaries as a separate community. In a passage that reflects the regeneration of both the size and organization of the Sevillan Jewish community, the *repartimiento* mentions that three buildings that were formerly used as mosques had been converted into synagogues. Interestingly, this relatively detailed land register contains no reference to the establishment of a new Jewish cemetery at Seville. Later mention of a Jewish cemetery situated outside of the *judería* on the road leading out of the city most likely refers to one that pre-dates Christian rule.[27]

At Mallorca, the earliest references to Jewish settlement under Christian rule repeatedly associate the newcomers with the Muslim *almudayna*, the fortified citadel at the heart of the city. Such allusions to a specific Jewish quarter signals the continuation of a Jewish presence in the city of Mallorca, and indicates that the new arrivals from the peninsula settled in the same neighborhood where their coreligionists had always lived. This continuity is also suggested by a reference to the "Gate of the Jews" in the text of the *repartimiento*. If, as it seems, this refers to a landmark which predated the arrival of Catalan Jews, then it would indicate the existence of a Jewish community at the Muslim-controlled city (*Madinat Mayurqa*) that lived in its own walled section of the town, like the urban Jewish settlements found in mainland Iberian cities. Such continuity of settlement notwithstanding, Christian conquest also brought a significant expansion of land owned by the Jews of Mallorca. The grants that the new Jewish settlers received col-

---

[26] This could be the royal palace (*alcázar*), or royal marketplace (*alcacería*). In some towns, such as Murviedro (Catalan Morvedre) in Valencia, new *juderías* were established where none had previously existed. Mark Meyerson, *Jews in an Iberian Frontier Kingdom*, 10.

[27] ACS, section XI, caja 4, no. 36/1, in Manuel González Jiménez, *Diplomatario andaluz de Alfonso X* (Seville, 1991), no. 4, pp. 6–8. In the early fourteenth century, the archbishop and the *cabildo* of Seville gave a mosque in their possession to the royal rent collector Don Yehudah Abenhabed, but there is no evidence that it was turned into a synagogue. ACS, section IX, caja 101, no. 8/1. See also González, *Repartimiento de Sevilla*, 1:363, and for the Jewish cemetery, pp. 362, 543.

lectively were not confined to any urban neighborhood, but were strewn throughout the various areas of the island under royal control.[28]

In assessing the initial Jewish resettlement of southern Iberia during the mid-thirteenth century there remains the provocative question of whether or not we can characterize this process as a "return" of a people to their ancestral home. The presence of Toledan Jews in the early settlement of Seville may indeed signal a return, at least of the leading families of Andalusi Jews, to the region their forefathers had fled in the previous century. Yet even here, there is a need to exercise caution in assuming such neat demographic patterns. Abraham ibn Daud records that Cordoban Jews fleeing the Almohads migrated to Saragossa, as well as to Toledo, and it is possible that the Andalusi refugees found safe haven in a number of other Christian towns.[29] Furthermore, those who did settle in Toledo integrated into a pre-existing Jewish community, and it is impossible to tell which, if any, retained their distinct Andalusi identities and their claims on lands and houses in cities such as Córdoba and Seville.[30] The original provenance of Jewish settlers to the Aragonese frontier is even more complex than that of Castile, and in the case of Portugal we have no evidence to suggest that those Jews who followed the royal court southward carried with them any conscious sentiment of reclaiming former lands.

The image of Jewish resettlement as a recuperation of their place in southern Iberia is further challenged by their choice of settlement. While the Jewish community at Christian Seville would develop in accordance with that city's position as the region's leading marketplace, the numbers of Jews who migrated to Córdoba would remain relatively modest, and the once great rabbinic center of Lucena would not be revived at all under Christian rule. Similarly, Jews do not appear to have been recipients of lands during most of the smaller Andalusian partitions that followed the conquest of Seville.[31] Rather, Jewish settlement patterns and the development of communities and intellectual centers in the thirteenth century owed far more to

[28] For the Gate of the Jews, see Soto i Company, *Còdex català*, fol. 43; Prospero de Bofarull y Mascaró, *Repartimientos*, 65.

[29] Ibn Daud, *Sefer ha-Qabbalah*, 72.

[30] The sole reference to such "reclamation" is at Seville, where a prominent Jewish settler, Rabbi Yuçaf Cabaçay, was granted a store together with its warehouse that was listed as being located behind those of the Jewish moneychangers, "as it had been in the time of the Moors." ACS, section IX, caja 101, no. 21/1; and Antonio Ballesteros, *Sevilla en el siglo XIII* (Madrid, 1913), no. 73.

[31] On these other *libros de repartimiento*, many of which have been lost, see Manuel González Jiménez, "Repartimientos andaluces del siglo XIII, perspectiva de conjunto y problemas," in *De Al-Andalus a la sociedad feudal: Los repartimientos bajomedievales* (Barcelona, 1990), 99.

Part I. The Jewish Settler and the Frontier

the opportunities created by their Christian host society than to any collective desire to return to and reestablish their former communities. Therefore, Jewish migration to southern Iberia in the decades following its incorporation into the various Christian kingdoms must be understood in the context of the wider process of resettlement.

CHRISTIAN COLONIZATION AND THE GROWTH OF JEWISH COMMUNITIES

Under the guidance of the great warrior kings of the early thirteenth century, the renewed push to "recover" control of *Hispania* had been a resounding and unprecedented success. Spurred on by the coordination of Castilian and Aragonese efforts, Christian conquest was swift and extensive, with the result that the balance of power in the peninsula had been turned once and for all in the favor of the Christian kingdoms of the north. Yet victory brought with it a new set of problems. The crusader kings soon found themselves to be demographically overstretched, their kingdoms precariously close to collapse under the weight of the new territories. The half-century following 1248 thus marks the end of the greatest phase of the *reconquista*, and the beginning of the even grander and more difficult undertaking of colonization. Castile halted its drive southward, choosing instead to focus on settling the territory it had conquered, and to collect a sizable tribute from the only remaining Muslim kingdom on the peninsula, Granada. The kings of the federated Crown of Aragon would continue to expand into the Mediterranean, annexing Sicily from the French in 1282. Yet within their Iberian territories they too turned their attention to the questions of resettlement and development.

All along the advancing frontier, the military successes of the thirteenth century were marked by symbolic references to the formal transfer of power from Muslim to Christian rule. Together with their knights and churchmen, the triumphant Christian kings led dramatic processions into city after city where Muslim governors were forced to swear fealty to their new masters. Mosques were converted to churches, and in a grand gesture that reflected the fulfillment of the reconquest ideal, Castile's Fernando III returned to the cathedral of Santiago de Compostela the bells that had hung in the great mosque of Córdoba since their capture by al-Mansur in 997.[32] However,

---

[32] On the various examples of Christian symbolism form this era, see O'Callaghan, *Reconquest and Crusade*, chap. 5.

such displays of dominance obscure the socio-political realities of the situation that prevailed on the frontier in the aftermath of Muslim capitulation. The victorious Christians had neither the ability nor the inclination to alter the existing structures of landownership and social organization in their new provinces, and followed the long-standing tradition of granting religious freedom to all those who freely recognized their sovereignty.

Traditionally, the *repoblación* has been understood as an extension of the *reconquista*, a result of the inevitable need for the partition of new territory among those active in its conquest, and the attraction of settlers to effect the process of colonization. In many areas of the frontier, the desperate need to attract settlers is attested to by the crown's issuance of a variety of privileges and exemptions. The Castilian privilege of *homicianos*, or amnesty for criminals, revived by Fernando IV in 1310, typifies the difficult conditions that hindered the process of resettlement.

> To all who went to Gibraltar and who became citizens or residents, be they bandits or thieves or assassins, or any other men no matter what wrong they may have done, or to any married woman who may have abandoned her husband . . . that they may be defended and guarded from death.[33]

With settlers induced by such royal incentives and drawn by the lands and new economic opportunities then available in the under-populated south, the second half of the thirteenth century became a period of unprecedented immigration and mobility among Iberian Jews. Recalling the rapid growth of the Jewish community at Seville, Alfonso XI would later explain that the crown invited many Jews to settle in the Andalusian capital, because the city had been left empty by the fleeing Muslims and "was in need of a great many people to inhabit it."[34] One of the principal prerogatives that helped fuel Jewish migration to the new territories was the right to move and travel freely, as can be seen in the privilege granted to the Jews of the kingdom of Valencia in 1239.

> We receive you all, collectively and individually, and your property under Our protection, custody and command, and under Our special safe-conduct wherever you may go, remain, or return in all the places

[33] Manuel González Jiménez, "Frontier and Settlement in the Kingdom of Castile," in *Medieval Frontier Societies*, 72. Though the privilege was intended to attract settlers to Gibraltar, its essence applies to the rest of the Castilian south that remained underpopulated throughout this period.

[34] Baer, *Juden*, vol. 2, no. 167.

of Our kingdoms and dominions on land and on the sea, and neither shall anyone dare to aggrieve you or your property in any place nor invade or seize you or your property, except in the case of your own debt or offense.[35]

This right was greatly prized among Iberian Jews, and reiterated in rabbinic texts.

[A Jew] may go and no one hinders him, and this matter is known and the custom reinforced so that in the courts of the kings and their castles, in their mouths and the mouths of their counselors and in their hearts it is placed and engraved that all the Jews in the places where they dwell are free to go where they choose. . . . The Jews are as free as the knights to go wherever they wish.[36]

The freedom of travel encouraged Jews to settle throughout the massive frontier that cut across the various peninsular states, and to migrate within this region as well. The conquest of Murcia drew Jewish settlers from Castile to the southwest corner of the peninsula, from where they entered into the neighboring lands controlled by the Crown of Aragon. The names of Jewish settlers arriving in the kingdom of Valencia in the decades following its conquest attest to the continuous migration of Jews from the northern cities of the Catalonia and Aragon. The count-kings of the Crown of Aragon also encouraged the immigration of Jews from Castile to their southern territories and issued letters of safe conduct to encourage the settlement of Jewish merchants.[37] Similarly, in the western regions of the frontier, there is also evidence that some of the Portuguese Jews who had followed the royal court southward from Coimbra in the late twelfth century later migrated eastward into southern Castile. A settler named Juçef of Lisbon appears among the Jewish courtiers who received land near Seville, and a certain "Don Çuleyman Portugales" is listed as a leading figure in the new Jewish community of Niebla. The border between southern Portugal and

---

[35] ACA, reg. 941, fol. 176v.–177; and Baer, *Juden*, vol. 1, no. 91.

[36] Baer, *Juden*, vol. 1, no. 224a, arts. 1–2. Though this text comes from Catalonia and dates from a later period, there is evidence that the freedom of travel was seen as an essential right by Jews living on the thirteenth-century frontier. In 1354, the *aljamas* of Valencia joined with those of Catalonia in petitioning the crown for confirmation of their "ancient right" to travel freely. Ibid., no. 253, art. 35.

[37] See, for example, Salomon de Torre de Azmel of Tarazona (ACA, reg. 59, fol. 131), Astruc of Gerona (reg. 63, fol. 39v), Astruga and Juceff of Barcelona (reg. 74, fol. 66), Mosses of Calatayud (reg. 199, fol. 11), and Mayr of Lérida (reg. 21, fol. 46v). For Castilian Jews, see ACA, reg. 42, fol. 230; reg. 60, fol. 56v. See also ACA, reg. 134, fol. 171; and reg. 256, fol. iv.

the Spanish kingdoms remained fairly permeable throughout the late thirteenth and early fourteenth centuries, and Jews from central and eastern Iberia also moved westward into Portugal.[38]

Too much mobility was not always welcomed by the crown and local lords seeking to stabilize the under-populated territories by attracting permanent settlers. As we have seen in the initial land partitions, those who were unwilling or unable to actively settle and work their lands would risk losing them. At one point, Valencian nobles warned the crown that Jews and Muslims who emigrated from their land without permission would forfeit their rights to the property.[39]

A key source of information regarding Jewish migration during this period is the royal *guidaticum*, or letter of safe conduct. Given to Christians, Muslims, and Jews alike these letters protected the traveler by setting a fixed monetary penalty to be paid to the crown by anyone who might molest the recipient. Many of these letters give the right of settlement as well as safe passage, and were issued to Jews throughout the peninsula and abroad. The majority of these royal privileges stem from the Crown of Aragon, whose prominent role in maritime commerce helped its Jews maintain strong contacts with their co-religionists in North Africa. Over the course of the late thirteenth century, Aragonese expansion and prosperity prompted many North African Jews to immigrate to its dominions.

This process is illustrated by a *guidaticum* issued by Jaime I to four Jews from Sigilmasa to come and settle in his lands with all their families and possessions. It would seem that these immigrants were able to obtain this writ through family connections at the Aragonese royal court, since the grant was given to "Salomon Benammar, Jew of Sigilmasa, brother of Ammar, our faithful Jew."[40] The Benammar clan continued to enjoy royal favor under Pedro III, who sent an open letter to all his admirals and others who might command royal ships to ensure safe passage to another family member from the North African city of Trebalos. The royal chancellery then records that simi-

[38] González, *Repartimiento de Sevilla*, 2:66. Another Jew associated with Niebla was Don Jacob Yahion, a royal rent collector for Castile, who was a member of the aristocratic ibn Yahia family of Portugal. See Isabel Montes Romero-Camacho, and Manuel González Jiménez, "Financieros judíos en la primera época de la repoblación del reino de Sevilla," *Anuario de estudios medievales* 29 (1999): 404–405, 371.

[39] See the case of the courtier Abraham Mascaram, ACA, *Cartas Reales*, Alfonso II, Ex. S., no. 133, fol. 10v, and ACA, reg. 19, fol. 85.

[40] In 1270, the king granted the same rights to the brothers Barchet and Maner Avenmenage who, along with their families, were emigrating from Alexandria. Robert I. Burns, "The *Guidaticum*: Safe-Conduct in Medieval Arago-Catalonia," *Medieval Encounters* 1 (1995): 81. For Salamon Benammar, see Jaime Villanueva, *Viatge Literario a las Iglesias de España* (Madrid, 1852), 22: 327–328. See also Régné, nos. 443, 691.

Part I. The Jewish Settler and the Frontier

lar grants were to be made for three other Jews from Trebalos: the *alfaquim* Isaac Jucef Benbolfarag, Ismael Bonhazan Aliepdoni, and Isaac Abenjucef Annafusi. Once Hayon had made contact with the Aragonese crown, most likely through Jews at court, he then seems to have been able to obtain matching grants for his three companions. An analogous example can be seen in the case of Jucef, son of Todros ha-Levi, who owed his *guidaticum* to settle in the kingdom of Valencia to his father, an influential courtier from Calatayud.[41]

Those Jews without connection at the royal court could utilize the auspices of the local community they wished to join in order to obtain royal letters of safe conduct. The permission for the Castilian Jews Nathan el Roman and his son Mahir el Costal to settle in the Valencian town of Alicante was the result of a petition made by its Jewish community to Jaime II. It would seem that, along with their desire to expand their community, the Jews of Alicante also had concerns regarding the general status and rights of such newcomers. Five days after granting his safe conduct to the two families from Castile, the king issued a letter declaring that all Jews living in Alicante, including those who would later come to settle there from abroad, would enjoy the same rights and privileges as the indigenous inhabitants.[42]

A guarantee of safe passage was often all that was needed by Jewish settlers who were drawn by the opportunity to establish businesses and trade routes in a new town or region. For others, the challenge and risks of starting life anew in an unknown region required more substantial incentives. Such inducement routinely took the form of an exemption from royal taxes for a determined period. Indeed, after the initial land partitions of the new territories, the primary incentive employed by the royal courts to attract new Jewish settlers to the towns of the frontier was tax relief. Although there was no standard allotment of time, these exemptions tended to run from one to five years. As with the *guidaticum*, the rights granted to these Jews were usually extended to include "all other Jews," and thus opened the door for settlement by a broader sector of the Jewish population. One such example is a letter written by Jaime I to Jaffias Maymo of Tortosa, allowing him to settle in the Valencian city of Morella, which was addressed to him and "to all other Jews who come to populate the town of Morella." It was through these sorts of letters that the crown took the opportunity to set out the basic privileges and rights that would be enjoyed by all Jewish settlers to a certain locale. Here, the grant exempted all Jews from any royal taxes and services for their first year of settlement, with a reduced tax of only 20 sous per household for the following four years. Upon settlement, the Jews of

---

41 This was Hayon Benammar Albarach, ACA, reg. 37, fol. 64.
42 ACA, reg. 256, fol. iv, and reg. 195, fol. 120.

Morella would enjoy the privileges given to the Jews in the charter (*furs*) of Valencia, and after five years in the town would follow the tax regulations of the other Jews in this region.[43]

These exemptions were only for crown taxes and did not absolve Jews from other obligations to the local community, or *aljama*. Nonetheless, there were some who sought to use their royal exemptions to get out of all communal responsibilities. In 1260, Jaime I wrote an open proclamation to the whole Jewish *aljama* of Játiva stating that royal exemptions did not release anyone from general communal obligations including responding to alarm signals. The possibility that some Jews might go so far as to not respond to public alarms highlights the sort of challenges confronting Jewish communal government in these frontier towns. In some cases tax exemptions were not given to the settlers themselves, but to the communities that were to receive them. Such was the case at Elche, where Jews did not have to pay taxes during their first year of settlement. In this instance the letter is written as a royal concession to the community of Elche, obviously in response to their petition, and includes a clause ordering that the exemption be upheld by the royal bailiff of the region. Here, the Jewish community's desire to attract settlers was greater than any concern over losing eligible taxpayers. [44]

The royal incentives, writs of safe-conduct, and the availability of new lands and marketplaces resulted in the steady growth of Jewish settlements in southern Iberia over the course of the late thirteenth century. Within a decade after its conquest Jewish immigration to Seville had already become sufficient for the king to address a letter to the Jewish community and its leaders, and by the close of the century, this *aljama* had become one of the largest in all of Castile. After Seville the next largest Jewish settlement developed at Córdoba where, in the generation following the fall and initial partition of the city in 1236, Jews are listed as contributing to the maintenance of the city's water works as a community. Their annual tax of 100 *maravedíes* (*mrs.*) was equal to the amount given by the town council, and more than that paid by the cathedral chapter (30 *mrs.*).[45]

Throughout the new territories, Jewish settlement patterns appear to have generally followed those of Christian colonists. In Andalusia, the great

[43] ACA, reg. 12, fol. 143. There is no mention of the existence or establishment of a separate Jewish quarter at Morella, but the grant allows Jaffias and his fellow Jews "to build their houses in the center of town."

[44] For Játiva ("nec possit se desistere de vestris catanis, nec de alarmis vestris"), see ACA, reg. 11, fol. 190; and Burns, *Diplomatarium*, vol. 2, no. 327, p. 278. For Elche, see Régné, no. 2864.

[45] Julio González, *Reinado y diplomas de Fernando III* (Córdoba, 1986), no. 685. For annual tax, see BCC, ms. 125, fol. 17.

Part I. The Jewish Settler and the Frontier

disparity in size between the principal Jewish community at Seville and others such as Niebla, Jérez, and Ecija, are in keeping with the widespread under-population and poverty of these towns in the late thirteenth century.[46] A similar pattern emerged in Portugal where Jews from the largest northern center at Coimbra migrated south to the new capital at Lisbon. A document from 1219 records a land sale that reflects the movement of a wealthy Jewish family along this trajectory. In it, Regina, the widow of Jucefe son of Almosarif (*almoxarife*), and Solomon, the son of Almosarif, sell a parcel of land that the family possessed outside the village of Villa Franca, near Coimbra. The fact that the sale was made in Lisbon, to one of its residents, seems to indicate that this family had relocated there, and the mention of the father's title of *almoxarife*, or royal rent collector, probably indicates his attachment to the royal court. The names listed as witnesses and sponsors of Regina's children also reflect this family's close contacts with relatives and other Jews from Leiria and Santarem whose presence in Lisbon might also indicate their settlement in the capital.[47]

By the thirteenth century Lisbon had become a major center for Jewish settlement. In the city itself, as elsewhere in the peninsula, the crown had established a Jewish quarter where the king rented commercial and residential property to his Jews. Here we see Christians selling houses to one another amid the stores operated by Jewish merchants and artisans. A number of documents from the thirteenth and early fourteenth centuries record Jews buying, selling, and receiving royal grants of land and houses in and around Lisbon.[48] Along with the community at the royal capital, Jewish set-

[46] For the economic problems suffered by both Christians and Jews at Niebla, see Romero-Camacho, and González Jiménez, "Financieros judíos," pp. 372–374. An idea of the distribution and relative size of the region's Jewries can be seen in the following list of taxes paid by these communities in 1294: Seville, 150,333 *mrs.*; Córdoba, 38,333 *mrs.*; Jaén, Úbeda and Baeza, 25,500 *mrs.*; Niebla, 7,000 *mrs.*; Ecija, 5,000 *mrs.*; Jérez de la Frontera, 5,000 *mrs.*; and Andujar, 1,500 *mrs.* See Mercedes Gaibrois Ballesteros, *Sancho IV de Castilla* (Madrid, 1928), 3:355–392, and González Jiménez and González Gómez, *Repartimiento de Jérez*, 65.

[47] This document was preceded by one dated November of 1217, which records the sale by Moses, son of Almosarif, of a parcel of land that he had inherited from his brother Abraham in the village of Villa Franca near Coimbra. This Moses was a brother of Solomon and the deceased Jucefe, and the two sales represent the brothers' divestment of their property farther north. Maria José Azevedo Santos, *Vida e Morte de um Mosteiro cisterciense. S. Paulo de Almaziva* (Lisbon, 1998), nos. 85 and 87. See also the record of a land-sale by the a certain Benjamin Coimbrão near Leiria from 1312. Maria José Pimenta Ferro, *Os Judeus em Portugal no século XIV* (Lisbon, 1970), 144, 356.

[48] As early as 1177, there is reference to a Jewish settlement by Lisbon's waterfront known as the "*aljizaria* of the Jews." ANTT, *Corp. Rel. Chelas*, m. 8, no. 142; *Chancel. de D. Dinis*, liv. 2, fol. 85v; and Gérard Pradalié, *Lisboa da Reconquista ao fim do século XIII* (Lisbon, 1975), 79.

tlements soon developed at most other urban centers of central and southern Portugal, including Santarem, Évora, Torres Vedras, and Estremoz.[49]

In his classic study *A History of the Jews in Christian Spain*, Yitzhak Baer made the following observation:

The territories reconquered during the thirteenth century—Andalusia, Murcia, Valencia, and Majorca—held no attraction for Jewish settlers at first, and played no significant role in Jewish cultural life during the period.[50]

Baer's comments regarding the thirteenth-century frontier reflect his interest in the cultural and intellectual development of Iberian Jewry, and underestimate Jewish settlement in these regions in the years following their conquest. Jewish migration to the new territories can, indeed, be traced from the time of the initial land divisions, and the steady growth of the Jewish communities of the frontier continued throughout the latter half of the thirteenth century as Jewish settlers from the interior of the peninsula and abroad began to drift into southern Iberia. The vast borderland created by the dramatic advances of the *reconquista* in the first half of the thirteenth century affords us the unique opportunity to witness the birth and early development of Sephardic communities from Portugal to Mallorca. One of the principal characteristics of this early growth was the formative role played by royal authority, a theme that would become increasingly dominant in the evolution of Jewish society in this region throughout the century and beyond.

The crown was active in reestablishing a Jewish presence on the frontier beginning with the initial land partitions themselves. As a result, the majority of the first Jewish recipients of land grants were those with close ties to the various royal courts, most of whom who saw the frontier as a place to extend their economic power rather than to settle.[51] In addition to the dona-

[49] In what appears to be a fairly typical process, the small Jewish settlement established just outside of Leiria in the twelfth century would, by the late thirteenth century, develop into an official Jewish quarter in the heart of the town. For the development of Jewish communal space at Leiria, see Saul Gomes, "Os Judeus de Leiria Medieval como Agentes Dinamizadores da Economia Urbana," *Revista da Facultade de Letras, Coimbra. Historia* 29 (1993): 2–6; and ANTT, *Alcobaça*, 1a inc., m. 19, fol. 37.

[50] Yitzhak Baer, *History*, 1:196.

[51] For a comparison to the settlement patterns of wealthy Ashkenazi Jews in the 14th and 15th centuries, see Michael Toch, "Jewish Migration to, within, and from Medieval Germany," in Simonetta Cavaciocchi, ed., *Le Migrazioni in Europa secc. XII–XVIII* (Florence, 1993), 642.

Part I. The Jewish Settler and the Frontier

tion of lands to these courtiers, Iberian kings also provided for the expansion of Jewish settlement in the region, renewing the rights to urban spaces in those cities where remnants of a Jewish community already existed, and elsewhere setting aside neighborhoods to accommodate new Jewish settlers, their synagogues and burial grounds. In the decades following the initial land divisions Iberian kings continued to shape the development of Jewish communities on the frontier through a combination of royal incentives including land grants, tax incentives, and the right to travel freely. It should also be emphasized that, in addition to encouraging the immigration of individual Jews and allocating territory for the growth and development of future Jewish communities, the crown did not seek to limit Jewish settlement or landownership in any way. In the following chapter I will discuss how Jewish ownership of both urban and rural property throughout southern Iberia helped to integrate them into the society of the frontier, and marked an important point of continuity for Jews in their transition from Muslim to Christian rule.

CHAPTER TWO
JEWISH LANDOWNERSHIP

Sir, I leave you all the lands on this side of the sea which the Moors won
from King Roderick of Spain. All this now lies within your power, one
part of it conquered and the other laid under tribute. If you should manage to hold it all in the way in which I leave it to you, then you are as
good a king as I; and if you should enlarge it, you are better than I; and if
you should lose any of it, you are not as good as I.
—King Fernando III of Castile-León to his son Alfonso, c.1252.

The lands granted to Jewish courtiers and settlers in the
wake of the thirteenth-century *reconquista* formed part
of a long-standing tradition in medieval Iberia, where
Jews had owned urban and rural property for centuries
under both Christian and Muslim rule. Jews owned large tracts of land and
whole villages in Muslim al-Andalus during the eleventh century, and had
also bought, owned, and sold land without royal approval in the Christian
territories of old Catalonia and Aragon prior to the thirteenth century.
Thus the proliferation of Jewish landholdings on the frontier in the thirteenth century and the degree to which these properties helped to integrate Jews into the social and economic life of rural Iberia were points of
continuity between periods before and after the thirteenth-century reconquest. In this later period, however, the ability of Jews to sell, alienate, or
inherit such property became increasingly subject to royal approval and
restrictions due to the renewed assertion of royal sovereignty over the
Jews.[1]

---

[1] Alfasi, *Responsa*, no. 131. On Jewish landownership under Muslim rule in general, see
Joseph Rivlin, *Bills and Contracts from Lucena (1020–1025 CE)* [Heb.] (Ramat-Gan, 1994).
For rural Jewish settlements prior to the thirteenth century, see Francisco Ruiz Gómez,
"Juderías y aljamas en el mundo rural en la Castilla medieval," in *Xudeus e conversos na his-
toria*, ed. Carlos Barros (Santiago, 1994), 2:116–120.

Like their northern European counterparts, the Jews of the Iberian kingdoms principally dwelt in urban centers. However, to equate this fact with
their isolation from the world of agriculture and rural landownership is to
misconstrue the nature of urban society in medieval Iberia. The political,
economic and social divisions between larger towns and rural villages were
often ambiguous, a fact which explains why the presence of an essentially
urban population such as the Jews is to be found throughout the rural landscape of thirteenth-century Iberia.

The peasants who made up the majority of settlers during the first
decades of *repoblación* were allotted parcels of land both in the original partitions and in successive, individual grants. These grants were generally characterized by small gardens (*huertas*), or vineyards (*viñas*), that may have con-
sisted of little more than a few trees or vines, and the land beneath them.
Though small, such garden plots were often quite productive, and whether
they were used for personal consumption or market-oriented agriculture
they formed the backbone of peasant economy in and around the urban centers of the frontier.[2] It is thus unlikely that those Jewish settlers who received grants of small orchards or gardens were members of an urban financial and mercantile "class" who held rural property solely as an investment.
To be sure, as we shall see below, many Jews were involved in the acquisition
and sale of lands, both urban and rural, as a form of business enterprise.
Nonetheless, the majority of Jewish settlers were not rich moneylenders
dealing in real estate speculation. Rather, they were more often individuals
of modest means, tilling their own gardens just as their Christian (and Muslim) counterparts did.

We have already seen that during the early stages of Christian colonization the essential structure of land division in southern Iberia frequently
tied urban property to such rural plots. The *libros de repartimiento* record
that a variety of properties were granted to individual Jewish settlers, as well
as to groups of royal officials and Jewish communities, in both the towns of
the frontier and their surrounding districts. Royal concessions of property
made to Jews both during these initial partitions and soon afterwards often
included several parcels of land to be used in a variety of ways. The following example from the Valencian town of Burriana typifies this practice:

[2] David Vassberg, *Land and Society in Golden Age Castile* (Cambridge, 1984), 128–132.

The lord king conceded and gave to Salamon Vidal, the Jew, in the settlement of Burriana, four jovates of land in the *regadío*, and a courtyard upon which to build, and a jovate and a half of land below the main irrigation canal for a vineyard, and a small piece of land for an orchard.[3]

The integral relationship between urban and rural properties meant that even those who lived in cities and derived the majority of their income from urban markets or workshops were not completely alienated from the surrounding countryside. It also indicates that Jews who came to possess urban property in the towns and cities of the frontier did so in a manner similar to their Christian counterparts. Indeed, one of the most significant developments of Iberian (particularly Castilian) society during the high Middle Ages was the rise of a class of urban, non-noble knights, or *caballeros villanos*. This group, which was formed from the upper echelons of the peasant, artisan, and merchant classes, helped populate and develop the burgeoning urban centers of the peninsula. However, while they chose to settle in these towns, they continued to hold land in the surrounding *alfoz* from which they derived a varying portion of their income. In the town and cities of the Crown of Aragon, the *caballeros villanos* had their counterpart in the growing urban patriciate drawn from increasingly prosperous merchant families. In addition to these "urban knights," members of the urban working classes known as *pecheros* also moved easily between town and country, whether by working the land in their municipal *termino* on a seasonal basis, or by owning small plots of land themselves. It is therefore important to note that the position held by urban Jews with regard to landholding did not marginalize them from mainstream society, but rather showed them to have participated in some of the most important social developments of the period.[4]

Though these vineyards, orchards, and other small plots of land were generally for private use, some Jews who held lands within the municipal *termino* did act as landlords in much the same way as did many Christians. In the kingdom of Valencia, the Jewish courtier Aharon Abinaffia was granted ownership of two whole villages, whose inhabitants seem to have been mostly Muslim. Likewise, the Cordoban Jew, Yehudah, appears to have col-

---

[3] ACA, reg. 19, fol. 102. The term *"regadío"* or "irrigated land" refers to the region's prime land that would be used for farming. For Jews owning small plots of land in southern Portugal, see ANTT, *Alcobaça*, m. 3, nos. 7, 28; m. 4, no. 9.

[4] For the development of the *caballeros villanos*, see Teofilo Ruiz, *Crisis and Continuity, Land and Town in Late Medieval Castile* (Philadelphia, 1994), 237–248; (for the *pecheros*, 268–271); and Carmela Pescador, "La Caballería popular en León y Castilla," *Cuadernos de historia de España* 33–34 (1961): 101–238; 35–36 (1962): 56–201; 37–38 (1963): 88–198; and 39–40 (1964): 169–260.

Part I. The Jewish Settler and the Frontier

lected rents from his lands in the same way as any urban *caballero*. In her challenge to Yehudah's right to the land itself, a Christian widow, Doña Pascuala, also laid claim to the rents (*terrazgos*) that she would have collected over the previous ten years if the land had been in her possession.[5] Further indication that Jews acted as landlords in a similar fashion to their Christian counterparts can be seen in the Church's attempt to enforce Jewish payment of taxes on formerly Christian land. Papal letters aimed at forcing Jews to pay the tithe referred to "the possessions which the Jews and Saracens cultivate or which they gave to others to cultivate." Evidence that Jews used non-Jews to work their land can also be seen in a law from the *Siete Partidas* that prohibited Jews from employing Christians as domestic servants, but allowed Jews to engage them as agricultural laborers. In addition to acting as landlords for Christian and Muslim tenants, Jews also acted as urban landlords for other Jews, as can be seen in a letter from 1302 that mentions a Jewish tenant of another Jew in Valencia who had found a treasure in his rented house. Elsewhere in Valencia, a document records that Vives, the son of the deceased courtier Jucef Avenvives, possessed land worked by tenant farmers outside of Játiva that the local *aljama* attempted to seize for debts he owed. The town's bailiff subsequently nullified the seizure on orders from Pedro III, who declared that Vives' tenants could not be responsible for his debts.[6]

JEWISH LANDOWNERSHIP IN RURAL IBERIA

In addition to the possession of gardens and vineyards near the towns of the frontier, Jews also owned farmland in more rural areas. On the Portuguese frontier, there is evidence of Jewish residence and landownership in a number of rural locales, including a region near Obidos that is referred to as the "Valley of the Jews."[7] The Christian custom of using land as a pledge or as repayment of a loan contributed to Jewish acquisition of rural proper-

---

[5] AHPC, Carp. 31, no. 1; Esther Cruces Blancos, "Datos sobre compravenas de tierras en Córdoba tras los primeros años de presencia Castellana (1242–90)," in *Andalucía entre Orietne y Occidente (1236–1492)*, ed. *Emilio Cabrera* (Córdoba, 1988), 225–226. For Abinaffia, see ACA, reg. 37, fol. 93; Burns, "The *Guidaticum*," 106.

[6] BCC, ms. 125, fol. 34r. See also ACA, reg. 199, fol. 34v, and reg. 46, fol. 82, and a similar document directed to the king of Portugal in 1273 in Solomon Grayzel, *The Church and the Jews in the 13th Century* (New York, 1984), 2:120–121, no. 32. For the *Siete Partidas*, see *Las Siete Partidas del rey don Alfonso el Sabio* (Madrid, 1807), 7.24.8.

[7] ANTT, *Alcobaça*, m. 26, no. 3; m. 3, no. 15. See also Pedro Gomes Barbosa, *Documentos Lugares e Homens* (Lisbon, 1991), 111.

ties during this period, and wealthy Jews with connections to the royal court were also actively involved in the lucrative land market that developed in the new territories, obtaining rural tracts through grants or direct purchase. In Córdoba, Jews like Moses d'Argot were often as active in the city's real estate market as they were in the business of credit, and on the Portuguese frontier, the Jewish courtier Guedelha, who succeeded his father, Judah, as the most powerful Jewish figure in the kingdom, owned several farm houses in the Val d' Oliva and in the area of Freilas. These truly elite figures were able to augment their holdings by requesting particular plots in reward for their services to the crown. In 1263, while holding the post of royal bailiff at Saragossa, Judah de la Cavalleria received a donation of irrigated farmland from Jaime I just outside of the city of Valencia. The grant was most likely the result of a request by de la Cavalleria, as the land was surrounded by plots that he already owned, having bought them up over time from the estates of various Christians. In another document the king prohibits anyone from trespassing or dwelling on any of Judah's farms or in any of his buildings without his consent.[8]

A letter from 1272 records an extensive land sale by a Portuguese Jewish couple, Moses and Avizibona, to a Christian settler, João Peres de Aboim. The transaction included farmland, storehouses, vineyards, and olive groves located in Leiria, Bombarral, Torres Vedras, Sintra, Rio de Mouro, Lisbon and Santarem. The appearance of Avizibona on the letter of sale is by no means rare. As was common with Christian families, Jewish women also appear in documents of sale, both with their husbands as well as on their own, usually as widows. One such widow appears in a document from 1304, selling land to a Christian lawyer at Obidos.[9]

Wealthy Jews who received rural property as a royal grant or accepted it as payment of a loan often treated such lands as a form of capital, keeping them only a short while and then selling them. However, some Jews did seem to have been directly involved in rural agriculture. Among the privi-

    [8] González, *Repartimiento de Sevilla*, 2:327–328. For Cordoba, see Manuel Nieto Cumplido, *Corpus Mediaevale Cordubense* (Córdoba, 1978), vol. I, no. 405; for Évora and Freilas, see ANTT, *Chanc. de D. Dinis*, liv. III, fol. 108; Pimenta Ferro, *Os Judeus* (1970 ed.), nos. 13, 18. See also ANTT, *Colleção especial*, caixa 86; *Alcobaça*, 2a incorp., m. 18, no. 406; and *Corp. Rel. Chelas*, m. 8, no. 141. For de la Cavalleria, see ACA, Reg. 12, fols. 103v, 106v; Burns, *Diplomatarium*, nos. 486a, 495a.
    [9] *Livro dos Bens de D. João de Portel*, no. 120; ANTT, *Alcobaça*, m. 24, no. 5. On the subject of Iberian Jewish women owning and inheriting land along with their husbands, see Rivlin, *Bills and Contracts*, 181–182; Elka Klein, "Protecting the Widow and the Orphan," *Mosaic* 14–17 (1993–99): 65–81; and for similar practices among Christians, see *Fuero Real*, bk. 3, tit. 3.

Part I. The Jewish Settler and the Frontier

leges granted to the Jews of Mallorca was the same access to water for irrigation that was granted to the rest of the citizenry. At Burriana, Salomon Vidal was awarded two small parcels of land by the Grand Canal for use as a vineyard and a garden, as well as four jovates of irrigated land. Since the other, smaller, plots of land were to be used as a personal garden and a vineyard, the larger plot located on prime farming land seems to be set aside for market-oriented agriculture. Vidal seems to be typical of many Jewish settlers who did not live by agriculture alone, but who nonetheless did possess some farmland.[10]

Perhaps the greatest confirmation of Jewish participation in agriculture on the frontier comes from a privilege given by Jaime II to those Jews who wished to come to Alicante in order to work in the fields there. The royal grant, given to the Jews of Alicante, stated that

We give and concede to the aforementioned Jewish harvesters of Alicante . . . who come from our sovereignty to the aforementioned places of Alicante in order to harvest there, the same privileges granted to all other inhabitants of the town of Alicante.[11]

Further evidence that Jewish settlers were involved in agriculture is indicated by two royal charters given to the Jews of the kingdom of Valencia in 1261 and 1262. In the first, the Jews of Valencia as well as their successors are granted the right to purchase all manner of lands including fields, vineyards and farms. The second states that all Muslims who make their residence on Jewish lands are exempt from paying the annual poll tax of one besant required of all Muslims. This law also points to an important underlying condition that aided Jewish landownership in the new territories, particularly in the regions conquered by the Crown of Aragon. Throughout medieval Europe, the ancient prohibition against Jews owning Christians slaves usually signaled their exclusion from all but subsistence agriculture. In Iberia, by contrast, the conquests of the thirteenth century left behind a large, and generally rural, Muslim population, giving would-be Jewish landowners a third labor option.[12]

---

[10] ACA, reg. 63, fol. 30; and Régné, *pièces justificatives*, no. XX. On irrigation, see the various studies of Thomas Glick, collected in *Irrigation and Hydraulic Technology, Medieval Spain and its Legacy* (London, 1996). For Burriana, see ACA, reg. 19, fol. 102.

[11] ACA, reg. 195, fol. 120; and Juan Manuel de Estal, *Alicante, de villa a ciudad (1252–1490)* (Alicante, 1990), 210–211.

[12] ACA, Reg. 12, fols. 202v, 44v; Burns, *Diplomatarium*, nos. 366, 393.

Under the Christian monarchs of the thirteenth century, royal dominion over both the Jews and their possessions meant that Jewish lands, houses, and shops were held as a sort of royal tenure. The principal issue with which the Christian kings were concerned was control over their own taxable property, a fact that was routinely demonstrated by prohibitions against Jews selling or otherwise alienating their lands without royal consent.[13] The royal monopoly that the Iberian monarchs held over Jewish taxes did not extend to the other estates of the realm, and the sale of Jewish land to other lords would constitute a royal loss of the revenues to those properties. The crown granted Jews lands in order that they might act as guardians of royal property which might otherwise be acquired by other barons, the Church, or municipal *concejos*. Even those grants made to Jews as a reward for their faithful service to the crown helped to fulfill this objective, so central to royal policy. Thus, a grant of houses in Lisbon made to Salamon Negro in 1301, contained the following admonishment against selling it away from royal control:

And you Solomon and your wife and your successors are not to sell, nor give nor in any way alienate the aforementioned houses nor any part thereof, to any bishop, nor clergymen, nor order, nor to any religious person, nor to any knight, nor lady, nor squire.[14]

While all of the Jews of the Crown of Aragon were required to obtain royal approval in order to sell or alienate land to Christians, Jews were nonetheless allowed to sell their lands among themselves, since such transactions would not alter the ultimate status of the property as belonging to the crown.

Furthermore, no Jew nor Moor shall sell or alienate land that he possesses and which belongs to the crown to any Christian except with the permission and authorization of our bailiff. But if the Jews or Moors

---

[13] In Portugal, Dinis declared the crown's sovereignty over the Jews to be: "tamben os corpos come os averes deles." ANTT, *Chanc. de D. Dinis*, liv. III, fol. 104. For examples of such prohibitions, see Gunnar Tilander, *Los Fueros de Aragón* (Lund, 1937), law no. 274; José Luis Lacruz Berdejo, "Fueros de Aragon hasta 1265," *Anuario de Derecho Aragonés* 2 (1945): 327.

[14] ANTT, *Chanc. de D. Dinis*, liv. III, fol. 21v. See also ANTT, *Chanc. de D. Dinis*, liv. II, fol. 120v. For similar cases in Valencia, see ACA, reg. 229, fol. 247; and reg. 83, fol. 69v.

make sales and purchases among themselves, one with another, they may well do so without the permission of our bailiff.[15]

A reiteration of this law can be seen in a case from Murviedro, where Jucef Avençaprut was given three jovates of land near the main road of the town with the right to alienate them to anyone except clerics, nobles, or municipalities. In Castile, the monarchy proved equally reticent to allow Jewish property to be sold out of royal control. In 1278, Alfonso X received a formal complaint from the *cabildo* of Córdoba that stated that Moses d'Argot had sold to them some stores and a bodega that, they later determined, were not his to sell. The *cabildo* had purchased the buildings that stood at the entrance to the *judería* two years earlier, in celebration of the anniversary of Córdoba's bishop. They were soon presented with a royal letter that indicated that these properties did not belong to d'Argot, but rather to the entire Jewish community of Córdoba, to whom they had been granted by the crown. Despite the *cabildo*'s claim that it had purchased the stores before they were granted to the *aljama*, the king ordered that d'Argot repay the *cabildo* its money, and that the *aljama* retain ownership of the property.[16]

Restrictive conditions regarding the resale of Jewish land were only one of several ramifications that resulted from an increase in royal control over Jewish property over the course of the twelfth and thirteenth centuries. Iberian monarchs also maintained the right to repossess Jewish land at will in order to grant it to another party. Such instances were not uncommon throughout the peninsula, though the king in question usually tried to compensate Jewish landholders for their loss. This was the case in 1158, when the newly crowned Sancho III of Castile gave five *yugadas* of land to the Jewish courtier Boniuda who had served as *almoxarife* to his father, Alfonso VII. The land, given permanently to Boniuda and his descendants, was in recompense for the village of Ciruelos near Ocaña, which Boniuda had possessed but which Sancho had given away to the Order of Calatrava. Similarly, the land registers record a number of instances in which the king assigned the same plot of land to different people.[17]

As in the case of the Castilian *almoxarife* Boniuda and the Portuguese courtier Salamon Negro, some Jews were able to secure grants that gave them ownership of land in perpetuity. Yet despite these and similar ex-

<hr />

[15] Antonio Gargallo Moya, ed., *Los Fueros de Aragón* (Saragossa, 1992), bk. 8, tit. 307, p. 159.

[16] For Avençaprut see ACA, reg. 19, fol. 65rv. For d'Argot see BCC, ms. 125, fol. 33 and ACC, caja F, no. 386 and caja G, nos. 147–148.

[17] AHN, Clero, c. 3017/9; pub. in Baer, *Juden*, vol. 2, no. 34, Pilar León Tello, *Judíos de Toledo* (Madrid, 1979), vol. 1, no. 1.

amples, the practice of granting property to Jews and their descendants was not standard, and Jewish land was not necessarily inherited by the following generation. In cases where the inheritance was no more than a house or other small amounts of urban property, the matter was usually resolved under the auspices of the Jewish community. However, in the case of wealthy Jews who left large amounts of land upon their death, the property often reverted back to the crown until the proper heirs could be determined.[18]

In Portugal, special exemption was needed for Jews to be allowed to pass on property received as a royal grant to their own descendants. A Jewish couple in Lisbon were given a house with the added permission that they may leave it to whomever they choose. Without such permission, the crown was free to grant the property of deceased Jews to other favorites, as is illustrated by a grant of land and several houses formerly owned by Jews in Lisbon to Manuel Pezagno, a Genoese merchant. In some cases, however, the crown assumed control of Jewish estates in order to safeguard the inheritance of Jewish minors. After the death of Astruc de Gerona, a Jewish settler in Murviedro, Alfonso III of Aragon ordered that the inheritance he had left to his daughter and nephew be protected against seizure. Similarly, when the sons of the royal *alfaquim*, Aaron, lost a suit over land their father had possessed at Játiva, the king made amends to the would-be heirs by granting them a plot of land in the same town as compensation for their loss. Iberian monarchs, who generally treated the Jews as their personal financial reserves, had an interest in rewarding them and keeping them prosperous. This policy generally applied to landownership as it did to other privileges and exemptions. Nonetheless, Jewish property, especially Jewish inheritance that owed its origins to a royal grant, was always at the mercy of kings who often found themselves financially overextended.[19]

Additions or emendations to Jewish property, such as the construction of a doorway or a bath, were also subject to royal approval, and in Valencia, a Jew seeking to construct a bridge between two of his houses had to first obtain

---

[18] See also the case of a Jewish settler who received houses owned by the crown in the *judiaria* of Évora along with "his wife and all his heirs." ANTT, *Chanc. de D. Dinis*, liv. II, fol. 120v; and Pimenta Ferro, *Os Judeus*, (1st ed.), no. 3. For royal involvement in cases regarding the inheritance of wealthy Jews in the Crown of Aragon, see Yom Tov Assis, *The Golden Age of Aragonese Jewry* (London, 1997), 274–278. For the *kahal* resolving disputes over the inheritance of urban property in Valencia and Mallorca, see Adret 2:385, and 3:54, respectively.

[19] João Martins da Silva Marques ed., *Descobrimentos Portugueses*, (Lisbon, 1944), vol. I, no. 53. For Pezgano, see ANTT, Gaveta 3, M.1, no. 7; for Astruc de Gerona, see ACA, reg. 63, fol. 39v; Robert I. Burns, *Jews in the Notarial Culture: Latinate Wills in Mediterranean Spain, 1250–1350* (Berkeley, 1996), no. 28; for the sons of Aaron the *alfaquim* see ACA, Reg. 12, fol. 92v; Burns, *Diplomatarium*, no. 482a.

Part I. The Jewish Settler and the Frontier

royal permission. As with their houses, the nature of Jewish property owner-ship also varied with respect to the shops they possessed in these towns. Laws governing the Jews of Játiva and the city of Valencia held that they could have their houses, but not their shops, seized for nonpayment of taxes.[20]

In cases where a Jew was found guilty of treason against the king, or other capital offenses, the latter would assert his right over the Jew's land, and it would automatically be made forfeit. Perhaps the most famous of such in-stances is that of the Castilian courtier Çag de la Maleha, whose vast hold-ings were confiscated by Alfonso X when the former diverted royal funds to the rebellious Infante (Prince) Sancho. Jews convicted of murder would also have their property seized by the crown. In 1258, the buildings that the Va-lencian Jew al-Mubarak al-Ma'dani had formerly held in Alcira were auc-tioned off by the crown to Pere Barceló, a Christian resident of the town. The property had become forfeit when al-Ma'dani was found guilty of mur-dering a Muslim, and executed.[21]

Finally, the crown also repossessed frontier lands if their Jewish owners failed to work them, a fact attested to by several *libros de repartimiento*. In most cases, Jews who sought to hold land on the frontier were required to see that it did not lie idle, as was also the case with Christians. Jewish settlers were expected to work the lands they owned, and in some cases, such as at Elche, Jews needed a special dispensation in order to own land without in-habiting it themselves.[22]

JEWISH LANDOWNERSHIP AND THE
ECCLESIASTICAL TITHE

The nature of Jewish landownership during the thirteenth century is fur-ther reflected in the contentious issue of Jewish payment of *diezmos*, or tithes. The *diezmo* was levied upon all land owned by Christians, and was one of the principal sources of income for the medieval Church. While tithes were also collected on a variety of other goods, such as bread and

[20] Jerome Lee Shneidman, "Protection of Aragonese Jewry in the Thirteenth Cen-tury," *Historia Judaica* 1 (1962): 56–57; ACA, reg. 20, fol. 325v; ACA, reg, 196, fol. 172.
[21] Norman Roth, "Two Jewish Courtiers of Alfonso X Called Zag (Isaac)," *Sefarad* 43 (1983): 75–85. For a similar case on the Aragonese frontier, see ACA, reg. 256, fol. 36. For al-Ma'dani, see ACA, Reg. 10, fols. 55, 66bis rv; Burns, *Diplomatarium*, nos. 118a, 131.
[22] ACA, reg. 19, fol. 85; José Hinojosa Montalvo, "Bosquejo histórico de los judíos en tierras alicantinas durante la baja edad media," in *Actes Ir. Colloqui d'historia dels Jueus a la Corona d'Aragó* (Lérida, 1989): 212–213.

wine, it was the tithe on land that became the focal point of tensions between the Jews, the crown, and the Church. Since they stood outside of the Christian community, Jews were not automatically required to pay this tithe on land they acquired by purchase, royal grant, or as payment of a debt. However, as Jewish landownership became more common, the Spanish Church and, through it, the papacy, became increasingly alarmed at the potential loss of revenues on these formerly Christian lands. In a steady series of complaints to the kings of Portugal, Castile-León, and the Crown of Aragon, the papacy and bishops from throughout the peninsula demanded that the Jews be forced to pay tithes to their local church on any land they obtained from Christians.[23]

As a rule, these monarchs wrote letters ordering the Jews to comply with the Church's demands. However, the persistence of this issue throughout this period suggests that most kings were not particularly rigorous in their enforcement of this principle. This lack of royal zeal is understandable when one considers that the property in question, and the taxes to be paid on it, ultimately belonged to the king. Furthermore, these monarchs often relied on Jewish capital as a source of extraordinary revenue needed to finance military campaigns and other royal expenses. Thus, any taxes paid out to the Church would, in turn, diminish the Jews' capacity to come up with extra funds for the crown. As a result of this conflict over taxable land, the issue of Jewish payment of the *diezmo* became a bitter and long-running dispute between the Church and the various Iberian monarchies, forming part of the larger battle over valuable revenues and sovereignty over the Jews.[24]

The assertion of a renewed ecclesiastical program aimed at the restriction of Jewish influence and status is usually attributed to the outcome of the Fourth Lateran Council. Yet in the Iberian Peninsula, papal efforts to limit landownership among Jews, and to compel them to pay the *diezmo*, began even prior to 1215. In 1205, Innocent III wrote to Alfonso VIII of Castile to admonish him for not enforcing the Jewish payment of the tithe, and allowing the Jews to continue to acquire more land.

And although in the matter of your not allowing the Jews and Saracens of your kingdom to be compelled to pay the tithe from their possession we have already had apostolic letters sent to you, you nevertheless have not only refused to have them compelled to pay the tithe, but have even granted them greater rights in buying of more extensive possessions.

[23] Grayzel, *Church and the Jews*, nos. 21, 31, 33, 36, 37.
[24] Peter Linehan, "The 'Gravamina' of the Castilian Church in 1262–3," *English Historical Review* 85 (1970): 730–754; Robert I. Burns, "A Mediaeval Income Tax: The Tithe in the Thirteenth-Century Kingdom of Valencia," *Speculum* 41 (1966): 438–452.

Part I. The Jewish Settler and the Frontier

Thus while the Synagogue grows in power the Church becomes weaker, and the handmaid is openly preferred.

Ecclesiastical complaints of dishonor notwithstanding, there was a general lack of royal enthusiasm for enforcing this law, an attitude which produced a great deal of frustration and ill will both in Rome and among the local clergy. These sentiments would soon lead the same pope to order the bishop of Toledo to demand that Jews be separated from all contact with Christians until they agreed to pay the tithe.

By removing from them all communication with Christians, and this without any chance of appeal, you compel the Jews of those parts to pay in its entirety the tithe from those possessions which they had either bought or had by some other legal means acquired from Christians, and from which possessions this dean and Chapter used to get the tithe.[25]

Another papal letter written ten years later added the further detail that this separation was to be maintained "especially in matters of commerce."[26] Yet the struggle over Jewish tithes, the papacy's threats and admonishments carried relatively little weight. Innocent's advice to the Toledan Church that it enforce separation "without any chance of appeal" would have been received with a measure of exasperation considering the close relationship between the Jews and the crown, and the frequency with which the former appealed nearly all non-royal legislation. Indeed, Innocent's attempt at enforcing payment met with little success in Castile, and Honorius III was forced to make explicit the threat of excommunication of any Christians who did not observe this separation. Not to be deterred, Castilian Jews attempted to avoid the issue by destroying houses they had acquired from Christians, and building new ones.

Know that it has reached our ears that the Jews who dwell in your Province [Toledo] exert themselves by means of subterfuges, to get around the decree of the General Council . . . by building new houses, for which they refuse to answer, in accordance with the said decree, to the churches in whose parishes the houses are constructed.[27]

The Church's struggle to see that Jews paid the required *diezmo* was not limited to the frontier. In the early years of his reign, Alfonso VIII had to

[25] Grayzel, *Church and the Jews*, nos. 17 and 21.
[26] Ibid., no. 31, pp. 142–143.
[27] Ibid., nos. 33, 36. For the quotation, see ibid., no. 37.

settle a dispute over Jewish payment of tithes to the bishop of Calahorra in the Rioja region. In 1177 and again in 1285, the issue surfaced in the northern Castilian centers of Valladolid and Burgos, and in 1175, the question of Jewish tithes was raised in the Aragonese capital of Saragossa.[28] However, it was Castile's new territory in Andalusia, and in particular the bishoprics of Córdoba and Seville, which became the focal points of much of the conflict during the thirteenth century. In 1239, just three years after the conquest of Córdoba, Pope Gregory IX wrote to the bishops of Córdoba and Baeza ordering that they force Jews there to pay tithes on land formerly owned by Christians. In a letter sent the same day, the pope also intimated that, aside from the Jews' legal acquisition of Christian land referred to in the letters of his predecessors, they may also be involved in obtaining land through deception while Christians were away at war.[29]

In March of 1250, Pope Innocent IV sent letters to Córdoba and Jaén stating that, due to complaints from the *cabildo* in Córdoba, they should pressure Moses de Alcaraz, Yn Huda Albiunez, Jucef Acedo and all other Jews to pay their tithes. A few months later, a letter from the papal legate Gil Torres to the ecclesiastic and secular officials at Córdoba reiterated that both Jews and Muslims "must pay tithes in full to the churches to which they correspond, as would Christians if they had cultivated them."[30] Yet it took four years before Alfonso X added his own support to Jewish payment of tithes, ordering that Jews and Muslims were not only required to pay taxes to Cordoban churches on rural land, but also on any houses they acquired within the city, stating:

> If they [the Jews and Muslims] should obtain some houses from the Christians, from now on they should give that tribute which the Christians would have paid for the houses if they had owned them, and if they bought houses outside of [their] neighborhood, they should have

[28] Ildelfonso Rodriguez de Lama, *Colección diplomática medieval de la Rioja* (Logroño, 1989), vol. 2, no. 206; Julio González, *El Reino de Castilla en la época de Alfonso VIII* (Madrid, 1960), no. 287. For Burgos, see Baer, *Juden*, vol. 2, no. 88. For Saragossa, see Angel Canellas López, *Colección diplomática del concejo de Zaragoza* (Saragossa, 1972), vol. 1, nos. 18–19, 31, 61.

[29] In general, see Joaquim Moya Ulldemolins, "El Diezmo eclesiastico en el obispado de Córdoba," *Axerquia* 13 (1985): 73–103; and the bibliography presented on 73. Gregory's letter to Córdoba and Baeza is in ACJ, *Códice gótico*, fols. 2v–3; BCC, ms. 125, fol. 3r; Grayzel, *Church and the Jews*, vol. 1, no. 99.

[30] BCC, ms. 125, fols. 3v and 34. It is unclear as to why the pope chose to single out these three Jews, (a rarity in legislation concerning Jewish tithes), but it is probable that they were among the largest Jewish landholders in Córdoba.

Part I. The Jewish Settler and the Frontier

the custom of giving tribute to the Church just as those [Christians] did when they owned them.[31]

Alfonso extended this law to the bishopric of Seville the following year. It is noteworthy that the king's letter refers only to those houses obtained "outside of [their] neighborhood" (*fuera del barrio*), indicating that Jewish property in the *judería* itself was exempt from tithes, ostensibly because the crown was the true owner of the land. A reiteration of this principle can be seen in the Crown of Aragon, where a contemporary legal compilation noted that Jews and Muslims where expected to pay a tithe on land obtained from Christians, but not on land which had never belonged to Christians.[32]

In Seville, the local cathedral chapter sought to extend the concept of Jewish tribute beyond the ownership of urban or rural land. Alfonso X granted the *cabildo* and archbishop the right to collect the annual sum of fifteen *dineros* from any Jews who did not have enough property on which to pay tithes.

Know that the archbishop and deacon and the *cabildo* of the Church of the aforementioned city of Seville complained to us and said that they had the custom to collect *las [c]uartas* annually from all the Moors and Jews that dwell outside of the *judería* and do not have possessions upon which to pay tithes, from whom they say they are to take fifteen *dineros* according to what they [archbishop and *cabildo*] would receive from Christians had they been the ones to dwell there.[33]

Payment of a special tax, *la cuarta*, by those Jews who did not have sufficient property upon which to pay tithes was later reiterated in 1336 in a document by Alfonso XI.[34] In addition to these taxes on Jewish property, the Church of Seville was also granted the right to collect a general poll tax of thirty *dineros* annually from each member of the city's Jewish community. The Jews of Seville resisted paying this tax throughout the second half of the thirteenth century, leading to repeated petitions to the crown on behalf of

[31] ACC, caja P. fol. 76, and BCC, ms. 125, 8r.
[32] ACS, caja 5, no. 48; and González Jimenez, *Diplomatario andaluz*, no. 158. The copy of this letter published by González Jiménez reads "*banno*," or "bath" rather than "*barrio*," meaning neighborhood or urban district. However, it is clear that the word should read "*barrio*," which is the way it appears in the resubmission of the same law the following year. See also Gargallo Moya, *Fueros de Aragon*, 28.
[33] ACS, caja 6, 2/5.
[34] ACS, sección IX, caja 182, no. 1.

the city's Church. An early complaint is recorded in a letter sent by Alfonso X to the elders of the Jewish community, dating from 1256.

Let it be known that the *cabildo* of the church of Santa Maria of Seville has sent to me the complaint that you do not want to give to them the thirty *dineros* which you are supposed to give annually, just as the Jews of Toledo give to the church of Toledo.[35]

Though the king went on to order the payment of the annual tax, the issue was far from settled. Under his successor, Sancho IV, the Jews appear to have been successful in reducing the tax from thirty to twelve *dineros* per person, and that even this amount was further limited to those Jews who possessed property.

The aforementioned *aljama* obtained a letter from our chancellery in which we ordered that the Jews were not required to pay but twelve *dineros* each, and that this amount was only to be paid by those who owned property for the next nineteen years, because they said that this was the custom in the time of the King Don Sancho my grandfather, may God forgive him [his sins]. And about this issue our canon of Seville, Lope Martinez, came before us . . . saying that the letter [of the Jews] silenced the truth, by reason that the Church of Seville always had the [same] privileges of the Church of Toledo.

As was often the case, however, possession of a royal writ was no guarantee that the crown would uphold a certain privilege, especially in cases such as this, in which a Christian authority produced a counter privilege. Alfonso XI, before whom this case appeared, brought an end to the long-standing debate with the following decisive ruling in favor of Seville's *cabildo*.

From now on at no time shall one of our letters, which may be shown to you [and] which is contrary to this, impede the aforementioned archbishop and deacon and *cabildo* . . . the collection of the aforementioned thirty *dineros* of the usual money that each of the said Jews must pay annually according to the collection of times past.[36]

---

[35] ACS, caja 6, no. 2/1; and González Jiménez, *Diplomatario andaluz*, no. 187. The issue is dealt with in a series of documents in caja 6, listed as 2/1–12.

[36] ACS, caja 6, no. 2/3.

Part I. The Jewish Settler and the Frontier

If the churches of Andalusia were frustrated by an inability to enforce Jewish payment of the *diezmo* even with royal support, their counterparts in Valencia lacked even this last, essential, tool. There is evidence from the Crown of Aragon that, in the latter half of the thirteenth century, the monarchy openly denied the Church the right to collect tithes from Jewish land. A letter from 1279 notes that the Jewish *aljama* of Murviedro had complained to the king that the bailiff of the bishop of Valencia was collecting tithes from them on formerly Christian lands. The Jews pointed out that they should not be obliged to pay the tithe, as it had never been their custom to do so. In his response, Pedro III sides with the Jews, telling his bailiff at Murviedro not to permit the bishop's bailiff to continue his collection.[37] Here, the struggle between crown and Church can be seen more clearly, with the Jews benefiting from their protective relationship with the former.

Royal enforcement of Jewish tithing was equally ambivalent in the kingdom of Portugal. In 1265, Pope Clement IV sent a letter to Afonso III in order to address a number of complaints he had received from members of the Portuguese clergy, including that the king had been permitting them to be released from having to pay the tithe. His successor, Pope Gregory X, also wrote to Afonso, cataloging many of the same complaints of royal laxity in implementing canon law regarding the Jews. The last in the list of accusations was that the king did not compel Jews or Muslims to pay "the tithes or first fruits" from possessions which they had acquired from Christians either by way of purchase or as the result of an unpaid debt. Despite such complaints, or perhaps in response to them, there is evidence that the Church did receive at least partial support in this matter from Afonso III. It was this king who enforced Jewish tithing in the diocese of Silves in the Algarve, a policy later continued there by his successors. Afonso's son, Dinis, also took steps to compel Jewish payment of the tithe throughout Portugal by writs issued in 1289 and again in 1309. Nonetheless, the repetition of such decrees, here as in the rest of the peninsula, seems to indicate that Jews continued to resist paying tribute to local churches.[38]

In his *Social and Religious History of the Jews*, Salo Baron remarked that the issue of ecclesiastical tithes remained a point of contention between reli-

---

[37] ACA, reg. 41, fol. 98.
[38] Grayzel, *Church and the Jews*, vol. 2, nos. 23, 32. On the tensions between Afonso III and the papacy, see Antonio García y García, *Estudos sobre la canonística portuguesa medieval* (Madrid, 1976), 222–225; Fortunato de Almeida, *História da Igreja em Portugal* (Coimbra, 1910), 1:210.

gious and secular authorities throughout the eleventh and twelfth centuries, but that: "After, 1215, it seems to have been adjusted more or less to the satisfaction of the Church, notwithstanding the ensuing diminution of the Jews' taxable property available to the king." He goes on to note that, despite this rapprochement, "the Jews, understandably, continued to resist a tax which they considered a direct contribution to the support of an alien faith." These statements underestimate the protracted struggle between the Church and the various Iberian monarchs that took place over the course of the thirteenth century, and misinterpret the motivation behind Jewish resistance. As the preceding pages have attempted to demonstrate, ecclesiastical "satisfaction" with royal enforcement of the tithe was only achieved after several decades of pressure on the part of several popes and local bishops from throughout the peninsula. Furthermore, Iberian Jewry did not see the Church in purely theological terms as the representation of "an alien faith." On the contrary, medieval Spanish and Portuguese Jews displayed an enduring willingness to do business with the Church, including entering into the employ of their local bishops, monasteries, or crusading orders. Rather, Jewish resistance to paying the ecclesiastical tithe seems to have had a much more pragmatic origin, namely, the desire to avoid taxation whenever possible. Indeed, the argument for a more secular motivation is buttressed by the fact the Jews were not alone in their attempts to avoid ecclesiastical taxation. As it has been clearly demonstrated, the Iberian Church encountered similar resistance during this period from many Christians who, presumably, had no particular ideological problem with respect to supporting the Christian faith.[39]

One of the archetypal characteristics of medieval Jewry has always been its identification as an essentially "urban" community. Yet despite the growing scholarship on medieval cities and their complex relationship with the surrounding countryside, our understanding of what being an "urban" population meant to medieval Jews has remained relatively undeveloped and imprecise. A closer look at the nature of Jewish landownership on the Iberian frontier presents a portrait of an urban community that maintained close ties to rural land, a position that subsequently aided their integration into the socioeconomic fabric of frontier society.

[39] Baron, *SRHJ*, 10:355 n. 3. At the *Cortes* of Santarem in 1331, there were still complaints of Jews and Muslims who bought land. Pimenta Ferro Tavares, *Os Judeus* (2nd ed., 2000), 113. For Christian resistance, see José Manuel Nieto Soria, "La conflictividad en torno al diezmo en los comienzos de la crisis bajomedieval Castellana, *1230–1315*," *Anuario de Estudios Medievales* 14 (1984): 215–216; Burns, "A Mediaeval Income Tax," 439.

Part I. The Jewish Settler and the Frontier

Indeed, one of the most striking characteristics of Jewish landownership in the new territories is that it appears to have been relatively unexceptional. Not only were Iberian Jews permitted to own land, but the types of lands owned by Jews, as well as the social and economic status which they derived from these properties, closely paralleled those of other urban groups on the frontier. Under Muslim rule, urban property had been tied to gardens, vineyards and orchards located outside the towns' walls, and the transition to Christian rule did little to alter this basic urban landscape. It was thus commonplace that Jews who settled the cities of southern Iberia were also involved in the cultivation of small plots of land, and came to own a variety of urban and rural properties in much the same way as other settlers. The availability in some regions of a large Muslim labor force even allowed Jews to act as landlords in a style which mirrored that of Christian urban patriciate. Additionally, some Jewish settlers possessed larger tracts of farmland beyond the municipal *termino* while others participated directly in the exploitation of rural farmland as did their Christian and Muslim counterparts.

The struggle over Jewish payment of the ecclesiastical tithe is yet another area in which the Jewish experience mirrored that of other groups. Papal indignation regarding the Iberian churches' inability to collect the *diezmo* was not confined to the Jewish community, since Muslims and even Christians were often remiss in their payments. Rather, it was part of a larger frustration of ecclesiastical weakness throughout the peninsula that was made more acute by the general reluctance of Iberian kings to effectively and consistently protect the rights of the Church.

Jewish landownership on the Iberian frontier was thus an extension of the Jews' unique social and legal relationship to the crown, a relationship which generally protected the former from extraordinary taxation by the Church and their local municipalities. Iberian monarchs would continue to defend the Jews' right to own land in the face of mounting ecclesiastical and municipal opposition, while closely controlling Jewish property that they would confiscate, protect, or redistribute at their pleasure. Jews with connections to the royal court continued to be those who benefited most from such royal control, and the largest parcels of Jewish land on the frontier were granted to the wealthiest and most powerful Jews as a reward for their services. Yet, as conquest passed into colonization, many more Jewish settlers would come to possess both urban and rural land through a variety of means, and landownership would remain an integral part of Jewish social and economic life throughout this period and beyond. At the Castilian *Cortes* held at Alcalá de Henares in 1348, Alfonso XI explained that the Jews would continue to be allowed to own land:

Because it is our desire that the Jews remain in our dominion, as is commanded by the holy Church, since they might still turn to our faith and be saved as prophesied, and so that they might have sustenance and a way to live and flourish in our dominion, we order that they may possess and buy land for themselves and their heirs in all the cities and towns or our realm.[40]

[40] *Cortes* of Alcalá de Henares of 1348, chap. 57; Manuel Colmeiro, ed., *Cortes de los antiguos reinos de León y de Castilla* (Madrid, 1861), 1:533.

CHAPTER THREE
MONEYLENDING AND BEYOND
Jews in the Economic Life of the Frontier

> The burgher told the Hebrew his business, "Sir, I believe that you indeed
> know my situation; I would like very much to obtain a loan from you,
> since I never thought I would see myself in this predicament."
> —Gonzalo de Berceo, *The Miracles of Our lady*

Our discussion of the Jewish experience in the Iberian reconquest began with the observation that the Jews have traditionally been seen as having no significant role in the grand martial drama by which the national identities of Spain and Portugal were forged. If, however, there exists one image that has come to symbolize Jewish involvement in the *reconquista*, it is that of the Jewish moneylender, profiting from the great contest of arms without ever becoming directly involved. This depiction of Iberian Jews as a sort of necessary, if reviled, feature of the business of crusade and conquest has its origins in contemporary literature and folklore, particularly in the figures of the avaricious Jewish moneylenders Raquel and Vidas in the grand epic poem of the *reconquista*, *The Song of the Cid*. In recent decades, scholars have begun to move beyond the dominant cliché that medieval Jews represented something of a distinct social "class" set apart from the greater Christian milieu in terms of economic activity and faith. Unfortunately, this older view has yet to be replaced by a new understanding of the texture of Hispano-Jewish economy during the period of *repoblación*. It is to this end that the following chapter will be dedicated.[1]

For the individual Jew, the frontier created by Christian expansion in the late twelfth and early thirteenth centuries also represented a new frontier of economic opportunities. Drawn to the new territories by royal land grants, tax exemptions, and guarantees of free travel, Jewish settlers became rapidly

---

[1] For the most comprehensive, if somewhat de-contextualized study of Jewish economy during this period Yom Tov Assis, *Jewish Economy in the Medieval Crown of Aragon* (Leiden, 1997).

[55]

engaged in a wide range of occupations. Indeed, their participation in the economic life of the developing towns and cities of the frontier was the principal vehicle through which they became integrated into Iberian society of the thirteenth century.

MONEYLENDING

Negative literary portrayals notwithstanding, Christian association of Jews with the business of credit reflects a certain social reality. Like their co-religionists throughout medieval Europe, Iberian Jews were actively involved in moneylending, and by the twelfth century had become almost synonymous with the profession in the eyes of their Christian neighbors. Thus, though the Jews of the frontier participated in a variety of occupations, it was with the business of credit that they were most readily identified in the popular Christian imagination. This association is also reflected in the municipal *fueros* of the period, which treated Jewish loans to Christians as the primary point of interaction between the two groups. In the charters belonging to the family of Cuenca-Teruel, as well as those granted by Afonso II of Portugal, Jews were forbidden to sell lands given to them by Christians as pledges. The *fuero* of Cuenca notes: "If a Jew puts the sureties of a Christian on sale, and this can be proved in the royal marketplace or outside it, he should return double the sureties." Similarly, Christians were also prohibited from selling or alienating any land that they had given as a pledge until they had paid the amount owed to their Jewish creditors.[2]

Throughout the late thirteenth and early fourteenth centuries, Jewish lenders played as important a role in the developing towns and villages of the frontier as they had in their former communities of the interior, and their contributions to the stabilization of the local economy helped to expand their civic status. So important were these Jewish lenders to the economic well-being of Murcia during the period in which the region was under Aragonese rule that Jaime II ordered that the brothers Moses Juceff and Albolazar be afforded the same rights and protection as Christian citizens of their town. In addition to collecting on their own loans, the Portuguese Jews also performed that service for the crown. A letter from 1276

---

[2] James F. Powers, ed., *The Code of Cuenca* (Philadelphia, 2000), chap. 29, rub. 21. For a similar situation in Portugal, see *PMH, Leges*, 232. On the practice of Jewish moneylenders receiving pledges see Haym Soloveitchik, "Pawnbroking, A Study in *Ribbit* and of the Halakah in Exile," in *Proceedings of the American Academy for Jewish Research* 38–39 (1970–71): 203–268.

Part I. The Jewish Settler and the Frontier

lists a Jewish official from Lisbon as being charged with the collection of a loan made by the king to the crusading Order of Avis. The loan had been made years earlier in the form of grain and was given to the Order to help sustain their men at the castle of Albufeira.[3]

The subject of Jewish credit also became the greatest bone of contention between Jews and local Christian authorities, both ecclesiastical and municipal, who raised the issue at nearly every meeting of the *Cortes* during this period. Throughout the thirteenth century, representatives of the Castilian municipalities lodged repeated complaints that Christians suffered numerous financial abuses and deceptions at the hands of these Jewish tax collectors and repeatedly petitioned the crown for their removal.[4] In response to such pressure, Iberian kings did little more than reissue standard regulations regarding the rate of interest allowed to Jewish moneylenders. In Castile, the accepted rate of interest varied from one municipality to another, but in 1258 the *Cortes* of Valladolid set the limit and 33.33 percent annually, a rate that was generally accepted at later *Cortes* and in the royal legal codes of the thirteenth and fourteenth century. In the Crown of Aragon, Jaime I fixed the rate of interest for Jewish loans at 20 percent in 1228, a level that was later reiterated by the *furs* of Valencia. Nonetheless, the Aragonese municipalities frequently complained that Jewish moneylenders exceeded the legally mandated rate, and formal protests to this effect were lodged in subsequent meetings of the *Cortes*.[5] Such complaints regarding Jewish moneylenders had little impact on royal policy, despite the strident objections raised by the Church. When the bishop of Tortosa began an inquest into Jewish moneylending in that city, Jaime II warned him that the matter was out of his jurisdiction. Similarly, the ban on usury issued at the Council of Zamora in 1313 was ignored by the Castilian crown, as was most ecclesiastical legislation regarding the Jews of this period.[6]

---

[3] ACA, reg. 340, fol. 276r; Juan Manuel del Estal, *El Reino de Murica bajo la soberanía de Aragon* (Alicante, 1985), nos. 127–128. The town in question is Mula. For the Order of Avis, see ANTT, *Ordem de Avis*, no. 188.

[4] See the *Cortes* held at Haro in 1288, in Colmerio, *Cortes de los antiguos reinos*, vol. 1, tit. 21, pp. 104–105; Valladolid, 1293, ibid., tit. 9, p. 110; Valladolid, 1295, ibid., tit. 5, p. 131; Burgos, 1301, ibid., tit. 16, p. 149; Zamora, 1301, ibid., tit. 14, p. 155; Medina, 1302, ibid., tit. 5, p. 163. Also see the *Fuero Real*, 4:2.6.

[5] The restriction of Jewish credit was one of a number of statutes regarding the Jews that were promulgated at this session of the Catalan *Corts*. See Manuel Dualde Serrano, ed., *Fori antiqui valentiae* (Madrid, 1967), rub. lxvii, tit. I, p. 99; and the *Cortes* held at Gerona, in 1241, Lérida in 1300; and Saragossa, in 1301.

[6] ACA, *Cartas Reales*, Jaime II, caja 7, no. 999; and José Manuel Nieto Soria, "Los judíos como conflicto jurisdiccional entre monarquía e iglesia en la Castilla de fines del siglo XIII: su causistica," in *Actas del II congreso internacional, Encuentro de las tres culturas* (Toledo, 1985), 251.

Royal controls on the rate of interest notwithstanding, the long process of collecting on debts made the system vulnerable to abuses from lender and borrower alike. In Valencia, the Jewish settler Jahuda Azaron conspired with a Christian notary to register a loan to a Christian of the city that was never actually made. The two had expected the "debtor" to repay the bogus loan, rather than spend the time and money on a lawsuit. Conversely, Christian borrowers would often refuse to repay their debts until forced to do so and could thus effectively obtain a long-term loan at the much lower rate of a short-term loan. For their part, Jewish communal leaders were sensitive to the possibility that charging interest higher than the normal amount might incur the wrath of Christian debtors, but they were no more effective in preventing such abuses than their Christian counterparts.[7]

In an attempt to bring order to the contentious financial dealings between the Jews and Christians of his realm, King Dinis of Portugal decreed that all contracts between members of the two groups would have to be witnessed by two Christian officials, an *alvazil* and a *tabelion*. However, like so many royal reforms of the period, the king's bureaucratic solution proved impractical and equally subject to corruption. The following year, representatives of the Jewish community of Santarem complained that this policy was unfair and prevented them from collecting on debts, as they were never able to find the two officials in town at the same time. In addition to providing a loophole for Christian debtors, the necessity of having both officials present for all transactions also prevented both parties from establishing new loans, leading the Jews to protest that "now they say that whenever they want to make a contract with a Christian that they cannot."[8]

Throughout medieval Europe, high rates of interest and a nearly perennial shortage of liquid capital were constant hindrances to borrowers' ability to repay their loans. In addition to the many natural obstacles faced by an agricultural society, persistent warfare and raiding also exhausted capital, destroyed resources, and generally impeded economic productivity. On the Iberian frontier, the abandonment of agricultural property by the retreating Muslim population added to the economic instability caused by the battles

---

[7] The case of Jahuda Azaron is cited by Elena Lourie, "Complicidad criminal: un aspecto insolito de convivencia Judeo-cristiana," in eadea, *Crusade and Colonisation* (Brookfield, VT, 1990), 94. See also Nina Melechen, "Loans, Land and Jewish-Christian Relations in the Archdiocese of Toledo," in *Iberia and the Mediterranean World of the Middle Ages*, ed. Larry Simon (Leiden, 1995), 198–199; and Adret, 5:183. For the attitude toward excessive interest held by Jewish moralists of the period, see Baer, *History*, 1:251.

[8] Pimenta Ferro Tavares, *Os Judeus*, 2nd ed., 82, 83. The *alvazil* was a royal magistrate, and the *tabelion* was a keeper of accounts, or financial representative.

of the reconquest and the internecine fighting among Christian lords. When the Crown of Aragon took control of a portion of the kingdom of Murcia from Castile toward the end of the thirteenth century, the process exacerbated the already fragile economic situation in that frontier region. At Orihuela, the inability of the general populace to repay loans made by both Christians and Jews prompted James II to forgive half of the debts of the town's citizenry and grant them an extra two years to repay the remaining half. Similarly, a policy initiated by King Dinis of Portugal exempted those who went on crusade from having to repay their debts. Such measures were not uncommon throughout the new territories, and were no doubt a great strain on Jewish financiers.[9]

In much of Andalusia as well the latter half of the thirteenth century was a time of economic crisis, as years of drought and poor agricultural yields pushed the frontier population to the brink of starvation. At Niebla, the economic situation had deteriorated to the point that, in 1306, the city council and the Jewish community had to set up a temporary interest-free payment schedule so that Christians could repay their debts to Jewish creditors. The *concejo* noted that "the state of the land was greatly diminished, and the citizens very poor and in debt, and that they were in danger of being driven off the land."[10]

These conditions often prevented Jews from collecting on their loans, and in many cases Jewish lenders enlisted the aid of the crown in recovering debts from Christians. Royal orders of payment, whether of private loans or taxes owed to the crown, generally came via individual letters rather than municipal law. At times, however, the crown might also direct municipal legislation with regard to Jewish debt collection. In 1301, the town council of Montenegro, Portugal, attempted to bar the Jews from settling in the municipality as well as from collecting debts there. The *concelho* inserted into its royal charter the following addition: "And no Jew shall be a resident in this town nor in the surrounding area, and if there are some in this area who owe them money, that money is to be lost [to the Jews]." Though the king recognized the *concelho's* right to bar Jews from settling in Montenegro, he nonetheless protected the latter's right to collect money owed to them. Two years later, doubtless after a petition from the interested Jewish parties, the

---

[9] Ibid., 90. For Orihuela, see AME, Arm. 2, Códice no. 72, fol. 88 rv; del Estal, *El Reino de Murcia*, vol. 1, pt. 2, no. 55.
[10] Miguel Angel Ladero Quesada, *Niebla, de reino a condado. Noticias sobre el Algarbe andaluz en la Baja Edad Media* (Madrid, 1992), 29–30. Due to the crown's position as lord over all the kingdom's Jews, money owed to them was, ultimately, money owed to the crown.

king replaced this ruling with the following modification: "And no Jew shall be a resident in this town nor in the surrounding area, nor collect from them without the consent of the council."[11]

The Jews' biggest clients, and thus their largest debtors, were the great landed nobles including the various monarchs themselves. During the 1260s and 1270s, the Aragonese prince, Pedro, came to owe the Jewish lender Vives of Valencia the considerable sum of 64,000 *solidi*. When royal debtors were unable to repay their loans they often gave their creditors the rights to crown revenues, and there are several records of royal grants being issued to Jewish lenders in lieu of monetary payment of debts. Jewish lenders received houses, lands, and the rights to local businesses as payment for royal debts. In 1263, with money in short supply, Jaime I granted the Jewish courtier Astrug Jacob Xixon control over the castle-town of Peñiscola as well as the rights to several royal mills on the outskirts of the city of Valencia as a means of repaying large debts owed by the crown.[12]

JEWS IN THE URBAN ECONOMY OF THE FRONTIER

In addition to their role as moneylenders, Jewish settlers also participated in a variety of other economic activities and occupations. Documents from this period show an economically diversified Jewish population involved in long and short distance trade, acting as doctors, teachers, artisans, and proprietors of a variety of shops, mills, and baths.[13] Nor was the "urban" economy of the towns and cities in which the majority of these Jews settled divorced from the world of agriculture. Just as the structure of landownership

---

[11] ANTT, *Chanc. de D. Dinis*, liv. III, fol. 16v; ibid., liv. V, fol. 22v.

[12] Irene Llop Jordana, "Jewish Moneylenders from Vic according to the *Liber Judeo-rum* 1341–1354," *Hispania Judaica Bulletin* 2 (1999): 75–76. For the debt to Vives, see Joaquim Miret y Sans, ed., *Itinerari de Jaume I* (Barcelona, 1918), 406–407, 491–493; and for royal grants in lieu of payment, see ACA, reg. 14, fol. 19rv; María de los Desamparados Cabanes Pecourt, ed., *Los Documentos de Jaime I* (Valencia, 1976) vol. 5, nos. 1323, 1331 and 1572.

[13] See the grant allowing Jews to operate bathhouses at Murviedro in the 1270s. ACA, reg. 19, fol. 19; Régné, *pièces justificatives*, 7. For Valencia, see ACA, reg. 20, fol. 152. Despite their lack of representation in the extant documentation, there is little doubt that a great number of Jews worked as artisans in the communities of the frontier. Sources from other Iberian cities record Jews working carpenters, tanners, shoemakers, dyers, blacksmiths, and silver smiths. See the indexes in Baer, *Juden*, vol. 2, *Sachregister: Handwerker*. For Jewish tanners and shoemakers in Portugal, see *PMH, Leges*, 743.

in medieval Iberia often tied urban residences to rural plots of land, the economy of the market town was essentially an extension of rural agriculture. Jews owned and exploited their own gardens, vineyards, and other plots of agricultural land, along with participating in the real estate market that arose in the wake of conquest. Those Jews who were not directly involved in agriculture often formed a juncture of urban and rural economies, whether as bankers who lent money to Gentile farmers, merchants who traded in all manner of agricultural products, or as owners of flour mills, salt works, and presses for making olive oil and wine.

The famed *almoxarife* of Alfonso X, Don Çuleyma, received mills on the Guadaira River, near Seville, among his many grants of urban and rural property. That such royal grants were made to men like Don Çuleyma is not surprising, as they were courtiers of the first rank with strong ties to the crown in their respective kingdoms. The control of a mill, generally a hallmark of the seigniorial "class," reflected the status they had achieved as royal bailiff and *almoxarife*. However, grants of this sort were not restricted to intimates of the royal court. In the Algarve, in southern Portugal, Moses ben Vidal and his wife were granted a mill with the stipulation that they pay the king one quarter of what it produces. In the same region, another mill was granted to a group of Jews along with the rights to an oven, thus enabling them to control the entire process of the production of bread. Similar monopolies over the rights to bread baking and the production of salt were granted to Jews in Mallorca, Tortosa, Atougia, and the town of Arcos de Salinas in northern Valencia.[14]

Another way in which urban Jews were integrated into the world of agriculture was through the production and sale of comestibles such as wine and olive oil, often from their own vineyards and presses. The Jew, Bonet Avinvanez, ran a royal mill and oil press in the Valencian town of Murviedro, and in Mallorca, Jews pressed oil for the monastery of Santa Maria la Real. A Jewish wine merchant seeking access to the markets of the city of Valencia was awarded the right to sell whatever amount of wine he was able to harvest and produce from his vineyards at Murviedro. And in the Portuguese town of Évora, the city council protested the Jews' employment of Christians to make and transport their wine. It is tempting to discount the importance of the various references to Jewish ownership of vineyards and wine

---

[14] For Seville, see ACS, caja 4, no. 45/1, S. A. 1–7–83. Concerning Mallorca, see ACA, reg. 194, fol. 93v; for Tortosa, see Cabanes Pecourt, *Documentos de Jaime I*, vol. 5, no. 1496. For Arcos, see ACA, reg. 14, fol. 19rv, Burns, *Diplomatarium*, no. 466a. For Portugal, see ANTT, *Alcobaça*, 2a incorp., m. 114, 116, 121; m. 18, no. 406; and Maria Helena da Cruz Coelho and Armando Luís de Carvalho Homen, eds., *Portugal em Definição de Fronteiras* (Lisbon, 1995), 360.

cellars throughout the peninsula during this period with the explanation that these were merely for the production of wine for Jewish religious needs. However, the evidence that Jews sold some foodstuffs to Christians diminishes the likelihood that their wine, flour, and bread were only sold to a Jewish clientele.[15]

Jews were also proprietors of a variety of shops and small businesses within the towns and cities of the frontier. As indicated in most *fueros*, Jews were closely linked to the shops of the *alcacería*, or royal marketplace, from which they served Christians and Muslims, as well as Jews. Many shop owners were among the wealthiest and best-connected Jews of the frontier, and other settlers bought and sold shops as an investment in commercial real estate. Such was the case at Córdoba, where a local Jew, Baruc, was active in the dynamic market in urban land in the 1250s, and where documents from 1275 record two Jewish brothers selling shops to the dean of the local cathedral.[16]

TRADE

Territorial expansion of the Iberian kingdoms also greatly amplified the world of the Jewish trader. For these merchants, Christian conquest opened up a series of new markets to be integrated into the network of Iberian and Mediterranean trade. While the ever-fluctuating border between Christian and Muslim territory had always been somewhat permeable for merchants, the danger caused by warfare and the economic alternative of raiding often disrupted and limited trading between the two camps. For Jews, long the natural middlemen between the peninsula's Muslims and Christians, the Almohad persecutions had further restricted their access to markets in Muslim Iberia. The Christian conquests of the late twelfth and early thirteenth centuries brought a measure of stability to formerly turbulent frontier regions, and even those areas that retained a measure of volatility could not deter Jewish traders from taking advantage of new economic opportunities. In the kingdom of Valencia, which retained a large Muslim population after its conquest, rebellion and outbreaks of violence continued to be a threat to

15 For Mallorca, see ARM, 342, Prot., Civit et part. for. (1239–1261) fol. 36r; Mora and Andrinal, *Diplomatari*, nos. 23, 24. For Valencia, see ACA, reg. 44, fol. 180; for Évora, see Pimenta Ferro Tavares, *Os Judeus*, 2nd ed., p. 80.

16 See the *fuero* of Cuenca, chap. 29, rub. 16. For Jews in the *alcacería* of Valencia, see also Burns, *Diplomatarium*, vol. 3, no. 555; and ACA, reg. 42, fol. 235; and reg. 46, fol. 83. For Córdoba, see ACC, caja D, no. 588; and caja G, nos. 147–148.

Part I. The Jewish Settler and the Frontier

Christian rule. Yet for Jewish traders, these Muslim communities represented new markets to be explored. In 1276, Moses Maymo and other Jewish merchants of Valencia were given the right to trade with Montesa and other recently subjugated Muslim towns, as long as they did not sell any items of military importance.[17] Thus, as the Christian conquerors began to integrate these new territories into the economic life of their kingdoms, Jewish merchants began to extend their routes into the urban centers of the frontier, and from there into the rural villages which had been heretofore beyond their reach.

These Jewish merchants followed the path of Iberian trade beyond the confines of the peninsula and out into the Mediterranean world. One of the effects of the *reconquista* was the eventual decline of Andalusian trade routes that had connected the peninsula to the Muslim lands of the Mediterranean, and the subsequent growth of northern routes into Christian Europe. Yet, despite this eventual shift in the focus of Iberian trade, the Christian kingdoms continued to maintain economic ties with the Muslim world throughout this period, with Jewish merchants from the Iberian kingdoms continuing to play an active role in the process. Jews acting as translators and diplomats to the Crowns of Aragon and Castile in their continued negotiations with the Muslim rulers of Granada and North Africa must also be seen as potential merchants. As was the custom throughout the medieval Jewish world, these Jewish courtiers mixed public and personal business, taking advantage of their diplomatic missions to trade. Jews also served as factors for the crusading orders in their business in North Africa. A document from 1258 records that Aaron, a Jewish trader in the service of the Templars, died in Morocco while on business for the order. The Templars, who feared that they would be held liable for Aaron's life and the value of his merchandise, successfully lobbied Jaime I to defend the order, at the crown's expense, against Aaron's family and business associates. The king's statement that the crown would defend the Templars in any action, "whether it be presented in court or out of court," signals the commonality of private settlements in such cases.[18]

Such instances appear to have been relatively common. While the success of the Christian conquests brought a measure of pacification and stability to the frontier with Muslim Granada, Iberian merchants involved in long-distance trade continued to confront an abundance of dangers when

---

[17] ACA, reg. 38, fol. 63v.; cit. in Régné, no. 664.
[18] For trade with North Africa, see Yom Tov Assis, "Diplomàtics jueus de la Corona catalanoaragonesa en terres musulmanes (1213–1327)," *Tamid* 1 (1997): 7–40; Àngels Masià i de Ros, *Jaume II: Aragó, Granada i Marroc* (Barcelona, 1989), 23–28, 48, 151–152, 173–175, 257–259. For Templars, see ACA, reg. 10, fol. 83rv; Burns, *Diplomatarium*, vol. 2, no. 165a.

they entered the western Mediterranean. In the winter of 1274, a Catalonian trading ship was captured in the North African port of Carthage and its passengers held for ransom. Among the captured were Jews from the cities of Alicante and Murcia. Six years later, a wealthy Valencian merchant named Abraham Abingalel was the victim of pirates off the coast of Granada. In this instance, the pirates were Christians from Castile, and Abingalel used his connections at the court of Pedro III to pressure the Castilian king to compensate him for the loss of his merchandise.[19]

For Jewish traders, the menace of piracy faced by all long-distance travelers was compounded by the threat of crusading Christian armies that often failed to distinguish between Muslim and Jew. During his final years as the leading rabbinic authority of Toledo, Asher ben Yehiel received a letter which described the plight of a group of Jewish traders preparing to set out on a long journey from Andalusia to the Land of Israel. The responsum records the following account from the Jewish merchants:

We were planning to go, and we had to hire a ship from Córdoba to Seville, and it was reported to us that ships from the kingdom of Portugal were going by sea to plunder and loot [the ships of] all Jews and Muslims by order of the Pope.[20]

As the Crown of Aragon expanded into the Mediterranean, the Balearics became one of the most important centers of Iberian trade, linking the peninsular states to the rest of Christian Europe, as well as to Muslim North Africa and the Middle East. Mallorca's Jewish merchants formed an integral part of this trading entrepôt, prospering under the protection of the king for whom they often acted as agents. When Mallorca went to war with the peninsular states, its Jewish merchants were guaranteed the right to continue to trade freely and were reassured that their goods would not be subject to embargo.[21]

---

[19] ACA, reg. 19, fol. 95v-96; reg. 48, fol. 83v in Régné, *pièces justificatives*, no. 12. For the dangers posed to Iberian merchants in the twelfth and thirteenth centuries, see James W. Brodman, *Ransoming Captives in Crusader Spain: the Order of Merced on the Christian-Islamic Frontier* (Philadelphia, 1986), 1–40.

[20] Asher ben Yehiel, *Responsa*, 8:13. The incident most likely refers to the military campaigns launched by Alfonso XI against the Muslim kingdom of Granada.

[21] Fidel Fita and Gabriel Llabrés y Quintana, "Privilegios de los hebreos mallorquines en el códice Pueyo," *Boletín de la Real Academia de la Historia* 36 (1900): 128–129. See also the instance, in 1286, when Mallorcan Jews were given royal funds for the purpose of outfitting a trading ship. ACA, reg. 67, fol. 141.

The successes of the thirteenth-century *reconquista* led to an increase in the number of Muslims who became enslaved, as well as an increase in the involvement of Jews in the trade and ownership of these slaves.[22] Mallorca soon became the principal center for a burgeoning trade in captured Muslim and, along with the peninsular territories of the Crown of Aragon, one of the greatest markets for these slaves as well. Jewish merchants from southern France, a region controlled by the Crown of Aragon at various points during this period, also became involved in the Mallorcan slave trade from the very onset of Christian rule in the Balearics. The newly conquered port cities of Valencia also served as gateways to the Mediterranean for Christian and Jewish slave traders, as illustrated by a royal grant of 1258 giving Abraham Albanna of Tortosa permission to transport Muslims from Castile to North Africa through the Valencian port of Denia. Jewish merchants were also active in the sale and purchasing of slaves in Sicily after the island fell to the Aragonese in 1285.[23]

In the original privileges given to the Jews of Mallorca in 1231, the king guaranteed that Jews whose Muslim slaves were baptized by Christians would be reimbursed for their loss. Mallorca's Jews were also guaranteed compensation should their Muslim slaves be taken from them as a means of repaying a debt owed by these slaves. Yet despite such royal efforts to protect Jewish interests, the issue of emancipating converted Muslim slaves continued to be a source of rancor for Jewish merchants throughout the century as Christian missionary activity increased in Mallorca and throughout the Crown of Aragon.[24]

For Muslims enslaved to Jewish masters, baptism brought about an immediate change in status, due to the long-standing prohibition against Jews owning Christian slaves. As the royal charter granted to the kingdom of Valencia noted: "It is a great evil if a Christian, whom Jesus Christ redeemed through the blasphemies and disgraces that He suffered, should be in the service or power of a Jew."[25] However, the promise of manumission through

[22] See Stephen Bensch, "From Prizes of War to Domestic Merchandise: The Changing face of Slavery in Catalonia and Aragon, 1000–1300," *Viator* 25 (1994): 77; Olivia Remie Constable, "Muslim Spain and Mediterranean Slavery," in *Christendom and its Discontents*, ed. Scott Waugh and Peter Diehl (Cambridge, 1996), 280.

[23] For Mallorca, see AHN, Clero, carp. 86, no. 3; Larry Simon, "Muslim-Jewish relations in Crusader Majorca in the Thirteenth Century: An Inquiry based on Patrimony Register 342," in *Christians, Muslims, and Jews in Medieval and Early Modern Spain*, ed. Mark Meyerson and Edward English (Notre Dame, 2000), 125–140. For Sicily, see ACA, reg. 10, fol. 62v; for Jewish slave ownership in Tortosa, see Adret, 4:139.

[24] AHN, Clero, carp. 75, num. 17; and ACA, reg. 20. fol. 242.

[25] *Fori regni Valentiae*, lib. VI, rub. 1, chs. 15–16.

conversion brought into question the slaves' motivation. In 1246, the ecclesiastical council held at Tarragona rendered the following decision:

> Because we understand that some Saracen slaves insincerely come to be baptized, that they may escape the yoke of slavery, we decree that when this sort of Saracen shall flee to the church for baptism, he is to be kept for some days by the pastor so that [the latter] may know if he dwells in darkness.[26]

The concerns of the Church were not always shared by the Aragonese crown, which also sought to promote trade and to protect the rights of Jewish merchants. In 1273, Jaime I attempted to dissuade Christians from baptizing Muslim slaves belonging to Jews by declaring that all baptized Muslims would become property of the crown. This threat proved ineffective, and four years later a delegation of Jews came before the newly crowned Pedro III with the contention that, throughout the Crown of Aragon, Muslim slaves of Jewish masters were still converting to Christianity in order to obtain their freedom.[27] The problem persisted under Alfonso III with whom Mallorcan Jews once again raised the issue in 1288. Similar complaints went out from Jewish slave owners in other Iberian kingdoms as well. In Portugal, the crown declared that any Muslim slaves owned by Jews who underwent baptism would be forced to return to their masters, and that their former property would be confiscated. In response to this policy the Portuguese clergy wrote to Pope Gregory X who condemned it, but to little avail. While these examples of Jewish slave-ownership generally describe Muslims who were the temporary possessions of Jewish merchants, and not in permanent service to Jewish masters, some Jews did retain slaves for private use. Muslims were found in the employ of Jews throughout the newly conquered territories, and in Valencia Muslims were known to work and dwell on the lands owned by Jews.[28]

---

[26] Robert I. Burns, "Journey from Islam: Incipient Cultural Transition in the Conquered Kingdom of Valencia (1240–1280)," *Speculum* 35 (1960): 342.

[27] ACA, reg. 19, fol. 47v; ACA, reg. 74, fol. 107v; and reg. 40, fol. 16v–17; in Régné, *pièces justificatives*, no. 11. Pedro's decision also allowed for compensation of the Jewish owner, should the slave have been offered for sale within a period of three months after being acquired. This arrangement was also included in *Las Siete Partidas* (7.4.21), and followed the policy set forth canonical compilations of Raymond of Peñafort. *Decretales* 5.6.5, 8, 13; and *Summa* 1.4.3.

[28] Grayzel, *The Church and the Jews*, vol. 2, no. 32; ACA, reg. 12, fol. 44v; Burns, *Diplomatarium*, no. 393.

There is also evidence of Jews working in a variety of literate professions in the communities of the frontier. Along with the various legal experts, judges, and communal officials to be found in every Jewish community, some Jews also retained the services of other members of their community to act as legal advocates on their behalf and to represent them in court cases brought before Christian magistrates. Though some *fueros* make mention of Jews not being allowed to represent themselves or others during such legal proceedings, this was not the case in most places, and other charters, such as those of Salamanca and Ledesma, even make special note of the fact that Jews did have the right to representation.[29] Indeed, we have evidence from thirteenth-century Córdoba of a Jew acting as a legal representative for another Jew in case brought before a Christian magistrate. In the dispute, mentioned in the previous chapter, between Don Yehudah and the Christian widow Doña Pascuala over the ownership of some land in the city's *termino*, Don Yehudah was represented at court by Abraham Sobrino who is listed as his *personero*. In some cases, Jews hired legal experts Mallorca to represent them in the Christian courts. On the role of such lawyers, one Hebrew text from Mallorca notes that "This post is called 'advocate' in the language of the Christians."[30]

In the expanding urban landscape of twelfth and thirteenth-century Iberia, Jews also came to fill a number of specialized and administrative posts. The most famous of these were the relatively small percentage of Jews who formed part of the royal administration, a role that they had played for centuries under both Christian and Muslim rule. In the Christian kingdoms, members of the Jewish elite served in important administrative roles during earlier stages of the Castilian *reconquista* beginning with the reign of Alfonso VI (r. 1072–1109). Alfonso's physician, Joseph Ferruziel (aka "Cidellius"), wielded power at the royal court and within the Jewish community as

---

[29] Prohibitions against Jews representing themselves at trial are found in the *fueros* of Coria, rub. 219; Cáceres, rub. 220; Castello-Bom in *PMH, Leges,* 777. In contrast, see Salamanca, rubs. 259, 341; Ledesma, rubs. 176, 303, 390, 400; also Pilar León Tello, "Disposiciones sobre judíos en los fueros de Castilla y León," *Sefarad* 46 (1986): 285–286. Even in those towns where Jews were denied a voice at trial, they still had recourse to appeal to the king, a privilege that was frequently invoked by the Jews of this period.

[30] For Córdoba, see AHPC, carp. 31, no. 1; and Cruces Blancos, "Compraventos de tierras," p. 225. In Portugal, the post is referred to as that of *procurador.* Pimenta Ferro, *Os Judeus,* 1st ed., 167–170. For Jews representing other Jews in Gentile courts, see Adret, 3:141 and 5:287.

well, and was among the first to help resettle Jewish refugees from al-Andalus. In the Crown of Aragon Jews held the offices of bailiff and *repositarius*, or finance minister, as early as the 1120s.[31]

In the period following the Christian expansion of the early thirteenth century, Jewish courtiers served in all of the Iberian kingdoms as tax collectors, financial advisors, diplomats, or royal bailiffs, and had a particularly strong presence in the new territories of Andalusia and Valencia. While the success of the *reconquista* meant the cessation of major military campaigns against Muslim held territory, both Castile and Aragon continued to maintain economic and diplomatic ties with the kingdom of Granada and the Muslim lands of North Africa throughout the thirteenth and fourteenth centuries. During this period, the role of diplomatic envoys to these Muslim courts would continue to be filled by Arabic-speaking Jews.[32] Throughout his long reign Alfonso X employed a great many Jews in the civil service of Castile, most of who were drawn from the elite of the Jewish community of Toledo. The royal *almoxarifes* Don Mayr and Don Çuleyma had been among the first of these Toledan Jews who came to play a key role in the government of the new territories in southern Castile. Don Çulema's son, Çag de la Maleha, came to replace his father as one of Alfonso's leading administrators, and his association with the rebellious Infante Sancho led to his fall from grace and eventual execution. The reprisals against de la Maleha and other Jewish courtiers thought to be associated with Sancho were felt most acutely in the frontier city of Seville where the Infante sought refuge in a local monastery. Most of the surviving Jewish courtiers were eventually returned to favor when the latter ascended the throne as Sancho IV in 1284. The leading figure among these courtiers was another Toledan, Abraham Barchilon. In 1287, the king entrusted Barchilon with the minting of gold coins for the entire kingdom and a number of other financial responsibilities, including the collection of revenues from Toledo, Murcia, and the frontier region bordering the kingdom of Granada.[33]

In the new Aragonese territory of Valencia, the court Jews who were active at the time of the conquest, such as Judah de la Cavalleria and Salomon

---

[31] For Cidellius, see Baer, *Juden*, vol. 2, no. 29; idem, *History*, 1:50, and the bibliography cited on p. 387. For Aragon, see Baer, *Juden*, vol. 1, nos. 15, 21; for the period from 1151 to 1213, see Thomas Bisson, ed., *Fiscal Accounts of Catalonia under the Early Count-Kings* (London, 1984), vol. 2, nos. 4, 10, 13, 26.

[32] For Jewish bailiffs in the Crown of Aragon see Jerome Lee Shneidman, "Jews as Royal Bailiffs in Thirteenth-Century Aragon," *Historia Judaica* 19 (1957): 59–66. For Jewish diplomats, see Assis, "Diplomàtics jueus," 7–40; for the documents published by Àngels Masià i de Ríos, *Jaume II*, 2: 23–28, 48, 151–152, 173–175, 257–259, 480.

[33] For Don Çuleyma, also known as Solomon ibn Zadok, and his son as Çag (Isaac), see Baer, *History*, 1:124–133; idem, *Juden*, vol. 2, nos. 87, 93.

and Moses Alconstantini, were followed by other members of the Jewish elite from the north. Rich and influential courtiers such as Muça Portella and Aaron ibn Yahia would assume important roles in the administration of the city and kingdom of Valencia, and also come to extend their economic influence into this new territory through a variety of royal concessions and the acquisition of urban and rural property.[34]

The position of tax collector was one based on personal wealth and recourse to capital in which the collector, who usually obtained the job by outbidding rivals, guaranteed a certain amount to the crown and retained any taxes he could collect above that amount. As a result, the business of tax farming remained in the hands of a few prominent Jewish families whose wealth and connections to the royal court became self-perpetuating qualifications for the job. These clans, though often in competition with one another, also developed relationships that transcended the political boundaries of the kingdoms that they served. This was especially true on the frontier, where the sparseness of the populations and the vastness of the territories to be covered prompted business alliances between Jews from as far apart as Murcia and Seville in order to complete the task of tax collecting.[35]

In addition to acting as civil servants in the royal administration, Jews also participated in the management of their local municipal and communal governments as scribes, notaries, and tax collectors. Jews, like Christians, were able to bid on different sorts of monopolies related to communal and political administration, from the composition of notarial documents, to the collection of taxes for certain districts. In some cases, individuals from the two religious communities shared a monopoly. In one such case, two brothers, David and Vidal Astruch, purchased the right to collect the taxes of the city of Valencia and the surrounding area at a public auction. They were to carry out their collection in accordance with two Christian notaries, Gener Enbaça and G. de Vernet, but were allowed to present their total before a Jewish notary, A. Astruch, who appears to have been a relative of the two Jews.[36]

In Valencia, Jahuda de Adarra won the right to a monopoly on Hebrew notarial records, and in turn farmed out the actual work to two other Jews. In a style representative of the general audacity of the Valencian Jews in the

---

[34] The careers of these and other Jewish notables of the era have been studied by David Romano, *Judíos al servicio de Pedro el Grande de Aragón (1276–1285)* (Barcelona, 1983).

[35] AHN, Santiago, Encomienda de Montiel, c. 214, no. 19. The post of tax collector was often passed down from father to son among the elite. For examples of sons taking up the duties of tax collection while their fathers were away, see Adret, 6:159; and 1:915.

[36] ACA, reg. 50, fol. 121.

late thirteenth century, these two took advantage of their monopoly by overcharging their clients, sometimes refusing to complete their work until a second fee was paid. Outraged, the *aljama* made a formal complaint to the king, begging him to intervene on their behalf. In response to this plea, the king ordered the bailiff of Valencia to work together with Jewish officials in order to ensure proper business practices. Though he chose to include the *aljama* in the resolution of the problem, the king's response also led to a decrease in the previous level of autonomy enjoyed by local Jewish scribes. From that time onward, all decrees or documents made by the *aljama*, whether regarding taxes or other business, were "to be done by a Christian notary and not by a Jew . . . so nothing can be added to its value or detracted or changed."[37]

Finally, among the Jewish settlers to the new territories were physicians who were employed by a wide variety of Christian patrons. At times, this made for some interesting professional and social relationships. In the kingdom of Valencia, a Jewish doctor by the name of Homer tended to the Franciscan brothers there, and in Játiva a Jew was hired by a local house of preachers to teach them Hebrew. To these relatively unique situations must be added the more routine contact which ecclesiastics and laymen had with a variety of Jewish landlords, merchants, and moneylenders.[38]

One of the distinguishing characteristics of Iberian Jewry that sets its members apart from their co-religionists in northern Europe was the degree to which the former were able to maintain a high level of economic diversity throughout the Middle Ages. The economic activity of the Jews of the thirteenth-century frontier can be seen as a microcosm of such diversity. While the majority of the professions in which Jewish settlers became engaged remained available to them throughout the peninsula, the economies of the new territories opened up a vast region into which Jews might expand. Aided by a variety of government incentives Jews migrated to the towns and cities of the frontier to take advantage of new lands, markets, and trade routes that had reopened with the extension of Christian rule into southern Iberia.[39] The rapidly developing economy of the frontier also created a need for credit, and the absence of a native population of moneylend-

<hr>

[37] ACA, reg. 229, fol. 274v; Burns, *Notarial Culture*, no. 43.

[38] ACA, reg. 196, fol. 296; reg. 195, fol. 94; Jerome Lee Shneidman, *The Rise of the Aragonese-Catalan Empire* (New York, 1970), 2:424.

[39] While it is not possible to know the exact motivation for Jewish migration to the frontier, we can assume that economic opportunities were a major factor. See Baer, *History*, 1:210. For similar motivations among early Ashkenazi Jews, see Michael Toch, "Jewish Migration," 641.

ers helped to attract Jewish settlers who, along with Christian lenders, were able to provide this service. As in the case of landownership, the urban economy of the market towns of the frontier was also inextricably tied to the agriculture of the countryside; the Jews who worked as merchants and shop owners also cultivated vineyards, and operated wine and olive oil presses, saltworks, and flour mills.

For several decades after the initial Christian conquests, Jewish merchants on the frontier were also active in the trade of Muslims who had become enslaved as a result of the *reconquista* and subsequent rebellions. Ecclesiastical objections to Jewish ownership of converted slaves is a prism through which one can see the crown's ongoing protection and support of its Jews over and against the strident and repeated protests of the Church.

The allure of the economic possibilities of the frontier was such that it drew Jewish settlers to the region despite areas of low agricultural production (Andalusia), and social instability caused by ongoing conflicts between native Muslim populations and their Christian overlords (Valencia, Mediterranean piracy). The royal chronicle commissioned by Alfonso X depicted the newly Christianized city of Seville as a trading center of unlimited economic potential.

There is no town so pleasant or well situated in all the world. It is a town to which the ships come daily up the river from the sea. Ships and galleys and other sea vessels dock there inside the walls with all kinds of merchandise from all parts of the world.[40]

Though written to promote immigration to the under populated south, this description of Seville nonetheless captures the allure of the new territories for both Christian and Jewish settlers from the interior. For the latter, the variety of trades and professions open to them during the thirteenth century led to their integration into the economic and social life of the new territories.

[40] Menéndez Pidal, ed., *Primera Crónica General*, 2:769. The above translation is from Angus Mackay, *Spain in the Middle Ages: From Frontier to Empire* (New York, 1977), 75.

PART II
THE JEWISH COMMUNITY
AND THE FRONTIER

For over half a century, Jews throughout the Iberian Peninsula continued to benefit from the demographic and economic needs that had been created by the thirteenth-century *reconquista*. The royal grants and privileges that drew settlers to the frontier also helped their nascent settlements to flourish and mature into full communities. The following chapters will examine the political and social contours of these communities as they developed out of the interplay between royal policies regarding Jewish rights, and Jewish customs of public administration.

As we have already seen, the re-establishment of Jewish settlements in southern Iberia did not follow the standard pattern of communal transition from Muslim to Christian rule that had typified northern centers. Far from being inevitable, the nature of the Jewish communities of the thirteenth-century frontier and the structure of their central institutions were as much a product of the broader currents of Iberian history as of the long-standing internal traditions of Jewish government and communal organization. The legal position of Iberian Jewry during the thirteenth century grew out of well-established Christian traditions of royal protection and control of religious minorities. In the wake of the military successes of the *reconquista* the Jews' relationship with the various peninsular monarchies would enter a new phase as royal programs aimed at expanding the scope of central authority led first to the greater elaboration of royal sovereignty over the Jews, and eventually to an increased royal presence in Jewish communal government. Over the course of the thirteenth century, Iberian kings would also attempt to exert greater control over the physical and social boundaries of the Jewish community, enforcing the reestablished Jewish quarters of the frontier as the only legitimate area of Jewish settlement, and exhibiting an unprecedented interest in regulating relationships between Jews, Christians, and Muslims.

In his analysis of the broad Iberian frontier created by the *reconquista*, Luís Adão da Fonseca has observed that "The frontier, as a border, (in the medieval sense), an undefined and imprecise space where people are separated by beliefs . . . would progressively become, in the second half of the thirteenth century, a reality of the past."[1] For the Jews who had come to settle in the newly Christianized territories and take advantage of the economic opportunities there, restrictions on settlement, potential occupations, and social interaction signaled the end of an era. Yet throughout the twilight of the Iberian frontier, Jewish society would continue to be characterized by the intrepid spirit of individual settlers who openly resisted such constraints.

[1] Luís Adão da Fonseca, "Portugal na Península Ibérica. Horizontes marítimos, articulação política e relações diplomáticas (sec. XIXVI)," in *Las Españas Medievales*, ed. Julio Valdeón Baruque (Valladolid, 1999), 87.

Part II. The Jewish Community and the Frontier

CHAPTER FOUR
ROYAL AUTHORITY AND THE LEGAL
STATUS OF IBERIAN JEWRY

The thirteenth century is the greatest of all medieval centuries, superior
to the sixth, and equal in many respects to the sixteenth.
—Vicente de la Fuente, *Historia eclesiástica de España*

Behind the problem of Jewish status in medieval Iberia
lurks the larger and more unwieldy issue of marginal-
ization. As a result, most discussions regarding the status of Jews in the Middle Ages become bound up with
the question of whether or not they represented a "persecuted" or "alienated" minority, and in doing so often ignore the broader political context in
which this status was forged.[1] In Iberia, as elsewhere in the medieval world,
legislative efforts to protect minority groups represent a small portion of
royal initiatives, and should not be misconstrued as evidence of majority
tolerance, let alone the cessation of violence and the establishment of socio-
religious tranquility. After all, the Christian kingdoms during the high reconquest have been termed "a society organized for war," and one in which
violence played a fundamental role in the construction of social relationships. Rather, these laws should be seen as representing a measure of secu-
rity for these groups, at least as far as they were successfully implemented.[2]
    The unique social and religious make-up of Iberian society presents
something of a challenge to the classic view of the medieval Latin West as a
civilization divided into those who work, those who fight, and those who

---

[1] Of the many studies on this topic, the following works offer varying attempts at syn-
thesis: Robert Ian Moore, *The Formation of a Persecuting Society* (Oxford, 1987); Kenneth
R. Stow, *Alienated Minority: The Jews of Medieval Latin Europe* (Cambridge, 1992); David
Nirenberg, *Communities of Violence;* Jeremy Cohen, *Living Letters of the Law* (Berkeley,
1999).
[2] The term was coined by Elena Lourie in her article "A Society Organized for War:
Medieval Spain," *Past and Present* 35 (1966): 54–76. See also James F. Powers, *A Society Organized for War: The Iberian Urban Militias in the Central Middle Ages* (Berkeley, 1988). On
the role of violence, see Nirenberg, *Communities of Violence.*

pray. This paradigm becomes all the more inadequate in the period of growth and social and institutional transformation that followed the Christian victories of the late twelfth and early thirteenth centuries. Teofilo Ruiz has recently argued that, in Castile, the thirteenth century witnessed a 'reordering' of society reflected by a shift in attitudes regarding commerce, property and language.[3] Politically, the organization and administration of the Christian kingdoms during this period was also in a state of flux. As Iberian Christians found themselves to be masters of the peninsula for the first time in centuries, the crown, the nobility, the towns and the church all sought to increase their own power and prominence. The big winners in this contest were the various crusader kings, and though their victory would prove transient, their reforms would leave a lasting imprint on the legal development of their respective kingdoms, and on the status of their Jewish subjects. The Jews' relationship to the crown, and their subsequent status during the high Middle Ages, thus developed out of this broader campaign to assert royal power and jurisdiction over an ever greater area, and the reaction it provoked from the other estates of the realm.

LEGISLATIVE DEVELOPMENT AND JEWISH STATUS

In the Iberian Peninsula the thirteenth century was dominated by a series of monarchs possessed of exceptional abilities, energy, and ambition. Fernando III and Alfonso X of Castile, Afonso III and Dinis I of Portugal, and the Aragonese kings Jaime I and Pedro III oversaw the unprecedented expansion of their dominions and undertook an equally sweeping transformation of the royal administration in their respective kingdoms. If territorial conquest and the attendant need to repopulate and reorganize the new provinces helped reestablish a Jewish presence in southern Iberia, other royal initiatives would have an equally significant impact on the civic status of these Jewish settlers. The *reconquista* and *repoblación* of the thirteenth century were greatly shaped by a changing conception of kingship that began to envision the monarch as a "head of state" who was the natural and spiritual leader of the realm, rather than a feudal lord who ruled through personal ties to his vassals.[4] This development was particularly pronounced in the

---

[3] Ruiz, *From Heaven to Earth*, chap. 1.
[4] For Castile, see Robert MacDonald, ed., *Espéculo, Texto jurídico atribuido al Rey de*

Part II. The Jewish Community and the Frontier

kingdom of Castile, where the notion that all inhabitants of the realm were naturally the vassals of the king gradually took hold over the course of the 12th and 13th centuries. In the other peninsular kingdoms as well the thirteenth century was marked by royal attempts at legal innovation and standardization that promoted the general expansion of monarchical power. As Teofilo Ruiz has remarked for Castile, "these legislative initiatives marked the intrusion of the Crown—of a more vigilant, expansive and organized royal bureaucracy—into the material concerns of everyday life."⁵

One of the principal legal innovations that helped to shape the social position of frontier Jewry was the proliferation and regularization of municipal charters, or *fueros*. *Fueros* were compilations of local law and custom, which were loosely based on the Visigothic *Liber Judiciorum*. During the eleventh and twelfth centuries a succession of kings reconfirmed these local charters and granted new ones to individual towns. By the thirteenth century, kings such as Castile's Alfonso VIII and Fernando III began to take a more active role in the development of municipal law by granting the same *fuero* to a number of different localities, helping to standardize municipal law within certain regions. The *fueros* granted to Cuenca, in Castile, and to the Aragonese city of Teruel served as models for many towns throughout the peninsula. Versions of the *Fuero de Córdoba*, or *Fuero Juzgo*, as it was also known, were later granted to all the major towns of Andalusia and Murcia, and thus came to form the foundation of municipal law in Castile's newly conquered territories. In Portugal, a similar program of systemization was undertaken by Afonso III, who issued a series of *forais* that gave the royal imprimatur to a host of customs in existence since the days of his father, Sancho II. During the thirteenth century, the proliferation of Portuguese charters based on the *fuero* given to the Castilian town of Coria, also fostered the regional character of municipal law in that kingdom.⁶

The kings of thirteenth-century Iberia also promoted the standardiza-

---

Castilla Don Alfonso X, el Sabio (Madison, 1990), 14, 23, 28. Though the situation was somewhat different in the more federated Crown of Aragon, Jaime I greatly advanced the authority and organization of the royal administration. See Thomas Bisson, " 'Statebuilding' in the Medieval crown of Aragón," in *Actas del XV Congreso de historia de la corona de Aragon* (Jaca, 1993), 1:141–158, esp. 141–149.

⁵ Ruiz, *Heaven to Earth*, 65. For royal intervention into the governance of the local Jewish community, see below, chap. 5. For the concept of *señorio natural* in Castile, see Robert S. Chamberlain, "The Concept of the *Señor Natural* as revealed by Castilian Law and Administrative Documents," *Hispanic American Historical Review* 19 (1930): 130–137; Aquilino Iglesia Ferreiros, "Derecho Municipal, derecho señorial, derecho regio," *Historia. Instituciones. Documentos* 4 (1977): 115–197.

⁶ *PMH, Leges*, 643, 683, 717–719, 721–723. For the diffusion of the *fuero* of Coria, see

tion of legislation throughout their domains by ordering the compilation of broad legal codes based primarily on Roman law. In the Crown of Aragon, Jaime I began to systematize and codify legal traditions throughout his expanding realms. The *Vidal Mayor*, or *Fuero de Huesca*, and its later, amplified version, the *Fueros de Aragon* are examples of this campaign, organizing the disparate strands of traditional Aragonese law and supplementing them with Roman legislation. Jaime also promoted the 12th-century Catalan legal code known as the *Usatges de Barcelona* as a supplemental code in the new territories of Tortosa (c. 1229), and Mallorca (c. 1231). In the kingdom of Valencia, he promulgated an even more comprehensive code, the *Fori regni Valentiae*, later revised in 1271 and translated into Catalan under the title *Furs de Valencia*. Unlike the *Usatges*, which was derived from Barcelonan customary law, the Valencian *furs* were based on older, Roman, legislation, primarily the *Code* and *Digest* of Justinian.[7]

In Castile, Alfonso X also sought to extend royal power through the creation of a standardized, kingdom-wide law code modeled on Roman and Visigothic law. The results were the *Fuero Real*, the *Espéculo de las Leyes*, and a revised and expanded form of the *Espéculo* that became the *Siete Partidas*.[8] The *Partidas* represents the fullest achievement of Iberian legal compilations, incorporating local customs with Roman and canon law. Translated into Portuguese, the code was widely employed during the reign of Dinis of Portugal long before its promulgation in Castile in 1348.

Such royal efforts to organize legal traditions and centralize them under the power of the crown met with resistance from the other great magnates of the realm as well as from the municipalities.[9] The former challenged the crown's attempt to extend its authority by withholding support for the

---

José Maldonado y Fernández del Torco, ed., *El fuero de Coria, estudio histrórico-jurídico* (Madrid, 1949).

[7] María de los Desamparados Cabanes Pecourt et al., eds., *Vidal Mayor: edición, introducción y notas al manuscrito* (Saragossa, 1997); Gargallo Moya, *Los Fueros de Aragón*. For Valencia, see Dualde Serrano, *Fori antiqui Valentiae*; Germà Colón and Arcadi García, eds., *Furs de Valencia*, 4 vols. to date (Barcelona, 1970–). Despite the establishment of the *furs* as the principal code of Valencia, the *Usatges* continued to be used by Catalan settlers in the north of the kingdom of Valencia.

[8] Gonzalo Martinez Díez et al., eds., *Fuero Real* (Ávila, 1988); Robert Macdonald, ed., *Espéculo*; Alfonso X, el Sabio, King of Castile, *Las Siete Partidas* (Madrid, 1807). The relationship between the various Alfonsine codes remains a subject of much debate. For the development of these and other compilations attributed to Alfonso, such as the *Leyes de Estilo* and the *Leyes Nuevas*, see Jerry Craddock, "La cronológica de las obras legislativas de Alfonso X el Sabio," *Anuario Histeorico del Derecho Español* 51 (1981): 364–418; Joseph O'Callaghan, *The Learned King: The Reign of Alfonso X of Castile* (Philadelphia, 1993), 31–37.

[9] For Castile, see also Joseph O'Callaghan, "Kings and Lords in Conflict in Late Thirteenth-Century Castile and Aragon," in *Iberia and the Mediterranean World of the*

Part II. The Jewish Community and the Frontier

crown at the assemblies known as the *Cortes* (Catalan, *Corts*). Two notable examples of such protests took place at the sessions held at Saragossa in 1264 and Burgos in 1272, in which the nobility of Aragon and Castile openly and successfully challenged these royal programs of legal reform, and the expansion of monarchical power in general. Following the nobles' example, municipal councils also began to use the meetings of the *Cortes* as a forum in which to protest the erosion of their rights. In 1295, the *concejos* of Castile banded together in formal *hermandades*, or brotherhoods, in order to better safeguard and promote their rights and privileges.[10]

It is against this background of expanding royal authority and baronial and municipal reaction that the civic status of Iberian Jewry must be viewed. Royal systematization of municipal law had a similar effect on the laws governing Jewish status in these towns, especially in the Castilian provinces of Andalusia and Murcia. In addition to their town's charter, Jewish settlements of the frontier were also often given the privileges formerly granted to the Jewish communities of the interior. In 1239, Jaime I granted Valencian Jews the privileges that had been given to the Jews of Saragossa, and in 1244 those given to the Jews of Barcelona. The rights and privileges of the Barcelonan *aljama* also served as a model for those granted to the fledgling Jewish community of the city and island of Mallorca.[11] The thirteenth century witnessed a proliferation of royal privileges granted to various Jewish communities of the Crown of Aragon, and in 1278, the crown sought to bring some order to this maze of legal documentation. Pedro III ordered all his bailiffs to have the Jews in their jurisdictions produce whatever privileges they had in their possession, and declared that only those privileges presented and confirmed at this time would henceforth be considered valid. On several occasions Pedro sought to further organize Jewish privileges by at-

Middle Ages, ed. Paul Chevedden et al. (Leiden, 1996), 2:125–133; César González Mínguez, *Fernando IV de Castilla (1295–1312): la guerra civil y el predominio de la nobleza* (Vitoria, 1976), 205–210, 330–334. For the Crown of Aragon see Donald J. Kagay, "Structures of Baronial Dissent and Revolt Under James I (1213–76)," *Mediaevistik* 1 (1988): 66; for Portugal, see da Cruz Coelho, *Definição de Fronteiras*, pp. 94–99; 104–106. Teofilo Ruiz argues that the tension between the three groups grew steadily after the conquest of Seville in 1248; see his "Expansion et changement: La conquete de Séville et la société castillane (1248–1350)," *Annales Economies Sociétés et Civilisations* 34 (1979): 557.

   10 Joseph O'Callaghan, *The Cortes of Castile-León, 1188–1350* (Philadelphia, 1989), 162–166. On the *hermandades* of Castile, see Antonio Benavides, *Memorias de D. Fernando IV de Castilla* (Madrid, 1860), vol. 2, no. 3. They would be followed promptly by the *concejos* of León and Galicia. Ibid., no. 4.

   11 ACA, reg. 941, fols. 176v–17; reg. 12, fols. 43–44v; pub. in Baer, *Juden*, vol. 1, no. 91. For Mallorca, see AHN, Clero, carp. 75, no. 17, and in Cabanes Pecourt, *Documentos de Jaime I*, vol. 1, no. 155.

tempting to create a broader Jewish charter that would encompass all the communities of the Crown of Aragon. These various attempts met with failure, however, and the development of any greater supra-communal Jewish legislation was never realized.[12]

The primary way in which the extension of monarchical power came to affect the legal position of Iberian Jewry was the increased assertion of royal authority over the Jews and the attendant rights to Jewish taxes. The question of sovereignty over the Jews was a contentious issue throughout Europe in the thirteenth century, and in the Iberian Peninsula the various monarchies had claimed sole jurisdiction over the Jews since the twelfth century. As early as 1141, the *fuero* given to the Castilian town of Calatalifa by Alfonso VII distinguished the Jewish and Muslim inhabitants of the town from the *vecinos*, or citizens, on the basis that the former groups belonged to the crown.[13] In Aragon, the *fuero* granted to Teruel in 1176 stated that: "The Jews are serfs of the king, and are always counted as part of the royal treasury," and in Portugal, an English crusader chronicling the sack of Lisbon in 1190 described the pagans and Jews fleeing that embattled city as *servos regis*.[14] Examples of the crown's claim to sovereignty over the Jews are also reflected in some of the municipal laws regarding the *caloña*, or fine, paid for killing a man. While such fines were normally paid to the relatives of the victim, the Jewish *caloña* was received by the crown. This concept was made explicit in the *fuero* of the Castilian frontier town of Baeza, which states: "And it is a known thing that the Jew has no part in his *caloña*, since Jews are serfs of the king and given to his treasury." The *fuero* of Baeza also set the penalty for the murder of a Jew as high as that of a nobleman, though this reflects the value of Jews to the Crown as human property, and not of any particular social rank.[15]

It should be pointed out that assertions of jurisdiction over the Jews often represented a royal contention rather than an established fact, and some statements in this regard betray concerns about seigniorial opposition to royal authority. This wariness is reflected in the *furs* of Valencia, which stated that Jews were automatically, and always, the possession of the crown, unless the latter made an express donation of the former to another lord:

---

[12] ACA, reg. 40, fol. 84; reg. 40, fol. 111v; reg. 41, fol. 50v.

[13] Tomás Muñoz y Romero, ed., *Colección de fueros municipales y cartas pueblas* (Madrid, 1847), 1:532, also in Baer, *Juden*, vol. 2, no. 27.

[14] Baer, *Juden*, 1:1043. On Portugal, see Baer, *History*, 1:395 n. 16.

[15] Jean Roudil, ed., *El Fuero de Baeza* (The Hague, 1962), nos. 669, 572. See also the earlier *fuero* of Castrojeriz which states: "Et si homines de Castro matarent Judio, tantum pectet pro illo quo modo pro christiano." Muñoz y Romero, *Colección*, 38.

Jews, although they take refuge with another lord, either ecclesiastical or secular, or shall make a home or dwell in another's domain, they are not freed from our dominion for that reason alone, but are ours forever, unless the lord of that place has from us or ours a statement of termination and of donation of said Jew.[16]

This sentiment was echoed by legislation in the other peninsular kingdoms. The *Libro de los fueros de Aragon* states that all Jews were under the special guard of the king, and not the protection of other lords, and King Dinis of Portugal asserted his power over all the kingdom's Jews by stating that the Jews belonged to the crown, and should appear before its judges, or else their own *arrabis*.[17]

In Castile, the recognition of the crown's control over the Jews in a passage from the non-royal *Libro de los fueros de Castilla* reflects the need to clarify this relationship. The section states that:

The Jews belong to the king; although they might be under the power of nobles or with their knights or with other men or under the power of monasteries, all should belong to the king under his protection and for his service.[18]

Royal concern over competing claims of sovereignty over the Jews was not unfounded. The services and taxes provided by Jews were prized by other lords who viewed the crown's declaration of jurisdiction over all Jews in their kingdoms as a spurious innovation. The archival information for the thirteenth century reveals a struggle over the rights to Jewish taxes and property that belies the unequivocal decrees issued from the royal court. In a letter to Alfonso II of Aragon, a group of noblemen and knights from Valencia warned the king that any Jews or Muslims who emigrated from their dominions without their permission would thereby forfeit all their possessions. Other lords sought to fine and even extort Jews living in their lands, ignoring their claims of royal protection and immunity. In 1290, Alfonso III of Aragon was informed that the count of Ampurias had taken legal action against the Jewish moneylenders in his domain. The king ordered the count to stop the inquest on the grounds that only the king had the right to judge the Jews, adding that any attack on the Jews was an attack on the crown it-

---

[16] Dualde Serrano, ed., *Fori antiqui valentiae*, 21.
[17] Gargallo Moya, ed., *Libro de los fueros de Aragon*, 67. ANTT, *Chanc. de D. Dinis*, liv. III, fol. 50; Pimenta Ferro Tavares, *Os Judeus* (2nd ed.), 87. On the office of *arrabi*, see below, chap. 5.
[18] Galo Sánchez, ed., *Libro de los fueros de Castiella* (Barcelona, 1924), 54.

self. Later that same year, a group of Jews who resided in the bishop's palace in Gerona wrote to the king complaining of a series of abuses at the hands of the bishop, including extraordinary taxes and an inability to collect debts owed to them. Alfonso reminded the bishop that, regardless of where they dwelt, all the Jews of Gerona were property of the crown alone. A similar situation arose in 1284, when the Jewish *aljama* of Barcelona complained to Pedro III that Christian preachers had begun to conduct inquests and search Jewish homes after accusing the Jews of harboring recent converts to Christianity. The king ordered his vicar and bailiff in Barcelona to oversee matters themselves, reminding them that, since the Jews belonged to the crown, the Church had no authority over them.[19]

THE JEWS AND OTHER LORDS

The persistence of royal concern regarding jurisdiction over the Jews reflects both the limits of monarchical authority and the practical necessity for Jews to develop social, economic, and political ties to a variety of lay and ecclesiastical lords. Though the crown aggressively promoted its sovereignty over the Jews, their services, and their property, it could, should it choose, award these rights to another lord or municipal council. One such example is found in the *fuero* of Calatayud in which the king grants the town's *concejo* the right Jewish property in the case of a Jew abandoning the town's general area, or *termino*.[20] Similarly, in the Leonese *fueros* of Ledesma and Salamanca, jurisdiction over the Jews is mentioned as being entrusted by the king to the town council.[21] Elsewhere in Castile, the crown granted the abbot of the monastery of Sahagun dominion over the Jews there, and the lord of the town of Molina had the right to tax Jews for the use of his salt as he did the rest of the citizens of the town.[22] Thus it was not uncommon for the crown to give away its economic rights over individual Jews and whole

---

[19] ACA, *Cartas Reales*, Alfonso II, no. 133, fol. 10v; ACA, reg. 81, fols. 87, 23; reg. 43, fol. 30v.

[20] Jesús Ignacio Algora Hernando and Felicísimo Arranz Sacristán, eds. *El Fuero de Calatayud* (Zaragoza, 1982), no. 33.

[21] The *fueros* for Ledesma and Salamanca have been edited together with others from León in Américo Castro, and Federico de Onis, eds., *Los fueros Leóneses de Zamora, Salamanca, Ledesma, y Alba de Tormes* (Madrid, 1916). Ledesma, rub. 399; Salamanca, rub. 331. A similar situation is reflected in the *fuero* of the Aragonese town of Albarracin, where the lord of the city was granted jurisdiction over the its Jews. See Fernando Suárez Bilbao, *El fuero judiego en la España cristiana* (Madrid, 2000), 62 n. 119.

[22] For Sahagun, see Baer, *Juden*, vol. 2, no. 31. For the Jews of Molina, see ibid., no. 32.

Part II. The Jewish Community and the Frontier

communities to other lords, often as a form of payment. These rights to Jewish property or rents did not, however, abrogate the general principal that all Jews of a particular realm belonged to the king. Such donations of jurisdiction over Jews and the subsequent rights to Jewish taxes were meant to underscore royal control, emphasizing that such rights were the crown's to grant as it pleased.

Yet the important legal and economic bonds between Jews and other lords were not solely a result of Christian arrangements. In Iberia, as in the rest of medieval Europe, Jews relied heavily on maintaining strong ties to central authority, be it the king, nobles, bishops or other local lords and actively cultivated such relationships. Jewish legal experts such as Solomon ibn Adret viewed baronial authority to be equal to that of the king, noting that "Every noble is like a king in his own territory, for there is no greater authority there than he."[23] In most cases, these local lords were able to enforce Jewish rights and privileges, and represented a much more effective source of protection than a king living far away. Jews on the frontier served the military orders of the Knights of Santiago, Calatrava, and the Templars as merchants and tax collectors, services for which they were often rewarded handsomely. In Tortosa, Ramon de Montcada II and the Templar preceptor of the city granted a castle to a group of Tortosan Jews in recognition of the faithful service they had rendered. In other instances, Jews appealed to the heads of these orders to represent them at court. In 1316, when the Jews of the Toledan town of Maqueda could not pay the required 8,321 *mrs.* tax to the crown, the master of the Order of Calatrava, García López de Padilla, interceded on their behalf to get the amount reduced to 3,281 *mrs.*[24]

Jews also served as physicians, tax collectors and scribes for other members of the royal family who were involved in the administration of frontier territories. Moses ibn Shoshan collected taxes for the Castilian Infante Juan Manuel in Elche, where the prince also rewarded his Jewish *alfaquim*, Issach ibn Waqar, with formerly Muslim houses and lands.[25] When parts of

[23] Adret, 1:1105. In northern Aragon, Jews living on baronial land also resisted paying taxes to the crown. See Adret 2:344.
[24] ACA, reg. 10 fol. 83rv, also in Burns, *Diplomatarium*, vol. II, no. 165a; and AHN, Santiago, Encomienda de Montiel, caja 214, no. 19. For Tortosa, see John Shideler, *A Medieval Nobel Family: The Moncadas* (Berkeley, 1983), 205–206. For Maqueda, see AHN, OO. MM., carp. 429, no. 187.
[25] ACA, reg. 256, fol. 27; cit. in Régné, no. 2679. For Isaac Ibn Waqar receiving lands in Elche, see ACA, reg. 203, fol. 140; cited in Régné, no. 2854. Isaac also acted as mediator between Aragon and Castile for affairs regarding Elche. See references to him as "Dončac Alfaquim," in Andrés Giménez Soler, *Don Juan Manuel* (Zaragoza, 1932), 24–25, 61, 237, 432, 6669, 688. On Isaac and his brother Abraham ibn Waqar, see Baer, *History*, 1:404 n. 41; idem, *Juden*, 2:89 n. 3; and Régné, nos. 2753, 2886.

the kingdom of Murcia passed to from Castile to Aragon toward the end of the thirteenth century, Jaime II of Aragon recognized Juan Manuel's continued rights to the taxes of the Jews of Elche.[26] In 1294, the Aragonese courtier Salamon Alconstantini unsuccessfully attempted to use his connection to the Castilian queen, Maria de Molina, in his bid to be appointed judge over all of Aragonese Jewry.[27] The queen maintained close ties to a number of Jewish courtiers, and in 1295 sent her Jewish *almoxarife* to enforce an order that prohibited his fellow Jews from residing on her lands in Murcia.[28]

The development of strong ties between Jews and lords other than the king always had the potential of creating overlapping jurisdiction and therefore the possibility of tensions and conflict. Perhaps the most famous case is that of the Castilian courtier Çag de la Maleha. At the height of his power as an administrator for Alfonso X, de la Maleha was invested with an extraordinary level of authority. Already assigned the position of collecting revenues for the entire kingdom, he also had the power to enforce or issue exemptions for other legislation, including restrictions on fine clothing and luxury items. In 1278, de la Maleha was given the task of raising a large sum of tax revenues to be sent to aid the siege of Algeciras. However, the money was captured by Alfonso's son, the Infante Sancho, who used it as his own. Though de la Maleha appears to have lost the money against his will and not as part of any allegiance to the Infante, the king nonetheless treated his failure as if it were treason, and had him executed.[29] Prominent courtiers were not the only Jews who found themselves caught in a web of overlapping jurisdictions. In 1307, Jaime II imposed the considerable fine of 7,000 *solidi* on a group of Jews in the southern Aragonese town of Montalbán for having accepted the protection and safeguard of the town's commander.[30] The steady growth of municipal power in Christian Iberia over the course of the thirteenth century meant that *concejos* would join the crown and the nobility in vying for jurisdiction over the Jews in their towns.

---

[26] ACA, reg. 106, fols. 93v–94v; also in de Estal, *El reino de Murcia*, I/1, no. 151, rub. 10.

[27] ACA, reg. 252, fol. 50; pub. in Baer, *Juden*, vol. 1, no. 136.

[28] ACM, Morales, Comp., fols. 420–421; also in Juan Torres Fontes, ed., *Fueros y privilegios de Alfonso X el Sabio al reino de Murcia* (Murcia, 1973), 108, no. 101.

[29] Baer, *History*, 1:124–130. See also Baron, *SRHJ*, 10:123. On his death, see Caetano Rosell, ed., *Crónicas de los reyes de Castilla* (1878; Madrid, 1953), 1:53–55.

[30] ACA, reg. 204, fol. 73; cited in Régné, no. 2874. Yom Tov Assis correctly identifies the town in question here as Montalbán, not the Catalonian town of Montblanch, as suggested by Régné. Assis, *Golden Age*, 11.

ROYAL VS. MUNICIPAL JURISDICTION

Writing on the nature of municipal administration in the medieval
Crown of Aragon, Donald Kagay has described it as "a marriage of limited
local autonomy and general royal interference"; a characterization that
might also be applied to the rest of the peninsular states during the latter
half of the thirteenth century.[31] In Castile, the reigns of Fernando III and
Alfonso X would mark the deterioration of urban autonomy as the crown
exercised increasing control over urban government. If this is true for the
kingdom of Castile in general, it is all the more applicable for the nascent
towns of the frontier where the crown's intervention in urban government
caused particular rancor and heated debate regarding the issue of juridical
jurisdiction in cases involving Jews. As their political identity began to develop, these municipalities sought to impose their authority over local Jewries by appointing their own judges for cases between Jews and Christians.
This expression of municipal independence and control quickly brought
several frontier *concejos* into direct confrontation with equally ambitious
royal policies.

In all the Christian kingdoms of the peninsula, the towns were served by
between two to six magistrates known alternately as an *alcalde, alcaide, alvazil*
or *juez*. In Castile, these judges were generally appointed annually by the
town's parishes, but the *Fuero Real* stipulated that they be appointed by the
king.[32] During the latter half of the thirteenth century royal appointment of
municipal *alcaldes* became increasingly common, and in many cities these officials also acted as the crown's representative to protect its Jews and to handle matters between them and Christians. In Portugal, a special *alcalde* for
criminal cases involving Jews and Muslims had been a royal mandate since
the time of the country's first king, Alfonso Henriques, in the twelfth century.[33] In Castile the use of such separate judges (*alcaldes apartados*) for Jewish matters was becoming relatively standard practice by the reign of Sancho

[31] Donald Kagay, "Royal Power in the Urban Setting: James I and the Towns of the
Crown of Aragon," *Mediaevistik* 8 (1995): 162.
[32] *Fuero Real*, 1.7. 2; O'Callaghan, *The Learned King*, 86; Manuel González Jiménez et
al., *Sevilla en tiempos de Alfonso X el Sabio* (Seville, 1987), 138–150; and María del Carmen
Carlé, *Del concejo medieval castellano-Leónés* (Buenos Aires, 1968), 109–131.
[33] João Martins da Silva Marques, ed., *Descobrimentos Portugueses, Suplemento ao vol. I*
(Lisbon, 1944), 5–6. The Portuguese crown used these officials to handle legal matters of
other social groups, such as sailors and fisherman. See ibid., 8.

IV. However, when the *Cortes* met at Palencia in 1286, the decision was made that the *alcalde* who oversaw Jewish cases should be drawn from among the *hombres buenos*, or "good men" of the city, rather than from the royal court. The king agreed to this arrangement, adding only that any *alcalde* in charge of suits involving Jews would be mindful that these cases be handled with dispatch lest they delay the collection of royal rents.[34] In the Crown of Aragon, the trend of municipal courts exerting greater control over suits between members of the two religions can already be seen in the *furs* of Valencia, formulated during the mid-thirteenth century.

> On all questions that the Jews have with Christians, whether civil or criminal, they are to respond and accept justice in the town court, notwithstanding any privileges they may have, and if the Jews have any case between themselves, it is to be adjudicated by their judges.[35]

In 1294, the Jewish community of Murcia petitioned Sancho IV of Castile to renew the privilege to have their own *alcalde apartado* to adjudicate cases they had with Christians. The city officials protested that this and other royal privileges granted to the Jews contradicted those that the crown had given to the *concejo*. Sancho resolved the issue by striking a compromise between the two parties. The crown would not impose upon the city a separate royal *alcalde* for cases involving Jews, but the latter would be compelled to choose one of the existing *alcaldes* of the city for this purpose. One copy of the king's decision was kept by the *concejo*, and another by the *aljama* of the Jews.[36]

In some cases the *alcalde* was not a permanent office filled by a royal appointee, but rather a provisional post created to handle a particular suit. Such was the case in the family of *fueros* modeled on that of the Castilian town of Cuenca. Here, a system was developed in which multiple *alcaldes* were chosen from among the local citizenry to handle suits between Christians and Jews.

> If a Jew and a Christian litigate for something, two citizen *alcaldi* should to be designated, one of whom is to be Christian and the other Jewish. If one of the litigants is not pleased with the judgment, he should appeal to four citizen *alcaldi*, two of whom should be Christian and two Jewish. These four should have final judgment. Whoever appeals the

---

[34] Colmeiro, ed., *Cortes de los antiguos reinos*, 1:99.
[35] Dualde Serrano, ed., *Fori antiqui valentiae*, tit. XXXVII.6, p. 59.
[36] AMM, priv. orig. no. 55; also in Torres Fontes, *Colección de documentos*, 2:104–106.

judgment of these four should know that he will lose the case. The *al-caldi* should guard against judging anything else than what the Code of Cuenca prescribes.[37]

A similar situation existed at the Andalusian outpost of Niebla, where two townsmen were appointed by the municipal *concejo* to work out a schedule for cases between Christians and members of the Jewish community.[38]
Municipal resistance to the use of separate *alcaldes* for Jewish affairs came only in regard to those cases involving both Christians and Jews, and not with Jewish autonomy in affairs of its own community. The issue here was not the curtailment of Jewish rights, but rather the opposition to royal encroachment upon local juridical authority. Local officials saw royal magistrates who were appointed to their cities to oversee Jewish affairs as an infringement on their sovereignty. In Valencia, there existed an ongoing conflict between the royally appointed Bailiff-General for the kingdom and the local justice of the city of Valencia regarding the jurisdiction over Valencian Jewry. The king had granted jurisdiction to the Bailiff-General in 1275, but the decree was openly challenged by the Valencian justice who often refused to execute orders made by the former regarding Jews on the grounds that his office, and not that of the Bailiff-General, had jurisdiction in such matters.[39] In 1288, the Jewish *aljama* of Mallorca complained to the king that the city's *concejo* was forcing Jews in its employ to pay taxes to the city in addition to those they paid to the king. Alfonso III came to the Jews' defense, reminding the *concejo* that all Jews were exempt from municipal taxes. Twelve years later the issue of legal jurisdiction over the local Jewish community was once again raised by the *concejo*, which complained to the king that both the royal bailiff and the Jewish communal council were infringing upon its rights.[40]
Jurisdictional conflicts involving the Jews also arose in the kingdom of Portugal where the laws regarding jurisdiction for cases involving Jews varied throughout this period. The most common configuration was the one established by the country's first king, Afonso Henriques. In a letter written in 1204, his son and successor, Sancho I, decreed that the Jews of Lisbon should bring their complaints to the city's *alcaide* or *alvazil* as was the custom

[37] Powers, *The Code of Cuenca*, chap. 29, rub.
[38] Ladero Quesada, *Niebla, de reino a condado*, 29–30.
[39] Jaime I's decree of 1275 is published in Robert I. Burns, "Jaume I and the Jews of the Kingdom of Valencia," in *X Congreso de Historia de la Corona de Aragón* (Saragossa, 1976), vol. 2, no. 23.
[40] ACA, reg. 75, fol. 66v; *Cartas Reales*, James II, caja 5, no. 754.

under his father. The king later established the same rules for the towns of Beja, Santarem and Almada.[41] In 1289, King Dinis ordered that all cases between members of the two faiths, whether criminal or civil, were to be handled by his *alcaides* and *alvazils*, with the notable exception of cases involving debts owed to Jews, which were to be judged by the Jewish *arrabi*. This ruling, first given at Santarem, was confirmed two years later at Coimbra.[42] It would seem that this decree met with the disapproval of the city's council, because in 1292 the king wrote back to Coimbra saying that it could elect a committee consisting of 2 *alcaides*, a member of the knightly class (*cavaleiro*) and a townsman (*cidadão*) to judge cases dealing with Jews.[43]

For their part, the Jews' primary concern seemed to be not only that they receive fair treatment by the *alcalde*, but also that they have sufficient access to him in order to be able to settle their financial contracts with Christians in a timely manner. During this period, the Jews of Lisbon were involved in so many loans with Christians that they petitioned the crown to obtain their own official to oversee such cases. The Jewish community was granted their request in exchange for paying an annual fee of 100 royal pounds directly to the magistrate. In 1315, a similar complaint was brought to the king from Jewish community of Santarem who argued that Jewish creditors were unable to collect debts owed to them because they could never find the requisite two officials in town at the same time.[44]

By the early fourteenth century, the town council of Lisbon also began to protest to the king that the Jews there had been granted new privileges that infringed upon the jurisdiction traditionally afforded to the council. Specifically, it complained that Jews involved in criminal matters refused to bring these cases before the *alcaide* and *alvazil* of the city, as was ordered by the city's charter, but rather took the cases to their own Jewish officials, or *arrabis*. Over the course of the fourteenth century the crown struck a compromise with Lisbon's *concelho*. The crown and its officials maintained jurisdiction over criminal cases involving Jews, but in civil cases, when the defendant was a Jew, the case went before a Jewish official or *arrabi*, and when the defendant was a Christian, it went before a town judge.[45]

---

[41] Da Silva Marques, *Descobrimentos Portugueses*, no. 1, pp. 5–6; *Arquivo de Beja*, Beja, 1944, 1:62; *PMH, Leges*, pp. 410, 476. See also M. J. Pimenta Ferro Tavares, *Os Judeus*, 2nd ed., 85.

[42] ANTT, Chanc. de D. Dinis, , liv. I, fol. 266, liv. II, fol. 16.

[43] ANTT, *Estremadura*, liv. XI fols. 302–303.

[44] Pimenta Ferro Tavares, *Os Judeus* (2nd ed.), 86, 83.

[45] *Documentos para a historia da cidade de Lisboa. Livro I de misticos de Reis. Livro II dos Reis D. Dinis, D. Alfonso IV, D. Pedro I* (Lisbon, 1947), 175, and *Ordenações Afonsinas*, liv. II, 2nd ed. (1792; Lisbon, 1998), 510–512.

The delineation of the legal relationship between Jews and Christians was the focal point of all Iberian legislation with reference to Jews, and it is here that one can best see the royal policy of protecting the Jews and establishing a civic status for them that was equal to that of Christians. I have argued that the legal jurisdiction and royal efforts to assert exclusive sovereignty over Iberian Jewry were part of an ongoing process, much contested by the other estates of the realm, and that royal legislation on this subject represents political aspirations of the crown more than it does a pervasive historical reality. It can also be noted that repeated royal claims to exclusive rights over the Jews and their property did not, in any way, bring about a degradation of Jewish status. Elsewhere in Europe, the motivation for similar shifts in royal policy have been attributed to the "royal desire to control and exploit Jewish lending," with the effect of making Jewish status "clearly distinguishable from all other statuses."[46] Unlike their northern counterparts, whose economic activity had been all but limited to the practice of moneylending by the thirteenth century, Spanish and Portuguese Jews still remained economically diversified throughout this period. Nor did royal control over the Jews of Iberia lead to the creation of a unique social and legal position that set them apart from the rest of society. In the tripartite society of the peninsula, monarchical control over the Jews was paralleled by similar claims over Muslim communities. Iberian kings sought control over the rights to Jewish taxes (on individuals, merchandise, and land) much as they did over other groups such as Muslims and the municipalities. In return, the crown provided the Jews with royal protection and privileges.

The precedent for the protection of Jews and the promotion of their status on the frontier was established during the early forays of the *reconquista* in the eleventh century. In Castile-León, a royal charter from 1091 asserted that legal disputes between members of the two groups were to be settled by the highest royal or ecclesiastical official or, in their absence, two representatives or *bastioneros*. Eight years later, Alfonso VI gave the *fuero* of Miranda del Ebro to the entire populace of the town, including "great men, or peasants, or Moors, or Jews." This *fuero* was reconfirmed and amplified several times over the next two centuries. The royal campaign to establish legal equality among Jews, Muslims, and Christians was expanded in 1177, and

---

[46] Gavin Langmuir, *Toward a Definition of Antisemitism* (Berkeley, 1990), 188, 191.

again in 1189, in the *fueros* granted to Cuenca, which in turn served as the model for a host of thirteenth-century charters. In these *fueros*, Alfonso VIII sums up this view of civil equality:

I likewise grant to all settlers this prerogative: whoever may come to live in Cuenca, whatever condition he may be, whether Christian, Moor, or Jew, free or servile, should come in safety. He need not answer to anyone by reason of enmity, debt, bond, inheritance, *mayordomia*, *merindadico*, or any other thing he may have done before the conquest of Cuenca.[47]

Here, the crown envisions the frontier town as a place in which all are free to come and make a new start. This notion would continue to characterize royal attitudes in the other Iberian kingdoms as well. When Jaime II of the Crown of Aragon set out to incorporate the kingdom of Murcia into his dominions at the end of the thirteenth century, he used similar language in assuring a group of Jews from the Castilian town of Cartagena that they would be allowed to settle in Murcia regardless of their past civil or criminal infractions. He also guaranteed all citizens of Cartagena, Jews included, that they would continue to enjoy all the rights and privileges granted to them when the city was under Castilian rule. When Castile once again came to govern the city of Murcia, the *concejo* complained to Alfonso XI that the city's *fuero* did not include specific penalties for Jews who were found guilty of attacking Christians. The king set the amount at 500 *mrs.*, explaining that: "it was our wish that Christians and Jews be equal in this point as in other matters."[48] In Jérez de la Frontera, Jews were exempted from paying the *portazgo* tax anywhere in Castile-León, and further granted the same general rights as any Christian citizens of the town. And at Tortosa, Muslim and Jewish settlers were considered to be so important to the commercial well-being of the town that they were granted the unprecedented privilege of attending general assemblies of the *Cort*. The *Costums de Tortosa*, a legal code dating from the thirteenth century, granted Jews the right to attend these assemblies in order that they might take part in "the deliberation and resolutions of public business."[49]

[47] *Karta inter Christians et Judaeos de Foros Illorum.* See Muñoz y Romero, *Colección*, 89; Baer, *Juden*, vol. 2, 8; Powers, *Code of Cuenca*, chap. 1, rub. 10.
[48] ACA, reg. 340, fols. 283v–284, 280v. For Murcia see Juan Torres Fontes, ed., *Colección de Documentos*, vol. 6, no. 121, p. 136.
[49] Fidel Fita, "Jérez de la Frontera, su judería en 1266," *Boletín de la Real Academia de Historia* 10 (1887): 484. The *portazgo* was a transport tax levied on merchandise. For quote, see *Costums de Tortosa*, lib. 1, rub. 9, cost. 5; lib. 1, rub. 1, cost. 17. The only stipulation was that Jews and Muslims were required to sit apart from Christians. For the reinstatement of the law, see *PMH, Leges*, 296, 310.

In Portugal, Afonso III set rules for witnesses in cases between Jews and Christians, ordering that at least one member of each group be present. It would seem that this royal precaution was not always observed, and the crown was forced to repeat his decree in 1284, 1294, and 1313. In this last letter, the king explains that the presence of Jewish representatives at court is imperative, since Christians otherwise would be tempted to bear false witness.

And on this issue of the Christians, that they are not to receive testimony against a Jew without another Jew being present, I order that they adhere to the law given by my father Dom Afomso [Afonso II], and my forefathers, in which they authorized that no Christian testimony against a Jew be valid without the presence of another Jew, because they found that many were induced to give false testimony against the Jews, convincing themselves that they could do so without sin.

The repeated issuance of this decree was most likely a result of complaints on the part of the Jews that it was not being obeyed. After being partially revoked in 1321, this law was reinstated three years later as a result of a complaint by the *arrabi mor* Guedelha.[50]

Another significant feature of thirteenth-century legislation concerning the Jews was that the monarchs who sought to revive Roman law bypassed many of the more discriminatory elements of the Visigothic code. In the version of the *Fuero Juzgo* promulgated in the towns of Andalusia and Murcia, the old anti-Jewish laws had been reduced to little more than rhetorical flourishes. These included the decree that cases between Jews and Christians should be heard by Christian judges "for the honor of Jesus Christ and the Christians,"[51] and the requirement of an annual tax of 30 *dineros*, which the Jews were to pay to the chapter of their local church. The latter was a nominal fee meant to recall the thirty pieces of silver paid to Judas for his betrayal of Christ, and was resisted by the Jews of Seville for years.[52]

---

[50] AHCM, *Livro dos Pregos*, no. 33, fols. 8–9. See also *Ordenações Afonsinas*, 502–504.

[51] AMC, *Libro de privilegios*, fol. 2. Even in this case, the language that was included in the *fuero* of Cordoba was omitted when the same charter was granted to the Murcian town of Lorca. There, the *fuero* merely states: "Otrossi, mandamos que si algun moro o judio oviere pleito con christianos, vengan a juyzio ante los alcaldes christianos." Torres Fontes, ed., *Colección de documentos*, 2:126.

[52] Mathew, 26: 14. See also Norman Roth, "The Civic Status of the Jew in Medieval Spain," in Chevedden et al., eds., *Iberia and the Mediterranean World*, 2:156–157. For the *aljama* of Seville's refusal to pay the tax, see ACS, leg. 117, no. 13; pub., in Ballesteros, *Sevilla*, no. 87; González Jiménez, *Diplomatario andaluz*, no. 187; the collection of documents in ACS, caja 6, nos. 2/1–12. For payment of the 30 *dineros* in Córdoba, see BCC, ms 125, fol. 61.

Other laws that suggest the influence of long-standing religious attitudes regarding the Jews were those governing the sale of foodstuffs. The *fuero* of Castel Rodrigo, Portugal, forbade Christian butchers to sell any meats slaughtered by Jews, and the *fuero* of Madrid contained a prohibition against Christians selling meat rejected by Jewish butchers.[53] Along with a similar law forbidding Christian butchers to sell Jewish meat, the *fuero* of Salamanca also prohibits Christians from butchering meat for Jews during the periods of Carnival and Lent.[54] Likewise, the *fuero* of Sepúlveda states that no Jew is to sell meat to Christians for three days prior and three days after the feasts of Easter, Christmas, and Pentecost.[55] Similar to these laws on the sale of meat was the common prohibition against Jews purchasing fish on Fridays; a law which extended to any Christian who would make the purchase on the Jew's behalf.[56] It should be noted that this law appears to be more of a nod to the Church than a safeguard against any true social problem, since, in either case, the penalty for such an infraction was a mere 1 *sueldo*. Such laws were aimed at separating the religious communities, not degrading Jewish status, and in some cases were even to the benefit of the Jews. The prohibition against Jewish patronage of Christian butchers during Lent, for instance, also served the purpose of preventing possible violence against the Jews.

Royal interest in maintaining a general sense of judicial equality between Jews and Christians is underscored by royal disregard for the few

---

[53] *Foro* of Castel Rodrigo, chap. 6, rub. 27, in *PMH, Leges,* 882; Madrid, rub. 57. The issue of Christian consumption of meat that had been declared unfit by Jews carried deep theological implications. In the 11th-century charter granted to the Jews of the Rhineland city of Speyer, for instance, the city's bishop made a special allowance for Jews to sell such meat to Christians and for Christians to purchase it. The charter is published in Chazan, *Church, State, and Jew,* 59. See also William C. Jordan, "Problems of the Meat Market of Béziers 1240–1247: a question of anti-Semitism," *Revue des Études Juives* 135 (1976): 31–49.
[54] *Fuero* of Salamanca, rub. 346.
[55] *Fuero* of Sepúlveda, titles 143 and 228. The *fuero* makes an exception for the sale of goat meat. See, also, León Tello, "Disposiciones sobre judíos en los fueros de Castilla y León," *Sefarad* 46 (1986): 282–283.
[56] *Fueros* of Plasencia, rub. 439; Cáceres, rub. 74; Coria, rub. 218; Castello-Bom, *PMH, Leges,* 770; *Alfaiate,* 880; *Castello-Melhor,* 924; etc. In his analysis of Jewish-Christian relations as reflected in the Siete Partidas, Dwayne Carpenter has argued that "Christians were also at times prohibited from purchasing meat from Jewish butchers because of charges that sought to poison Christians." However, the idea that Jews might try to poison meat and other foods sold to Christians, though widespread in Europe at this time, did not seem to be a factor in royal legislation on this topic in any of the Iberian kingdoms. Dwayne Carpenter, "Jewish-Christian Social Relations in Alphonsine Spain," in *Florilegium Hispanicum, Medieval and Golden Age Studies presented to Dorothy Clotelle Clarke,* ed. John S. Geary (Madison, 1983), 63.

regulations that did diminish Jewish status. One of the most frequently flouted laws was the prohibition against Jews holding the position of tax collector or other royal offices that might give them power over Christians. This was an ancient prohibition, originating in Roman imperial legislation of the fifth century, that had been preserved by local Iberian charters and in canon law, and which was reasserted by the Church in the fourth Lateran Council of 1215. However, this law was blatantly ignored by a series of kings, bishops, and masters of the various crusading orders throughout this period.[57]

Iberian monarchs had placed Jews in important administrative roles since the eleventh century, a practice that had been continually contested by the papacy. Ecclesiastical condemnation of the crown's willingness to employ Jews in positions of authority continued throughout the thirteenth century, but was to little avail. In 1231, Pope Gregory IX responded to complaints from the bishop of Lisbon that the Jews there had obtained privileges which contradicted those of the *concelho*, and specifically that they had been allowed to hold positions of authority over Christians. However, the only counsel that the pope could offer the indignant Portuguese episcopate was to try to reason with the king as best they could. The recalcitrance of the Portuguese monarchy in this regard remained a source of ecclesiastical indignation throughout the century.[58]

Charters given to the frontier towns of Córdoba, Murcia, and Lorca prohibited Jews from holding offices over Christians with the exception of the position of royal *almoxarife*. Though the *almoxarifes* were, in the strict sense, tax collectors, they were often granted powers that greatly broadened their

[57] For the original law prohibiting Jews from serving in the Roman imperial administration, see Amnon Linder, *The Jews in Roman Imperial Legislation* (Detroit, 1987), 323–337. The prohibition was preserved in the Visigothic *Liber Judiciorum*, 12. 2. 14, and reinstated for Toledo by Alfonso VII in 1118, Muñoz y Romero, *Colección*, 364–366. It was later included in *Las Siete Partidas*, 7.26.4; and Carpenter's discussion in *Alfonso X and the Jews: An Edition of and Commentary on Siete Partidas 7.24 "De los judios"* (Berkeley, 1986), 67–69. The prohibition's inclusion in the fourth Lateran Council is found in canon no. 68, published in Latin and English in Grayzel, *The Church and the Jews*, 1:308–309. For late-medieval Iberia, see the *fueros* of Cuenca, chap. I, rub. 17; Alcaraz, lib. I, rub. 20; Alarcon, title 16; *Fori regni Valentiae*, lib. 3, rub. 6, c. 16.

[58] Grayzel, *Church and the Jews*, vol. 1, no. 64. Afonso III's policies concerning the Jews and his general disregard for the concerns of the Church brought about his excommunication just prior to his death in 1279. For a similar debate in Castile see Peter Linehan, "The Spanish Church Revisited," in *Authority and Power, Studies on Medieval Law and Government Presented to Walter Ullman on His 70th Birthday*, ed. Grayzel and Brian Tierney (Cambridge, 1980), 127–147. Like a great deal of anti-Jewish legislation that was incorporated in Alfonso X's *Siete Partidas*, the reappearance of the prohibition against the Jews holding public office (7.26.4) reflects little more than a royal gesture to ecclesiastical demands.

authority. During the reigns of Alfonso X of Castile, Jaime I, and Pedro III of the Crown of Aragon, the laws prohibiting Jews holding positions of power was undermined by the steady increase in the number of Jewish *almoxarifes* and the scope of their powers. Toward the end of the century the Church was aided in its campaign to expel Jews from public administration by the municipal *concejos* whose representatives sought to pressure the crown to enforce the prohibition against Jewish tax collectors, in particular, at the *Cortes* of Valladolid in 1295, as well as those held at Burgos in 1301 and at Medina del Campo in 1305. The combined efforts of the various estates eventually had an impact on royal policy, and during the final two decades of the century, the presence of Jews in the royal administrations of all the peninsular kingdoms began to wane. Nonetheless, Jewish officials continued to serve the kings of Castile, Aragon, and Portugal, albeit in limited numbers, until their expulsion from the peninsula at the close of the fifteenth century.[59]

The treatment of the Jews in Castilian legal codes was not significantly influenced by the negative attitudes of contemporary ecclesiastical doctrine until the compilation of the *Siete Partidas*, which was not promulgated until the mid fourteenth century. Even then, anti-Jewish sentiment was generally offset by protective measures. While the *Siete Partidas* gives credence to popular tales of Jewish ritual murder, ordering for that offenders be put to death, it also notes that only the king had the right to carry out this sentence.

And since we hear it said that, in some places, the Jews celebrated and still celebrate Good Friday, commemorating the Passion of Our Lord Jesus Christ by way of contempt, stealing children, putting them on a cross or, when they cannot find children, making wax images and crucifying them. We order that, henceforth, if such a thing should take place in some locale in our dominions, and if it can be proved, all those who are confirmed in this matter shall be seized, arrested, and brought before the king. And after [the king] verifies their guilt, he shall sentence them to death in a disgraceful manner, no matter how many there should be.

---

[59] Fernando Valls y Taberner, *Los privilegios de Alfonso X el sabio a la ciudad de Murcia* (Barcelona, 1923), 42. A version from 1272 is published in Baer, *Juden*, 2:62, no. 81; the version given to Lorca is published in Torres Fontes, *Fueros y privilegios de Alfonso*, 123–131. For Córdoba, see Victoriano Rivera Romero, ed., *La carta de fuero concedida á la ciudad de Córdoba por el rey D. Fernando III* (Córdoba, 1881), 17. For legislation at the *cortes*, see Colmeiro, *Cortes de los antiguos reinos*, 1:131, 149, 173, 183.

Similarly, the charter for the Portuguese town of Beja stated that any Jew attacking or injuring a Christian was to be put to death, but only by the crown, noting: "and this justice should be done by the king."[60]

For the Jews, such safeguards and protective measures were the principal benefit of royal sovereignty. The Castilian sage Meir Halevi Abulafia noted that protection provided by the king was certainly more effective than hiring mercenaries. A generation later, Asher ben Yehiel offered a somewhat more pessimistic view of royal protection:

It seems to me that all types of taxes must be considered defense expenditures. For what purpose do some of the Gentile nations find in preserving us and allowing us to live among them if not the benefit that they derive from Israel in their collection of taxes and extortions from them.[61]

In a responsum dealing with the proper treatment of Christian kings, Solomon ibn Adret compared them to the kings of Israel, and noted that the real meaning of the legal concept of "the law of the land is law" is best exemplified by Christian kings who work on behalf of Jews. On this subject ibn Adret was no doubt influenced by his teacher, Moses ben Nahman (Nahmanides), who wrote that

It appears to me that when we say that "the law of the realm is the law," we are referring to the royal legislation accepted throughout the entire realm which the king and all those kings who came before him have enacted, and which are written in the chronicles and statutes of the kings.[62]

Nahmanides' respect for such statutes was shared by the Jews of the frontier who often invoked the rights and privileges guaranteed to them by municipal charters and royal grants to protest of any legal abuses. In one such instance, a Jew from Córdoba referred to the rights of Jews contained in the

---

[60] *Siete Partidas* 7.24.2. For Beja, see "Foros de Beja," in *Collecção de livros inéditos de historia Portugueza*, ed. José Francisco Corriea da Serra (Lisbon, 1824), 5:506.

[61] *Yad Ramah Baba Batra*, (Warsaw, 1887), chap. 1, 87, also 85. Asher ben Yehiel, *Commentary on the Babylonian Talmud, Baba Bathra*, chap. 1, 29. The translation is taken from Septimus, *Hispano-Jewish Culture*, 13.

[62] Adret, 2:134. Nahmanides' quote is found in Adret, *Responsa*, 5:198, as well as in the responsa of R. Samuel b. Isaac ha-Sardi, *Sefer ha-Terumot* (Salonica, 1628?), chap. 46, section 8.

fuero of that city during a court case with a Christian, pointing out that the charter guaranteed the Jews the right to have Jewish witnesses present during any suit brought against them.[63] The importance that Jews invested in their towns' *fueros* is also illustrated by a case in which one community sought to have the local charter altered in its favor. Under Pedro III of Aragon, a delegation of Jews from the city of Valencia petitioned for a change to be made in the city's charter regarding litigation between Jews and Christians. The existing clause allowed for Christian witnesses to give testimony in such cases without a corresponding Jewish witness. Their appeal was unsuccessful, as the king refused to contravene any existing *fueros* without the approval of the municipality itself. Nonetheless, their petition would indicate that they viewed their *fuero* as a valid and important set of laws that had a critical impact on their lives. The following year, Jahuda Alazar, also of Valencia, invoked the rights given to Jews in the city's charter in a case brought against him. In another example from this region, the *justicia* of Murviedro was ordered to deal with a financial dispute between a Christian and a Jew there according to the charter of Valencia.[64]

Royal attitudes toward the Jews of thirteenth-century Iberia were, in large part, characterized by the continuity and extension of earlier policies. The crown's involvement in the development of municipal legislation which began in the northern towns of the peninsula in the late eleventh century established the concept of judicial equality for settlers of this earlier frontier, assuming an open society characterized by the continual interaction of Christians, Muslims and Jews. This initial attitude toward the legal relationship between members of the three faiths would remain the basis upon which local and regional charters were established throughout the peninsula during the twelfth and thirteenth centuries. Whatever popular animosity Christians may have harbored toward the Jews, royal legislation did not curtail their rights on the basis of religion. The Jews themselves seemed to view the municipal and royal legislation regarding their communities more as guarantees of their rights than as restrictions and did not hesitate to invoke them during legal cases involving Christians.

It must be noted, however, that royal protection of Jewish status on the thirteenth-century frontier took place within a context that was significantly different from previous centuries and other regions. In contrast to earlier periods of the *reconquista*, the Christian conquests and subsequent coloniza-

---

[63] AHPC, Carp. 31, no. 1; published by by Cruces Blancos, "*Datos sobre compraventas*," 225–226.

[64] ACA, reg. 46, fols. 152v–153; reg. 57, fol. 222v; reg. 89, fol. 47v.

tion of the thirteenth century were highly centralized, and Christian territorial expansion was closely bound up with the expansion of royal authority.[65] The crown's relationship with the Jews developed out of this broader campaign to assert royal power and jurisdiction over an ever-greater area, and must be seen as a continuous process that required constant reinforcement. This ambitious program aimed at extending monarchical authority achieved its greatest success in the cities of the frontier, where the nascent municipal councils had yet developed the local customs and political power found in the older Christian towns of the north. Nowhere in the peninsula was this process of royal control and regularization of local law more prevalent than in the frontier provinces of Andalusia and Murcia, where all of the major towns were granted versions of the same *fuero* by the Castilian crown.

This unprecedented royal influence on the development of municipal government in the new territories would also have negative results for Jewish communities there. The claims of the crown to sole jurisdiction over the Jews and their promotion of royal judges to oversee cases between Jews and Christians were both products of a pan-peninsular attempt to extend royal power and control into new arenas. While Jewish settlers initially benefited from the crown's growing interest in its proprietary relationship with its Jews, such royal policies also fueled tensions between the young municipal *concejos* of the frontier and Jewish settlers whom the former increasingly came to view as agents of the crown. This trend toward the royal appointment of officials to oversee the financial and judicial affairs of the Jews would also create problems within the *aljama* itself. As Jewish settlements on the frontier began to develop, royal authority would come to play an increasingly central role in shaping Jewish communal autonomy and organization.

[65] On the impact of royal authority on the reconquest and resettlement efforts of the thirteenth century, see Mackay, *Spain in the Middle Ages*, 95–105; Lomax, *Reconquest*, 142–159; and Peter Linehan, *The Spanish Church and the Papacy in the Thriteenth Century* (Cambridge, 1971), 5.

CHAPTER FIVE
JEWISH COMMUNAL ORGANIZATION
AND AUTHORITY

The residents of each city may punish and impose sanctions of all sorts—
in the case of one who refuses to recognize their local ordinances. If the
recalcitrant person is violent and disorderly in his disregard for the law,
we should cause him to be arrested by Gentiles who will tell him to con-
form to the Jewish demands.
—R. Asher ben Yehiel

The nature of Jewish communal life in the new territories
was, to a considerable extent, loose and fluid. Jewish settlers who migrated to the frontier did so without any assur-
ance that they would be able to replicate the social and religious institutions present in the older Jewish centers of the interior. Indeed,
the development of communal institutions such as synagogues, cemeteries, and
kosher butcheries was often slow, and varied greatly from one settlement to the
next. The emerging governing councils of these Jewish communities were beset
with a variety of obstacles to the imposition of their authority including the
resistance of independent-minded settlers, the factionalism and conflict of rival
Jewish clans, and the increasingly frequent intervention of the crown and royally appointed officials. It was this latter challenge that would come to have the
greatest impact on Jewish communal government in the thirteenth century, and
lead to the integration of the ostensibly autonomous Jewish community into the
rapidly expanding royal administrations of the various Christian kingdoms.

THE ESTABLISHMENT OF COMMUNAL
INSTITUTIONS

The mix of collective and individual grants that characterized the initial
land partitions presaged the diversity of Jewish settlements on the frontier

that developed throughout the late thirteenth and early fourteenth centuries. The prevalence of public institutions established by these settlers varied greatly, and as a result, those Jews who settled the new territories often did so at great social and religious expense. One of the most striking characteristics of Jewish settlement during this period was the willingness of Jews to move to areas that were devoid of the communal institutions available in larger, more established communities. To be sure, major Jewish centers such as Valencia, Seville, and Lisbon possessed Jewish cemeteries and synagogues, baths and butcher shops, if not already prior to Christian rule, then shortly thereafter. Yet there is evidence that, throughout this period, Jewish individuals and even whole groups chose to live outside of these larger, more organized communities and the services that they provided.

The central institution in these communities was the synagogue, references to which are to be found at nearly all of the larger Jewish centers on the frontier. In Andalusia, the reestablished Jewish quarters at Seville and Jérez contained synagogues from the time of the initial partitions, and evidence of the construction of a new synagogue at Córdoba came less than fifteen years after the city's conquest. In Mallorca, Alfonso III's confirmation of the rights of the Jewish community in 1290 included clauses granting them the rights to a synagogue and a bakery within their quarter, both of which seem to be held in common by the entire community. In the city of Valencia, the communal synagogue is mentioned in a series of documents from 1304, and in the Portuguese capital of Lisbon, the first synagogue was erected by Joseph ibn Yahia during the reign of Sancho I (r. 1185–1211), according to Joseph's descendant the chronicler Gedalia ibn Yahia.[1]

It should also be pointed out that references to Jews who hold the title of Rabbi in these communities should not be taken as evidence of a communal synagogue. The common use of the designation "Rabbi" as a general honorific during this period, and the loose relationship between the medieval synagogue and those who were, indeed, "masters of Jewish law" make such conclusions untenable. To be sure, the common references to synagogues in municipal *fueros* as a place where Jews might meet to swear oaths in legal cases presupposes the ubiquity of communal synagogues. Yet despite the importance and prevalence of communal synagogues in larger Jewish centers, this institution was still absent from some of the smaller Jewish settle-

---

[1] BCC, ms. 125, fol. iv. For Mallorca, see ACA, reg. 83, fols. 99v-100; and Régné, *pièces justificatives*, no. 22. The construction of the synagogue was later approved by the city's bishop, Ponç des Jardí. Fita and Llabrés, "Privilegios," no. 14; Villanueva, *Viatge Literario*, 332–333, and for Valencia, see ACA, reg. 202, fols. 202r–203v. For Lisbon, see *Shalselet ha-Qabbalah* (1587; Jerusalem 1962), 29a; José Amador de los Ríos, *Historia social, política y religiosa de los judíos de España y Portugal* (Madrid, 1875–76), 1:271.

ments on the frontier decades after their conquest. Nor did the existence of a communal synagogue preclude that of other, smaller prayer houses that were maintained for private use, often by wealthy Jewish families. Indeed, the general lack of references to communal synagogues might also be the result of a custom among some of the Jews of this period to establish sanctuaries in private homes. The use of private or family synagogues posed a potential threat to public houses of worship, especially in smaller communities where it might have been difficult to gather the necessary ten men to form a *minyan*. The popularity of private sanctuaries is also illustrated by the *aljama* of Seville, where there were some twenty-three synagogues in operation by the fourteenth century.[2]

The establishment of private synagogues offered convenience as well as the ability to assert greater control over the limits of one's social group or religious community. It is unlikely that this practice resulted from the ancient legal restrictions placed on the construction or expansion of synagogues. Such restrictions first appear in a law from the fifth century in which the Roman emperor Theodosius II declared that: "no synagogue shall be constructed from now on, and the old ones shall remain in their present condition." This prohibition resurfaced in both papal and royal legislation during the thirteenth century. An example can be seen in the ecclesiastical legal compendium, the *Decretales*, which contains the following statement:

> Be advised that you ought not permit the Jews to build anew synagogues where they have not had them. Indeed if old synagogues fall or threaten to fall, it can be tolerated that the Jews rebuild them. They must not, however, enhance them or make them larger and more pretentious that they were known to be previously. In any case, they should clearly have the right to be tolerated in their old synagogues and observances.[3]

[2] See the town of Burriana where Jews did not have their own communal synagogue until 1326. ACA, reg. 228, fol. 211v. For the prevalence of private synagogues, ACA, reg. 198, fol. 211, reg. 16, fol. 171v, and Yom Tov Assis, "Synagogues in Medieval Spain," *Jewish Art* 18 (1992): 6–29, esp. 12–13. For Seville, see Baer, *Juden*, vol. 2, no. 67.

[3] For *Codex Theodosianus*, 16.8.25, see Linder, *The Jews in Roman Imperial Legislation*, 288. For the quote, see the edition of the *Decretales* edited by Emil Friedberg, *Corpus Iuris Canonici*, (Leipzig, 1881), 2:773. The translation is taken from R. Chazan, ed., *Church, State, and Jew*, 30. The medieval Spanish version simply states that "los iudios non deuen auer nueuas synagogas, mas deuen auer las uieias." See Jaime M. Mans Puigarnau, ed., *Deretales de Gregorio IX: versión medieval española* (Barcelona, 1939), 1:141.

Nonetheless, laws regarding the prohibition of synagogue construction had relatively little impact in the Iberian kingdoms. Such laws were absent from influential legal codes, such as Alfonso X's *Fuero Real*, and while they were included in the *Siete Partidas*, the formulation there also includes a provision that allows for exceptions to be made by the crown. The pertinent passage states that: "The synagogue is a place of Jewish worship, and they are not to make anew any such house anywhere in our realm, *unless by our order*." The relative ineffectiveness of the prohibition of new or expanded synagogues on the Iberian frontier is also exemplified by a papal letter from 1250. In it, Pope Innocent IV admonished the bishop of Córdoba for allowing the Jews of his city to build a synagogue of excessive height. Indeed, rededication by Fernando III of three Sevillan mosques as synagogues was in direct contradiction of the ecclesiastical prohibition against the creation of new synagogues.[4] The kings of the crown of Aragon also appear to have been willing to make such exceptions, waiving restrictions on synagogue construction in exchange for the payment of a "fine." In Valencia, Jaime II granted permission for the Jews of the city to expand their community's synagogue and house of study beyond the legal limits for height and size. The expansion came at the stiff price of 16,000 sous, an amount that was large enough that the king organized a committee of seven Jewish collectors in order to assure payment. He also ordered Valencia's bailiff to see that all Jews who possessed seats at the synagogue, or any other urban property, contributed to the collection.[5] Though the private synagogue constructed by Samuel Nageri of Teruel violated the law banning new houses of worship, he was able to keep it by obtaining a royal pardon.

The existence of other basic, public, institutions also varied among the Jewish communities of the frontier. As with communal synagogues, the *aljamas* of the larger towns were granted land that was set aside for Jewish burial. The *libros de repartimiento* of Seville and Murcia both mention the existence of Jewish ossuaries, and a cemetery in Mallorca, though not listed in the island's initial land registers, was included among the privileges given to the Jews soon after the Christian conquest of the Balearics.[6] A letter from

---

[4] *Siete Partidas*, 7.24.4. My emphasis. For the papal letter to Cordoba, see BCC, ms. 125, fol. 1v; published in M. Nieto Cumplido, ed., *Corpus*, vol. 1, no. 356, and for Seville, see ACS, section XI, caja 4, no. 36/1; published in *Diplomatario andaluz*, ed. M. González Jiménez, 6–8.

[5] ACA, reg. 202, fol. 202r–203. Whether this was a new building or an expansion of a preexisting structure is unclear.

[6] See the *fonsario de los iudios* at Seville (ACS, caja 58, no. 33; published in *Diplomatario andaluz*, no. 408, ed. M. González Jiménez); the Jewish *osario* at Murcia (*Repartimiento de*

1268 lists the Jewish cemetery at Játiva as being among those sites to be protected from Christian mobs on Good Friday, and in Portugal the Jewish community of Lisbon is listed as having its own cemetery, located outside the city.[7] As with synagogues, however, communal land dedicated for Jewish burial was not found in all Jewish settlements. Due to the paucity of Jewish settlers in the Valencian town of Burriana, Jews did not have their own cemetery there until the fourteenth century. Until then, Jewish settlers at Burriana had the arduous task of having to transport their dead to the Jewish cemeteries in Murviedro or the city of Valencia. Transportation of the deceased to another community for burial could be dangerous, as well as costly and inconvenient. In 1291, Jews from the northern community of Cervera were attacked as they transported their dead to a town with a Jewish cemetery. The acceptance of such a situation underscores the degree of religious and social hardship that some Jewish settlers were willing to accept. The burial situation that was endured by the Jews of Burriana was, in all likelihood, common to many small settlements of Jews in the southern territories. A royal decree issued by Pedro III regulating Jewish dress in the kingdom of Valencia makes an exception for those areas with fewer than ten Jewish homes, suggesting a number of such small pockets of Jewish settlement in this region.[8]

A similar disparity between larger and smaller communities in the early institutional development of frontier Jewries existed with regard to separate slaughterhouses for kosher meat. At Valencia, it was possible for Jews to obtain a royal privilege to establish a butcher stall in the *judería* in exchange for a nominal annual fee, yet such grants were slow in coming to other Jewish settlements. Along the southern periphery of the Crown of Aragon, the Jewish population was still quite sparse well into the fourteenth century. A letter from 1312 notes that "in the aforementioned locale of Elche, where the Jews are in modest numbers" they are unable to maintain their own butcher shops. In recognition of this situation, the king ordered local Christian butchers to give the Jews two animals a day to be slaughtered according to the Jewish rite (that is, the laws of *kashrut*). A similar privilege was granted to the Jews of Mallorca, who were allowed to slaughter their own meat at Christian butcher shops, and to the Jews of Tortosa who shared

---

Murcia, ed. Torres Fontes, 221). For Mallorca see AHN, Clero, carp. 75, no. 17; and the mention of a Jewish cemetery there in Adret, 5: 136.

[7] ACA, reg. 15, fol. 95v; cited in Régné, no. 377. For Lisbon, see ANTT, *Corp. Rel., S. Gens,* m. 1, no. 2.

[8] ACA, reg. 91, fol. 163, and Adret, 3:291. For Valencia, see ACA, reg. 46, fol. 152v, and Adret 5:253.

butcher shops with the local Muslim community until well into the four-teenth century.[9] Most of these new settlements also lacked other social institutions, among them, hospitals, houses for the poor, and organized charitable funds that began to become popular during this period in larger northern centers of the Crown of Aragon, such as Saragossa and Barcelona. The *aljama* of Valencia is the only frontier community for which we have references of a communal fund (Heb. *heqdesh*) to support orphans, widows, and the poor, and similar institutions were even slower to develop in the Castilian *aljamas*. When Asher ben Yehiel and his sons arrived in Toledo at the beginning of the fourteenth century, the large Jewish community there was still without a charitable fund. Indeed, the building set aside for Jewish refugees in Jérez de la Frontera is the only one of its kind recorded for any of the Jewish centers in the new territories, and appears to have been a temporary institution.[10]

The slow and erratic development of many communal institutions illustrates the non-corporate character of Jewish migration to and settlement in the new territories in the first decades of *repoblación*. In a few cases, Jewish settlers appear to have lived somewhat outside the boundaries of the organized Jewish society. In one case, Salamon, a Jewish settler in southern Valencia, was granted permission to settle in the town of Cocentaina without joining the local Jewish community. In another, Jacob Menahem was granted an exemption from paying property taxes to both the Muslim community of Ella, where he lived, and the Jewish community of neighboring Elche. Menahem had previously been paying his taxes to the crown along with the Muslims of Ella. This one short entry in the royal Aragonese register speaks volumes about the nature of Jewish settlement on the frontier. Ella was a town located on the southernmost edge of Christian dominated territory, in which Jews had chosen to settle and to live in close proximity with the local Muslim population. These Jews were seemingly drawn to this remote locale by the promise of economic opportunities and land grants from the crown,

---

[9] ACA, reg. 229, fol. 226; cited in Régné, no. 3415. For Elche, see ACA, reg. 209, fol. 147. The Jews of Elche and Orihuela did not receive the general privileges accorded to the rest of Valencia until 1316. ACA, reg. 212, fol. 145. For Mallorca, see Fita and Llabrés, "Privilegios," pp. 26–27, no. 10. For Tortosa, see ACA, reg. 221, fols. 226v–227. In 1271, Valencian Jews were granted the rights to spaces along side Christian butchers at their stalls. ACA, reg. 16, fol. 248v.

[10] See Adret, 3:297 for the appointment of members of the Valencian community to oversee the charity fund, and ACA reg. 204, fol. 48 for a letter exempting a Jewish physician in Valencia from the obligation to support the poor Jews of his community due to his advanced age and prior service to the crown. For Toledo, see *Hebrew Ethical Wills*, ed. Israel Abrams (Philadelphia, 1926), 2:192. For Jérez see above, chap. 1.

attractions which apparently took precedence over the comforts and religious advantages of an established Jewish community. Here, a Jewish settler owned land in a predominantly Muslim town and paid his taxes alongside the local Muslims, rather than with the nearest Jewish community.[11]

It is unlikely that Jews who made the decision not to belong to any organized Jewish community did so out of desperation, since there were simply too many Jewish centers throughout the peninsula that offered at least the basic services and comforts of communal life. Rather, the high level of migration to the new territories (from the interior as well as from lands outside the peninsula) that took place at this time suggests a large number of individual Jews seeking greater economic opportunity, even if that opportunity came at the price of cultural and religious privation. That the majority of Jewish settlers did seek to establish public institutions such as cemeteries and synagogues as soon as their numbers were large enough to support them is, indeed, noteworthy. However, we must not ignore the fact that, for over half a century after Christian conquest, some Jews chose to immigrate to a number of frontier locales in which they knew they would be without the most essential components of Jewish life.[12]

THE STRUCTURE OF THE JEWISH COMMUNITY

With the development and proliferation of Jewish settlements on the frontier came the corresponding standardization of the Jewish community, commonly referred to in the documentation as *aljama* (Castilian), and *kahal* (Hebrew). Though Jewish communal organization remained somewhat varied during the thirteenth century, the *aljamas* of the frontier shared some basic structural characteristics with each other, as well as with the communities of the interior from whence they derived both their settlers and the models for their royal charters. As elsewhere in medieval Europe, the Jewish communities of the Iberian Peninsula were granted a high degree of political and legal independence. The use of the Arabic term *açuna* for Jewish law in many Christian documents from the thirteenth century indicates that the autonomy of the Jewish legal system in peninsular communities was a

---

[11] José Hinojosa Montalvo, "Bosquejo histórico de los judíos en tierras alicantinas durante dla baja edad media," *Actes 1r. Colloqui d'Història dels Jueus a la Corona d'Aragó* (Lleida, 1989), 210. For Jacob Menahem, see ACA, reg. 211, fol. 183v.

[12] ACA, reg. 228, fol. 211v.

Part II. The Jewish Community and the Frontier

feature that predated the Christian *reconquista*. Similarly, Jewish legal tradition provided a model for Jewish communal organization and administration, providing a system for autonomous rule long recognized by Gentile authorities.[13] However, the practicalities of Jewish self-government rendered such theoretical models woefully inaccurate. In order to gain any true insight into the nature of Jewish political autonomy and authority during this period, we must first reject those studies that present a static view of Jewish communal government. Arguments, such as Gerald Blidstein's assumption that "the community, basing itself upon Jewish ethics and law, was able to control the manipulation of non-Jewish power by Jews in its midst," mistake Jewish legal pronouncements for political reality.[14] Royal and rabbinic declarations of Jewish communal autonomy notwithstanding, Jews regularly contravened the jurisdiction of their *kahal* in order to promote their own interests. Moreover, there can be little doubt that the presence of Christian courts as a viable option for Jewish litigants influenced the course and eventual outcome of many cases brought before Jewish courts. Thus, after securing the rights of political and judicial autonomy from the crown, the governing councils of these nascent communities were then repeatedly forced to turn right back to the Christian authorities to petition their help in implementing local ordinances and judgments. Finally, royal recognition of Jewish autonomy did not preclude the crowns' intervention in the affairs of the Jewish community. Just as the various Iberian monarchs sought to regularize and control the territorial boundaries of Jewish settlements, they would also play an integral role in shaping the development of Jewish communal organization and political structures.[15]

References to Jewish *aljamas* first begin to appear during the late twelfth and early thirteenth centuries. The *aljama* was generally ruled by a communal council made up of representatives who were either elected or appointed for terms of varying duration, and who were referred to by a number of ti-

[13] Assis, *Golden Age*, 145. *Açuna*, or *azunna*, comes from the Arabic *sunna*, a term which refers to Muslim law, but which was also used by Christians to refer to Jewish law as well. For examples of the latter, see Régné, nos. 446, 1887.

[14] See his article, "A Note on the Function of 'The Law of the Kingdom is Law' in the Medieval Jewish Community," *Journal of Jewish Sociology* 15 (1973): 213–219; and Daniel J. Elazar, "The Kehillah: From Its Beginnings to the End of the Modern Epoch," in *Comparative Jewish Politics: Public Life in Israel and the Diaspora*, ed. Sam N. Lehman-Wilzig and Bernard Susser (Bar-Ilan, 1981), 35, 42, and idem, "Toward a Political History of the Sephardic Diaspora," *Jewish Political Studies Review* 5 (1993): 5–33, esp. 9–11.

[15] The confluence of Jewish political self-interest and royal intervention into the affairs of the *aljama* is discussed in the following chapter.

tles, including *adelantados* and *secretarii*, in Christian documents, and *berurim, ne'emanim, mukademim*, in Jewish sources.[16] Both Jewish and Christian texts also employ the term "good men of the city" (Latin, *probi homines*, Hebrew, *tovei ha-ir*). According to Solomon ibn Adret, the term *tovei ha-ir* referred generally to those representatives who were selected to handle the affairs of the community.

The seven good men of the city who are mentioned everywhere are not seven men who excel in wisdom wealth and honor. Rather, they are seven men who are chosen by the public as general administrators regarding matters of the city, and to act as agents over them.[17]

Sources from this period also make reference to Jewish "elders" (Castilian *viejos*, Hebrew *zekenim*) who functioned as communal leaders. In 1256, Alfonso X sent a letter addressed "to the elders and to the Jewish community of Seville," indicating that the crown viewed these men as being in charge Jewish communal government. Like ibn Adret's definition of the *tovei ha-ir*, the meaning of the Hebrew term *zekenim* did not refer to any particular communal officers, or to the entire body of adult males in a community. Rather, the term appears to have been synonymous with Jewish communal officials in general. Drawing heavily on the work of rabbinic authorities such as Isaac Alfasi (1013–1103) and Judah al-Bargeloni (late 11th-early 12th c.), both of whom predate the thirteenth century, Shalom Albeck has characterized the *zekenim* as wise men of the community who are experts in Talmud, but the term appears to have been employed to describe any communal leaders, regardless of their intellectual abilities or legal prowess.[18]

Communal councils made up of these various officials depended heavily on royal authority, especially in matters pertaining to finance. In some *alja-*

---

[16] In some communities of the Crown of Aragon, the Hebrew term *'eza* (pl. *yo'azim*) was also used to describe communal counselors. See Assis, *Golden Age*, 78–79, 97–99. For the lack of precision with which such terms were sometimes used, see S. D. Goitein's discussion on Jewish communal officials in *A Mediterranean Society* (Berleley, 1967),2:68–85. In particular, see the referenece to the great twelfth-century Andalusian poet Judah ha-Levi who was called "mukedam of the Jews," despite not holding any official communal post.

[17] Adret, 1:617. See, also, Babylonian Talmud, *Megillah*, 26a; Adret, 3:394, cited below.

[18] Shalom Albeck, "The Principles of Government in the Jewish Communities of Spain until the 13th Century," *Zion* 25 (1960): 115–117 [Hebrew]. See also Adret, 3:394; and Asher ben Yehiel, *Responsa*, 17:8, both cited below; Abulafia, *Responsa*, nos. 261, 267, and 303. For Seville, see ACS, c. 6, no. 2/1; pub. in González Jiménez, *Diplomatario andaluz*, no. 187. In nearby Córdoba, a letter from 1331 lists a certain don Çuleyman aben Sancho as *viejo de la judería*. Baer, *Juden*, vol. 2, no. 68, p. 54.

Part II. The Jewish Community and the Frontier

mas, communal leaders acted as royally appointed judges who were expected to inform the royal tax official of all cases that came before them so that he might receive the fines. The crown's interest in the financial management of the Jewish communities was also the motivation behind a royal privilege from the Crown of Aragon which granted Jews the right to choose their own *adelantados*, but added that the selection had to be done in consultation with the *aljama's* royally appointed rabbi (*arrab*).[19]

The authority of the crown also helped to reinforce the executive power of Jewish governing councils by granting them extensive powers over the members of their communities, including the right to institute bans and to excommunicate offenders. Leaders of the Mallorcan *aljama* received royal support for their power over the Jews of their community, including the right to collect taxes and the ability to expel from the island any Jewish criminals or vagrants who posed a threat to the stability of the community. These powers extended to the Jews of the islands of Menorca and Ibiza, who were considered to belong to the same community. The king also buttressed the leaders of the Mallorcan *aljama* in their attempt to assert greater control over a number of social regulations, including restrictions on Jewish dress and the lavishness of weddings, cracking down on sexual misconduct and adultery, and, as always, the power to punish those who refused to pay their taxes.[20]

In 1264, the Jewish community in the Aragonese capital of Saragossa wrote to Solomon ibn Adret regarding the internal dissent that had been taking place over the highly contentious issue of tax assessment and collection. Though the responsum focuses on the particular problems of the Saragossan community, ibn Adret's reply also includes some valuable information regarding elected officials (*mukademim*) and the general structure of Jewish government of the time.

And behold I reply as heaven inspires me, and I say that the customs of various places in these matters are not equal at all. There are places in which all their matters are conducted by elders and their advisors, and there are places in which even the majority does not have the power to do anything without consulting the entire community, and obtaining their consent. And there are places in which they appoint over themselves men for a certain amount of time who act on their behalf in all communal matters, and they are agents over them. I see that you act in

[19] Adret, 3:385, 388, and ACA, reg. 202, fol. 201r–v; and in Baer, *Juden*, vol. 1, no. 88.
[20] ACA, reg. 194, fol. 266; cit. in Régné no. 2623, and Fita and Llabrés, "Privilegios," nos. 29 and 30.

this last manner, since you elect officials to represent you known as *mukademim*. And in all places where this is the custom, the rest of the people are not used, and these people [the *mukademim*] by themselves agree to take care of the needs of the public, and these are what the sages would call seven good men of the city, which is to say that they elected them to handle all public matters.[21]

The system of electing communal representatives adopted by the Jews of Saragossa was shared by most of the Iberian *aljamas*. In another responsum, ibn Adret conceded that:

In most places today, the men of the community who are great in counsel and authority execute all the needs of the public, since it is not possible for women and minors and the feeble-minded to make such decisions, and these councilmen alone are as agents for them, to watch out over all their affairs.[22]

The communal representatives in each *aljama* developed their own policies with regard to the creation of new communal regulations. Despite a desire to respect their shared legal tradition based on Jewish law, Jewish officials who governed the majority of frontier communities often possessed little more than a rudimentary understanding of *halakha*. In many cases, local custom, not Jewish law, dictated Jewish communal policy. As a result, the legal customs developed by an individual community (*minhag*) were generally considered to have the same legitimacy and judicial power as Jewish law (*halakha*). When asked whether non-*halakhic* communal ordinances were to be considered binding in a case regarding tax assessment, ibn Adret replied:

It is correct to claim that it is the way of the [Jewish] communities to testify according to the ordinances of the men of the state. For were it not so, it would be an abrogation of all communal ordinances, and the customs of the communities in this and all such matters have the status of legislation derived from the Torah, which is to say that custom supersedes *halakha*.[23]

---

[21] Adret, 3:394. The full text of this *responsum* also offers insight into the communal strife that plagued the Saragossan *aljama* during the latter half of the thirteenth century.

[22] Adret, 3:428. Assis identifies the "intellectually weak" as the poor and politically disenfranchised masses. *Golden Age*, 78.

[23] Adret, 5:286. See also Asher ben Yehiel, *Responsa*, 55:10; and Adret, 5:283, in which he notes "that all communal affairs are dependent upon *minhag*."

The responsa literature from this period reflects both the support for the legitimacy of such local ordinances on the part of rabbinic authorities and a general uneasiness regarding such legislation on the part of the communal leaders themselves. This lack of confidence in the theoretical validity of their own legislation suggests more practical problems faced by Jewish communal leaders in the implementation of their authority. One such group of communal officers wrote to ibn Adret regarding how they might reconcile local ordinances with Jewish law.

The community decided to select *berurim* to eradicate crime, and we took an oath to do this. And it is written in the ordinances of this decision that we are empowered[24] to castigate and punish corporally and monetarily, as we see fit. Tell us: If close kinsmen of a certain member of the community[25] were to testify that he had broken his oath, and the witnesses are [otherwise] fit to rely upon, what are we to do? Or, if a woman and child testify and make an incidental statement,[26] do we have the authority to punish this man or not? Similarly if the witnesses, or at least one of them, was a relative of the accused, and we see reasons to believe them, if the witnesses tell the truth, do we have the authority to act according to their words, even though there is no valid testimony there?

Here, the selectmen of the *kahal* are essentially asking if they, in their judicial proceedings, are to be held to the same strictures of law as would a formal Jewish tribunal, or *beth din*. (The very fact that the *berurim* were unclear as to the extent of their own power is itself noteworthy). In his answer, ibn Adret assured them that there was no practical conflict in this situation, since the communal officials in question did not form a *beth din*, and thus were not bound to base their rulings on Jewish law. Rather, since their power was derived from the state, and not the Torah, they should do what they see is right according to the situation.

The answer is simple, in my opinion, for you are empowered to do as you see fit. Since the matter to which you refer is only relevant to a *beth din* which judges according to the laws of the Torah, as a sanhedrin or

---

[24] The phrase "by the authority of the state" is included in the edition of Adret's *Responsa* published by the Bar Ilan *Responsa* Project (based on ms. Pietrokow, 1883) but absent in other standard editions. See, for example, the collection published by *Makhon Or* (Jerusalem, 1997) (based on Salonica, 1808).

[25] In Jewish law, such witnesses are considered invalid.

[26] That is to say, a statement that is not equivalent to formal testimony. See The Babylonian Talmud, *Yebamot*, 121b.

such other institution. But anyone who bases law upon ordinances of the state does not judge according to the actual written laws which are in the Torah, but rather according to what he needs to do according to the exigencies of the moment. . . . And this is certainly true for you, since the core of the decree is that you only have to do what you see is fitting, as it states in the writ of the ordinance of which you spoke. And therefore the matter is simple amongst us, and in all places where there exist similar stipulations.[27]

In another case, ibn Adret was asked regarding the general validity of communal legislation:

Is the public authorized to make ordinances and decrees and safeguards among themselves, and to fine and punish according to these decrees which are not based on the laws of the Torah, or not? And what about if the signed witnesses of these ordinances were found to be unfit on account of contamination of their testimony, or their relationship [to those involved in the case]?

In his reply, he once again affirms the legitimacy of Jewish communal authority and its independence from Talmudic law.

The matter is clear, that the public has the authority to create safeguards and to enact ordinances and to make decrees as they see fit, and behold this is as valid as law derived from the Torah. And they may fine and punish all who transgress that which they have decreed among themselves, provided that they will decree with the power of the entire community, without restriction.
And this also holds true if all the men of a certain occupation of the city, such as butchers, painters, sailors, and so on, make a decree in matters regarding their work, since each faction whose members deal with the same matter are as a city unto themselves. . . . And thus every community has the authority to act in this manner for themselves, and to fine and punish on matters not derived from the laws of the Torah . . .
And furthermore, the signatory witnesses of the ordinances and decrees of the community are not judged to be unfit according to the standard prohibitions regarding witnesses. For if that were so, there would be no valid ordinances in any of the [Jewish] communities; not in

27 Adret, 4:311.

the appointment of representatives, or counselors, or selectmen, or the rest of the decrees, all of which were signed by the men of the city . . . And thus all Jewish communities in all the places where they are found follow this practice, and all witnesses who sign public ordinances and decrees are considered fit, except those who are physically unfit.[28]

That the various representatives of the Jewish *aljamas* were not always among the most learned members of the community was particularly true for matters of communal finance for which Talmudic knowledge, or even literacy, was not a prerequisite. Asked regarding the status of one such illiterate official who had been chosen as one of three men to oversee communal taxation, ibn Adret replied that the official

is as competent as the other two who are literate, since he is as well-versed in tax collection, payments, and loans, and in all other matters of public interest as are his learned colleagues, and perhaps more so. And in many instances, and perhaps most of the time, the large number of communal representatives is only due to worldly prestige, since all the families of the city want one of their members to be selected in order to bring honor to them all, regardless of whether that member is learned or not. And in many places there are illiterate people who are nonetheless appointed to office along with learned men. Go and see if this has been the practice in your community.[29]

The observation that the size of Jewish governing councils was often driven by the desire for prestige among leading families alludes to another important characteristic of communal government during this period: the prevalence of oligarchical rule. Like the Jewish communities of the interior, local government in the frontier *kahal* was dominated by an oligarchy whose authority derived from wealth and family lineage. The custom of appointing wealthier members of the community to the governing council had been practiced in the Muslim period and continued under Christian rule. One notable case is that of the Nasi Jacob ibn Jau, who rose to prominence as a tax collector for the Andalusi king al-Mansur, and who was later appointed chief judge for the Jews of the realm. The political power wielded by wealthy Jews continued into the thirteenth century, when Shem Tov ben Joseph ibn Falaquera portrayed the haughtiness of Iberia's wealthy Jewish elite in *The Book of the Seeker.* "The man unto whom God hath graciously

---

[28] Adret, 4:185.
[29] Adret, 3:399. See also Adret, 4:142, 185, 450, 1:617, 3:438, in which he states that: "Each community rules over its own locality as the *geonim* did over all Jewry."

bestowed wealth and prosperity," declares the character of the rich man, "is the ruler over the people of his generation, and is the most noble." Rabbinic responsa from the early fourteenth century indicate that, at least with regard to financial matters, decisions were still made by the wealthiest members of the community, not the majority.[30]

In some communities, ruling families maintained control over important government posts through the practice of naming their successors. A responsum describes this process in one *aljama* as follows:

The appointment of the communal representatives and the counselors shall follow the decision of the majority, but rather if any of the representatives and the counselors wishes to appoint another to replace himself, he has the authority to do so even if others do not agree with him in the appointment of that representative or counselor.[31]

In Tortosa, the right of communal officials to select their successors was formally granted to the town's Jewish bailiff in 1263, and in the city of Valencia, the custom was practiced until it was forcibly ended by a royal decree in 1300. In 1296, Jaime II renewed a list of privileges for the Jewish community of Mallorca that included the right to choose three communal officials annually from among the prominent men of the community to act as judges in all cases between Jews, with the exception of capital crimes.[32] In most Iberian *aljamas*, there was no separation between those involved in legislative and judicial activities, and both the communal councilors and the local judges, or *dayanim*, they appointed were drawn from the same pool of aristocratic families.

[30] Abraham ibn Daud, *Sefer ha-Qabbalah*, 69, English. See also Alfasi, *Responsa*, no. 173. For ibn Falaquera, see *The Book of the Seeker (Sefer Ha-Mebaqqesh)*, ed. and trans. M. Herschel Levine, (New York, 1976), 15, and on the continued dominance of the wealthy elite, see Ishbili, *Responsa*, no. 80; and Asher ben Yehiel, *Responsa*, 7:3; and Adret, 1:887.

[31] Adret, 5:254. Even those communities that were not completely governed by oligarchical rule often had to make concessions to the more powerful Jewish clans. In Tudela, a communal statute drawn up around 1300 made provisions for the community to be governed by a council of elected representatives, but added that any *takkanot* that they produced would have to be ratified by members of the eight leading families of the *aljama*. Baer, *Juden*, vol. 1, no. 586; and Abraham Neuman, *The Jews of Spain* (Philadelphia, 1942), 1:34.

[32] ACA, reg. 12, fol. 15; and Cabanes Peccourt, ed., *Documentos de Jaime I*, vol. 5, no. 1310. For Valencia, see ACA, reg. 197, fol. 153v; Baer, *Juden*, vol. 1, no. 146. For Mallorca, see ACA, reg. 194, fol. 266.

LEGAL SCHOLARS AND CROWN RABBIS

Royal involvement in the affairs of the Jewish community was not limited to occasional episodes of direct intervention. During the thirteenth
century, the expansion of royal administrations in all the Iberian kingdoms
led to the establishment and development of offices charged with managing
the fiscal and judicial affairs of the Jewish communities. These royal officials, or "crown rabbis," joined with rabbinic scholars and the various communal councilmen mentioned above in the governance of the Iberian Jewish *aljamas*.[33]
Medieval Christian documents employ various renderings of the Hebrew
term *rav* (lit. "teacher"), such as *rabi, arrabi, rab*, and *rap*, in a relatively fluid
and imprecise manner. In addition to these terms, the title "master" (*magister*), or "master of Hebrew law" (*magister in lege ebrayca*) was often used to
denote Jewish scholars.[34] These rabbinic authorities were Jewish legal experts who did not hold any official post, but whose power derived from the
community's acknowledgment of their learning and expertise. Both Christian and Jewish authorities alike would seek their opinions in cases involving
Jews, and the vast responsa literature from this period serves to illustrate the
importance of these scholars to the judicial system of the *aljamas*. Throughout the Middle Ages, Iberian Jewry produced a number of outstanding
scholars, or *hakhamim*, whose mastery of Jewish law allowed them to play an
influential role in communal government far beyond their own *aljamas*. In
the thirteenth and early fourteenth century, these included Moses ben Nahman and his pupil Solomon ibn Adret in the Crown of Aragon, and Meir
Halevi Abulafia, Asher ben Yehiel and his son Yehudah in Castile. However,
while their judgment and counsel were sought by Jews throughout the
peninsula and beyond, the effective legal and political power of these rabbis
was restricted by several factors. They held no specific office, and their au-

[33] The same was true for the local Christian communities, where the 'good men" of
the towns shared the duties of communal government with various royal officials. See
Burns, *Diplomatarium*, vol. 2, nos. 283a, 289a; Kagay, "Royal Power," 162.
[34] For "*rap*," see Baer, *Juden*, vol. 1, nos. 136, 153. For the Portuguese term *arrabi*, see
below. The title "*magister*" was particularly common in the northern Crown of Aragon,
and throughout southern France. See Joseph Shatzmiller, "Rabbi Isaac of Manosque and
His Son Rabbi Peretz: The Rabbinate and its Professionalization in the Fourteenth Century," in *Jewish History, Essays in Honour of Chimen Abramsky*, ed. Ada Rapoport-Albert
and Steven Zipperstein (London, 1988), 61–83, esp. 65–66; and Régné, nos. 6, 84, 319, 323,
324, 725 and 751 (= Baer, *Juden*, vol. 1, no. 116), 873, 1507, and 1508.

thority was thus dependent upon the willingness of Jewish leaders to obey their legal advice. While the Toledan sage Meir Halevi Abulafia "was not fearful of donning the robes of sovereignty," it is difficult to determine the exact nature of his role in communal government. Abulafia himself complained bitterly of his inability to alter the intellectual tastes and religious behavior of other Toledan elite. Regarding his tacit acceptance of the custom of interrupting the regular liturgy with additional poetic prayers (*piyyutim*), he wrote to a friend:

What you were told about my sitting among them, hearing and keeping my peace, was correctly reported to you. . . . But what you were told about my having the power to protest was not correctly reported.[35]

If a respected rabbi was powerless in matters of liturgical practice, then how much more must his authority have been curtailed in the realm of taxation and finance. At times, rabbinic intercession into communal affairs met with violent opposition from members of the great Jewish clans, who viewed themselves as the rightful rulers of their respective *aljamas* and who resented the royal appointment of outsiders to act as communal rabbis. One unfortunate scholar, who was asked by the bailiff of Saragossa to lend his legal expertise to a particular case, was severely beaten by members of the wealthy Alconstantini and Eleazar families.[36]

Even if the personal prestige of these sages brought them considerable practical authority in their own communities and in the surrounding region, it would have little effect on the daily governance of frontier communities. It was the local Jewish scholars who, as more accessible custodians of the Jewish legal tradition, played a more active role in the government of their own communities. These scholars were consulted for their legal opinions, and in some cases acted as judges, but their roles differed in each community. In Castile, we know that there were learned and capable Jewish legal scholars who participated in the government of the principal *aljamas* of the frontier. A responsum from the period praises the wisdom, learning, and piety of the elders of Córdoba, and mentions their close relationship with the equally erudite rabbis of nearby Seville.[37]

[35] The statement about Abulafia was made by the contemporary Jewish writer, Jonah ibn Bahlul, cited by Septimus, *Hispano-Jewish Culture in Transition*, 12. For the quote, see 34. The translation is Septimus'.

[36] ACA, reg. 48, fol. 134.

[37] See Adret, 1:179, where *dayyanim* were not, necessarily, rabbis, and the letter of February 7, 1288, which makes reference to the rabbis of the *aljama* of Calatayud in conjunction with the implementation of Hebrew law; ACA, reg. 74, fol. 78. The decision of *dayyanim* who were not well versed in the law to defer to legal experts remained volun-

The role played by great legal scholars and local rabbinic authorities in the governance of the Jewish community was often superseded by Jewish officials who bore the same title, but who were appointed by the crown. In Muslim al-Andalus, there was already evidence of royal appointment of Jews from among the wealthy elite to serve as legal and fiscal representatives for their communities. The rise to power of one such official, Jacob ibn Jau, is described by Abraham ibn Daud in his *Book of Tradition*.

King al-Mansur became very fond of Jacob b. Jau. Accordingly, the former issued him a document placing him in charge of all the Jewish communities from Sijilmasa to the river Duero, which was the border of his realm. [The decree stated] that he was to adjudicate all their litigations, and that he was empowered to appoint over them whomsoever he wished and to exact from them any tax or payment to which they might be subject. Then all the members of the community of Cordova assembled and signed an agreement [certifying] his position as nasi, which stated: 'Rule thou over us, both thou, and thy son, and thy son's son, also.'[38]

A document from fourteenth-century Castile provides a description of the office of rabbi that bears a striking resemblance to the post held by ibn Jau. Here, it is not the king, but the archbishop of Toledo who appoints his Jewish physician as judge over all the Jewish communities of his domain.[39]

And we, considering that Rabbi Haym, our physician, is a man of good lineage and wise and good, and very learned, so that he will easily be able to judge litigations and disputes which arise among you and swiftly bring about justice and the fulfillment of law for all parties: Therefore . . . we gave and give him to you as your judge in order that he might hear and judge, sentence and determine and resolve all litigations, suits, and complaints, both general and special as well as appeals, or in whatever other manner that henceforth occur between each and every one of you in those things that a Jewish rabbi and judge can hear

---

tary, and Baer's statement that they were "required to consult the local rabbinic authorities before passing judgment," greatly exaggerates the power of the latter. Baer, *History*, 1:212–213. For Córdoba and Seville, see Judah Ben Asher, *Zikhron Yehudah*, nos. 79, 82.

[38] Ibn Daud, *Sefer ha-Qabbalah*, 69. Ibn Daud's assertion that the appointment of ibn Jau was certified by the community of Cordoba should be viewed with skepticism. Crown rabbis did not need the support or approval of the rest of the community to assume their posts.

[39] This would include all Jews residing on lands belonging to the archbishop in the province of Toledo.

and judge between you, for which we give to him all our complete power.[40]

The key factor in both passages is the crown rabbi's connection to the seat of central authority, in this case the archbishop. In addition to mastery of Jewish law, the archbishop cites the importance of lineage in determining eligibility for this office, illustrating the continued influence of the Jewish elite. This reference shows the account to be a somewhat idealized description of the post, since a lack of Talmudic learning did not usually bar the wealthy and well connected from assuming office. That these crown rabbis were selected for reasons other than their proficiency in Jewish law is often underscored by an order that they seek sound legal advice before rendering their decisions. One such example can be seen at the Catalonian town of Lérida, where Jaime I appointed a certain Naci Azday (Nasi Hasdai) to act as the crown rabbi and judge of the Jewish community there. His appointment came with the condition that he seek legal advice from two learned men form the community. This general lack of legal knowledge led traditional *hakhamim* to adopt a dim view of many of these crown rabbis. In a query written to Solomon ibn Adret, the issue was raised as to whether or not the legal imperative to respect Jewish scholars was to be applied to those rabbis who were appointed by the crown, some of whom were "not even able to read properly." Ibn Adret replied that the latter were not true rabbis unless they were learned in Jewish law, and that while one should be careful not to offend them in deed, there existed no legal prohibition against verbal insults.[41]

Question: It was said, that in our land there are rabbis appointed by the king and they don't even know how to read properly. If one insults them without knowing it, what is the law?

Response: Regarding a *rav* who is a learned man, there is a fine of one *litre* of gold for anyone who should insult him. . . . But for one who is only a *rav* by crown appointment, this law does not apply, but rather we fine the offender according to his status and that of the insulted party. And this is certainly the case if they insulted him in deed, but not in words.[42]

[40] BN, ms. 13089, fol. 75; and Baer, *Juden*, vol. 2, no. 241.
[41] ACA, reg. 16, fol. 202.
[42] Adret, 1: 475, based on Maimonides' *Mishneh Torah, Pereq ha-Hovel.* On the subject of communal enactments against insults, see also Asher ben Yehiel, *Responsa,* 101: 1.

One of the primary functions of crown rabbis that appears in the grant to ibn Jau, but is absent from the later passage regarding the appointment of Rabbi Haym of Toledo, was the collection of royal (or baronial) taxes. Though not a prerequisite for the office, many of the crown rabbis of the thirteenth century did play an important role in the fiscal administration of their respective kingdoms. These include the Jewish courtier Jacob Sabadel, a leading figure among the Jews of Orihuela, who was referred to as "rabbi of the Jews" in the town's *libro de repartimiento*. Other examples of these courtier-rabbis on the frontier include Juçef Cabaçay, who appears as a recipient of lands at Seville and Jérez, and "El Rab" Don Todeoç, who is listed as a royal functionary in Murcia. The latter may also have been the same "Rab Don Todros" whose son Juçef "the *nasi*" owned property in Seville's *barrio de la mar.*[43]

In addition to their fiscal responsibilities, these crown rabbis also acted as the primary judges for legal suits as well as courts of appeal. The grant of power from a Christian lord such as an archbishop or the king meant that these rabbis were imbued with the executive powers to both pass judgment and to mete out punishment. It also meant that Jewish scholars had little choice but to recognize such authority, however grudgingly. A responsum from the Castilian scholar Yehudah ben Asher noted that punishments were "made by the crown rabbis (*rabbanei ha-malkhut*) since in their hand is the scepter of the rulers." It was to these royal magistrates that a thirteenth-century compilation of charters from the Crown of Aragon referred when it noted that the only summons to which a Jew was legally bound to respond was described as one written by his "rabbi." "No Jew shall be forced to respond to any writ unless it come from the hand of his rabbi; nor the Muslim, if it does not come from the hand of his *alamín.*"[44] Similarly, a contemporary legal code from Castile, *Las Leyes de Estilo*, notes that:

If a Jew wishes to bring suit against another Jew in a civil or criminal matter, this suit is to be adjudicated by his communal officers or by his rabbis. And if a Jew has a complaint regarding the communal officers,

---

[43] Torres Fontes, *Repartimiento de Orihuela*, 78; idem, *Fueros y Privilegios de Alfonso X,* no. 54; ACA, caja 39, no. 35/1; Ballesteros, *Sevilla*, no. 174.
[44] *Zikhron Yehudah*, no. 77, at the end of the responsum. The courtier's connection to the seat of power also gave local Jewish officials pause in challenging his authority or accusing him of wrongdoing. Adret, 1:915. For the Aragonese legal compilation, see Gargallo Moya, ed., *Los Fueros de Aragon*, 73, rub. 127. The Arabic term *almamín* generally referred to an official in charge of weights and measures, but also was used as a synonym for *alcalde*, as appears to be the case here.

the rabbi should judge the case, and if [the complaint] is with the rabbi, the king.[45]

Here, the post of rabbi appears to be that of a royal official who functions as a sort of court of appeals, and who is answerable only to the crown. Elsewhere, the rabbi appears as a royal representative who governed the *aljama* in conjunction with communal officials. In the Aragonese town of Calatayud, Jaime I authorized the Jewish *aljama* to choose its own *adelantados*, but added that the selection had to be made in consultation with the community's royally appointed rabbi.[46] In a section discussing the amounts to be paid by royal officials for the privileges of being granted certain posts, the *Espéculo* includes the following stipulation regarding the appointment of crown rabbis:

And when [the king] appoints a rabbi over a certain area [the latter] should pay 200 *maravedis*. And when [the king] appoints *almoxarifes* over large towns, each one of these [should pay] 100 *maravedis;* and when he appoints *almoxarifes* over smaller towns, they should pay 50 *maravedis*. And when he appoints a head elder, who according to the Jews and Moors is like a communal official who can either be appointed to a general area in order to hear legal cases and resolve litigation for that region, or be appointed to a particular *aljama*, this official should pay 100 *maravedis*.[47]

The jurisdiction given to these crown rabbis thus ranged from individual *aljamas* to several locales in a particular region or domain, as in the case of Rabbi Haym of Toledo. Not all such appointments went uncontested. When Jaime I decided to designate the Jewish notable Salamon Alconstantini as rabbi and judge over the Jews of Saragossa and the rest of the kingdom of Aragon, he inadvertently provoked a sharp protest. The opposition to Alconstantini's appointment came from rival Jewish clans in Saragossa headed by Judah de la Cavalleria and Salamon Avenbruch, together with the support of the leading rabbinic authority of the day, Moses ben Nahman.[48]

[45] *Las Leyes de Estilo,* law 88, in *Opúsculos Legales del rey don Alfonso el Sabio* (Madrid, 1836), 2:275; and in Baer, *Juden,* vol. 2, no. 62.

[46] ACA reg. 202, fol. 201r-v; and in Baer, *Juden,* vol. 1, no. 88.

[47] Robert MacDonald, ed., *Espéculo, Texto jurídico atribuido al Rey de Castilla Don Alfonso X, el Sabio* (Madison, 1990), 4.12.55, p. 178. See also *Las Siete Partidas* 2.20.8. In Portugal, the *arrabi mor* and local *arrabi menores* paid 100 and 5 *libras*, respectively, for the rights to their posts. ANTT, *Livro de Leis e Posturas Antigas,* fol. 85; and Pimenta Ferro Tavares, *Os Judeus,* 2nd ed., 143. On the office of *arrabi mor,* see below.

[48] ACA, reg. 16, fols. 261–2v. Bernard Septimus has noted that similar rivalries among the Jewish elite also existed in Barcelona. See his "Piety and Power in Thirteenth-

The jurisdiction of the position was eventually limited to just Saragossa, and awarded to Avenbruch.[49] According to a royal letter from 1294, Alconstantini was successful in obtaining the post of judge and rabbi for Aragon under Pedro III and Alfonso III, but was not able to retain the office under Jaime II. When Alconstantini convinced the queen of Castile to write a letter to this king on his behalf, the latter reasoned with her that "you should not wish that for the sake of one Jew we should lose the others." As a result of this rivalry, no Jew was named chief judge over the Jewries of the kingdom of Aragon until 1304, when Jaime II appointed the royal courtier Ishmael de la Portella to that post.[50] At no point did there exist a Chief Rabbi or judge for the entire Crown of Aragon, and in Castile, there was no such post until the late fourteenth century with the creation of the office of *Rab de la Corte*.

The dichotomy between crown rabbis and rabbinic scholars and their respective positions within the power structure of the Jewish community is vividly illustrated by an incident that took place in Córdoba in the early fourteenth century. The case, which is recorded in the responsa of the great rabbinic scholar Asher ben Yehiel, surrounds an attempt by Jewish officials to impose a death sentence on a member of the Cordoban *aljama*, Abraham Safiyah. Safiyah had already been imprisoned by the Christian authorities for an unspecified crime, but had obtained his release in exchange for monetary compensation. Apparently, it was in celebration of his freedom that he made remarks that were considered blasphemous by the leaders of the Jewish *aljama*.[51] The text of the responsum continues:

And the judges and important men of the community who heard this gathered and agreed to make a judgment in this matter, and they sent off to capture him but they could not find him, and they tried to obtain the necessary testimony that was not before them because he had fled. They were only able to find one witness and the others were missing, and their testimony was suppressed.

Century Catalonia," in *Studies in Medieval Jewish History and Literature*, ed. Isadore Twersky (Cambridge, 1979), 197–230, esp. 215.

[49] ACA, reg. 62, fol. 53v; reg. 46, fol. 184. Salamon's nephew Moses Alconstantini was later given the post of rabbi for the *aljama* of Calatayud, and is listed in a case regarding letters of credit exchanged as part of a marriage contract. ACA, reg., 81, fol. 67v; cited in Régné, no. 2084.

[50] ACA, reg. 252, fol. 50; pub. in Baer, *Juden*, vol. 1, no. 136. The king's comment refers to the other leading Jewish families who opposed Alconstantini, and should not be taken to reflect popular resistance to the creation of such an office. For de Portella, see ACA, reg. 235, fol. 79v; Baer, *Juden*, vol. 1, no. 153.

[51] Asher ben Yehiel, *Responsa*, 17:8.

Unlike the (ostensibly municipal) Christian authorities who had easily arrested Safiyah and just as easily let him pay his way free, these Jewish communal leaders appear unable to apprehend both Safiyah himself and the witnesses necessary to prosecute him. As a result, they were forced to appeal to an authority outside the *kahal* in order to enforce their will. This authority would be the crown rabbi Yehudah ibn Waqar, physician and aid to the Infante Don Juan Manuel, and scion of one of Castile's most powerful Jewish dynasties.

And now with us in the city is the famous and the exalted Rabbi Yehudah, may he be blessed, bar Yitzhak ben Waqar, and "he is zealous for the Lord with great zeal" and he exerted himself in the matter of the witness so that this repulsive one came into his power, and he captured him with the power of the State and he imprisoned him. And in this way, his power increased in strength over the rest of the witnesses who had not come forward, and he forced them and caused them to swear and obtained proper testimony in this case of blasphemy.

And although this blasphemy was made in Arabic, since this youth was uneducated and unfamiliar with the Holy Language [i.e., Hebrew],[52] the opinion of this honorable one was in agreement with the judges and the prominent men of the community that it was important that this blasphemy should be attributed to this contemptible one, since the noun in Arabic is a blasphemy just as it is in the Holy Language, for those who know it. And [they also sought] to make a fence around the matter, so that the evildoer would not burst through the vessels of the world and speak insolently against Heaven. And this man was hardhearted and his actions were very evil, and there could not be found anyone in the city who could teach him pureness, and there were powerful men who would strengthen his hand.

And around ten of the prominent men of the community, men of action, agreed with the honorable Rabbi Yehudah and with the scholars who are here and with the elders of the city, that he should be punished. And since the aforementioned were in agreement, it seems that those close to the evildoer went with bribes and they asked the great lord, Don Juan Manuel, who we received in this our place as the representative of the king, may his glory be exalted and his justice increased. And he sent one of his knights to us, saying that no judgment

[52] It is worth noting the persistence of Arabic language among Cordoban Jews nearly a century after the Christian conquest of the city. Arabic was the lingua franca of Jewish society, and only educated men were conversant in Hebrew.

Part II. The Jewish Community and the Frontier

should be reached until he said so. And the honorable Rabbi Yehudah exerted himself in this matter with all his power, and appeased this lord, so that he not impede us in rendering judgment before the Gentiles, and the lord decided to allow the evildoer to remain in his captivity until the answer of our teacher, may he live, should come regarding what to do.

Both the decision regarding the status of the crime and the ultimate decision to punish Safiyah were made by ibn Waqar in conjunction with a broad coalition of Jewish leaders. The text distinguishes between communal officers or "elders of the city," and "prominent men of the community, men of action," from whom a committee of ten was formed to help in this case. The latter appear to have been members of the communal oligarchy who did not hold any official post nor legal credentials, but whose designation as "men of action" points to their capacity to bolster the executive powers of the communal elders. The final segment of this coalition is formed by local scholars, whose role would have been that of legal advisors.

Of all the various leaders who participated in rendering this decision, it was ibn Waqar alone who undertook the task of implementing it. The powerful courtier was forced to take matters into his own hands when Safiyah's supporters turned to ibn Waqar's master, Don Juan Manuel, and attempted to buy his support. Here we are given further indication that the case against Abraham Safiyah extended to a whole segment of the Cordoban *al-jama* which possessed sufficient wealth, organization, and connections to the Christian authorities to mount a serious opposition to the incumbent Jewish communal authorities. Faced with appeals from both factions, Don Juan decided to refer the case to another outside party, the Toledan legal expert Asher ben Yehiel. The decision to involve yet another Jewish authority, and one from outside of the Cordoban community, further demonstrates the relative impotence of the local *kahal* to manage its own affairs. The text of the responsum continues with the *kahal's* petition to Rabbi Asher:

And now, Adonai be praised, we petition our teacher, who is zealous for the Lord with great zeal, and may our messenger hurry before the lord changes his mind, and we are devastated in our shame and our disgrace. And he sent to us his judgment with an explanation and with proofs regarding what and how we should proceed. And similarly, in his mercy, let goodness be strengthened and let him strengthen the hands of the honorable Rabbi Yehudah, and regarding what he attempted to do in this matter and what he is going to do, and may The Holy One, blessed be He, be the help of our teacher and lengthen his days in goodness and repose.

Asher ben Yehiel, who arrived in Castile as a refugee from central Europe in 1305, belongs to a small group of Iberian rabbis whose abilities and influence straddled the divide between the crown rabbi and the legal scholar. Though his authority stemmed from his renown as a legal expert rather than from a post within the royal administration, the crown's recognition of his stature and appeal to his knowledge in such cases added weight to his decisions. In this case, however, Asher's response was greatly constrained by the involvement of the crown rabbi ibn Waqar, whose connection to the seat of royal authority was stronger than that of the great sage. Faced with a decision orchestrated by this powerful courtier, the "explanations and proofs" that Rabbi Asher might offer to "strengthen the hand of Rabbi Yehudah," amounted to little more than legal justification for a *fait accompli*. While he was empowered to render the ultimate decision as to the fate of the accused, his answer reflects an unwillingness to contradict the authority of ibn Waqar and what he perceived to be royally sanctioned customs regarding capital punishment. In his carefully constructed reply, Asher attempted to uphold the integrity of Jewish law as best he could, condoning the practical need to "remove" Safiyah, without giving the decision legal legitimacy:

May the perfect, pleasant, pious and delightful notables accept the blessing of abundant peace! I wondered at your question to me regarding capital cases, because in all countries with which I am familiar, capital cases are not judged [by Jews] except here in Spain. I was greatly surprised when I came here, that it was possible to judge capital matters without the existence of the Sanhedrin. They said to me, that this was due to the permission of the king, and also, that the [Jewish] community judges with a view to saving lives; a great deal more blood would be shed if such cases were judged by Gentiles. Given their argument, I accepted this custom for them, but I never agreed with them in the destruction of life. In truth, I see that you are in agreement to remove this evildoer from your midst, and clearly he profaned the Lord in public, and the matter is already known among the Gentiles, and they are very strict with speech against their religion and their faith, and the profanation would be greater if it were not punished. And we do find that in order to sanctify the Lord of Heaven they raised their hands against the sons of the king on behalf of the proselytes, and let their bodies hang overnight from the stake. And we also find that in order to make a fence around the matter, they stoned to death one who rode a horse on the Sabbath,[53] and it is also fitting that the Lord be sanctified through the removal of this evildoer, and you should therefore act as you see fit.

The variety of Asher's reasons supporting the death penalty reflects his uneasiness with this decision, and he closes with an aside to the prosecuting committee in which he offers them an alternative to capital punishment:

And if it were up to me, I would be inclined to advise you to cut his tongue out of his mouth, cutting off the majority of it used for speaking, and thereby silencing his lips. And in this way you would give him a punishment that fits his deeds, and one which is a common punishment which one sees every day. Act, then, in this matter as you see fit, since I know that your intentions are to sanctify the Lord of Heaven.

The details of this case help to depict the intricate power relationship that existed at this time between scholars, courtiers, the local Jewish community, and the crown. The involvement of so many Jewish authorities in the prosecution and sentencing of Abraham Safiyah underscores the limits of the local *kahal*, and reflects the internecine conflict and factionalism that plagued the Jewish communities of the frontier. Safiyah and his supporters demonstrated an appreciation and awareness of the power represented by Christian municipal and royal officials, and had little compunction about bribing the latter in order to gain their assistance. Their willingness to avail themselves of various authorities outside of the *kahal* forced communal officials and their rabbinic advisors to do the same. As a result, the only Jewish leaders who posses real and effective power in this case are the courtier ibn Waqar and the independent scholar Rabbi Asher, whose authority derived from their close ties to the crown rather than from the occupation of any official post. Finally, though the effectiveness of their decisions contrasts sharply with the relative impotence of the Cordoban *kahal*, each of them appears dependent on the authority of the other.

[53] The Babylonian Talmud, *Yebamot*, 90, 2. The preceding citations serve to cite precedent in support of capital punishment.

THE CROWN RABBI AT ITS APOGEE: THE
PORTUGUESE ARRABI MOR

The ascendancy of crown rabbis and the extent of their authority within the Jewish community can perhaps best be seen in the kingdom of Portugal. During the course of the twelfth and thirteenth centuries, the Portuguese monarchy began to develop a centralized system of legal and fiscal administration for the entire realm. Beginning in the late thirteenth century, this system would also come to encompass all of Portuguese Jewry by organizing the kingdom's communities under a broad network of Jewish magistrates and tax collectors. This network was headed by an *arrabi mor*, or "chief rabbi," who acted as the royal tax collector in much the same way as did Castile's *almoxarife mayor*. Seven other ministers known as *arrabis*, or *ouvidores*, served under the *arrabi mor* and were responsible for the taxes of various regions of the kingdom, called *arrabiados*. In addition to these regional *arrabiados*, local *arrabis* seem to have been appointed to individual communities as they were in Castile and Aragon. This system of *arrabiados* appears to be modeled on that of the *almoxarifados*, the administrative districts developed under Afonso III.[54]

The term *arrabi* is found in Latin and Portuguese documents from the twelfth century onward. It is mentioned as a communal post with judicial connotations in Portuguese municipal legislation of the late twelfth century where Jews were required to swear oaths in their synagogues "in the presence of their *arrabi*." Similarly, a document from 1293 mentions a certain Isaac who was "arrabi of the Jews" at Leiria. On rare occasions, the title appears as *Rabi*, as in a document in which the king sends greetings "to the *rab[b]i* and the community of my Jews" at Lisbon. These three documents all suggest the existence of a singular post of *arrabi* per community, indicating that these local royal officials were distinct from traditional Jewish legal scholars. References to the office of *arrabi mor* first appear under Afonso III,

---

[54] The post of *arrabi mor* the was part of the general rise of a new breed of chancery servant in Portugal after 1211. Maria João Branco, "The Kings Counsellors' two Faces," in *The Medieval World*, ed. Janet Nelson and Peter Linehan (Groningen), 526. The term *ouvidor*, from the Latin *auditore*, refers to "those who hear [cases]." The *arrabiados* were centered around O Porto, for the region of Entre Duero and Minho; Torre de Moncorvo, for Tras-os-Montes; Viseu and Covilha, for the Beira region; Santarem, for Estremadura; Évora, for the Alentejo; and Faro, for the Algarve. *Ordenações Afonsinas*, 476–491. The "arrabiado" of Beira is mentioned in a document from 1316, pub. in Pimenta Ferro, *Os Judeus* 1st ed., no. 10.

though its integration into a broader, kingdom-wide system does not appear to have taken place until the reign of his son, Dinis.[55] As with the Castilian *almoxarifes* under Alfonso X, the post of *arrabi mor* was filled by wealthy Jews, and tended to be controlled by family dynasties. The first *arrabi mor* to appear in the royal documents of the thirteenth century is Don Judah, who served Dinis in the early part of his reign, and who was followed by his son, Guedelha. Another characteristic which the *arrabi mor* shared with the *almoxarifes* and crown rabbis of the other peninsular states was that he also collected taxes for the crown, members of both communities were repeatedly commanded to view his seal as that of the king. Further indication that the Portuguese *arrabis* formed part of the kingdom's royal administration can be seen in legislation that Afonso III enacted in 1266. The king prohibited Jews from appealing decisions made by their *arraby mor*, "except where the king should want to intervene."[56]

However, as the last example indicates, the *arrabi mor* also filled a judicial role with respect to the kingdom's Jews, as did the network of local *arrabis* acting as royally appointed magistrates for individual communities. In a letter asserting royal dominion over all of Portugal's Jews, King Dinis informed his brother Afonso that the Jews belong to the crown, and should appear before its judges, or else their own *arrabis*. A law from the legal compilation *Ordenações Afonsinas* notes that the *arrabi mor* was not to judge: "simple suits nor grievances nor appeals nor any case of verbal injuries, for this jurisdiction belongs to the communal *arrabis*." Similarly, the charter of the town of Beja notes that the local *arrabi* was to act as a judge in conjunction with Christian magistrates, and that he had the right to appeal to the king any decisions concerning Jews which were made by the Christian *justiça* of the town.[57]

The judicial role played by the Portuguese *arrabi* developed over the course of the thirteenth and early fourteenth centuries. Before this period, cases between Jews and Christians had traditionally been brought before municipal courts. It was during the reign of Afonso III that there was a shift toward a more centralized legal system which became dominated by royal

[55] *PMH, Leges*, 71. For Leiria, see ANTT, *Alcobaça*, m. 19, no. 37, and for Lisbon, ANTT, *Ordem de Avis*, no. 188. On the development of Portuguese royal administration under these two kings, see da Cruz Coelho, *Definição de Fronteiras*, 123–144.
[56] *Ordenações Afonsinas*, 1998 [1786], 476–491. On the legislation of 1266 see *PMH, Leges*, 286–287.
[57] ANTT, *Chanc. de D. Dinis*, liv. III, fol. 50; cited in Pimenta Ferro Tavares, *Os Judeus*, 2nd ed., 87. The king grudgingly allowed Afonso's judges to oversee those cases in which Jews sued Christians from the latter's lands. *Ordenções Afonsinas*, 482. For Beja, see *PMH, Leges*, 640.

magistrates, both Jewish and Christian. In this system, judicial jurisdiction was determined by the party bringing suit, with Jewish officials judging cases brought by Jews, and municipal courts hearing cases brought by Christians. This move toward increased royal control over the judicial process was further developed by Dinis who, in 1291, declared that all cases between Jews and Christians were to be judged by the royal *alcaide* or *alvaziis*, and that all other Jewish cases were to be handled by the *arrabi mor*.[58] The king had already begun to establish this system two years earlier during the *Cortes* held at Santarem, stating:

> Regarding the grievance brought to me concerning the cases of the Jews and Moors . . . the Jews are to bring their cases before their *arrabi* and the Moors before their magistrate [*alcaide*].[59]

Here, Dinis equates the offices of *arrabi* and *alcaide*, treating both as judicial posts within the royal government. Though the *arrabi mor* was only given jurisdiction over cases between Jews, he kept a watchful eye on legal proceedings between Jews and Christians as well. He acted as an intermediary between other Jews and the crown, and was often present when the former petitioned the king for grants or help collecting debts from Christians. It was at the request of the *arrabi mor* that the number of *alcaldes* for cases between Jews and Christians at Lisbon doubled from two to four in the years 1285–1295. Half of these judges, who were elected annually, were to dedicate themselves to handling cases between Jews and Christians.[60]

By the early 14th century, the Jewish *arrabi* had come to replace the Christian *alcaide* or *alvazil* in charge of Jewish affairs for the Lisbon community. In a letter written by Afonso IV, the town council of Lisbon complained to the king that the Jewish community there had begun to refuse to appear before these Christian officials in criminal cases between them and Christians, as had long been the custom. Instead, the Jews had presented the council with a royal privilege from the king that, they declared, allowed them to bring such cases before their own officials or *arrabis*.[61]

Over the course of the fourteenth century, the judicial, executive, and financial authority of the *arrabi mor* would continue to grow. The extent of

[58] ANTT, *Chanc. de D. Dinis, liv.* III, fols. 104–105.
[59] ANTT, *Chanc. de D. Dinis, liv.* I, fol. 266. The dual function of the *arrabi* as court official and Jewish magistrate would continue throughout the fourteenth century. For all Jewish officials and judges ordered to comply with the decisions of the *arrabi mor* Moysem Navarro, c. 1360, see Amador de los Ríos, *Historia social,* 2: 567–568.
[60] CML, *Livro dos Pregos,* fol. 19.
[61] *Livro I de místicos dos Reis D. Dinis, D. Afonso IV, D. Pedro I.* In *Documentos para a historia da Cidade de Lisboa* (Lisbon, 1947), 175.

Part II. The Jewish Community and the Frontier

this power can be seen in a royal letter from 1373 in which Fernando I confirmed for his *arrabi mor*, Judah Aben Menir, a list of privileges referring to the post.[62] The confirmation affords special insight into the role which the *arrabi mor* had come to play in the governance of the Portuguese Jewish communities.

> Dom Fernando, etc., to whomever views this letter, let it be known that the Jew Dom Yehudah asked us that we afford him our favor in appointing him *arrabi mor* for all the communities of the Jews of our realm, and [said] that the *arrabis* of our realm who came before him judged and resolved matters within certain jurisdictions which were given and authorized to them by the kings who came before us, and petitioned us for our favor that we might authorize him by our writ, sealed with our seal, in order that he may use it to make law and do justice as pertains to his office. And we, seeing that what he asked of us pertained to the requirements of his office, agree and command that he may pass sentences in civil matters which take place between one Jew and another, and that these writs be made in our name and signed by him or whomever he appoints, and sealed with our seal and not with his, and therefore let there be no restriction against any similar letters given to Jews by us or by our judges or our district administrators.

As an agent of the crown, the *arrabi mor* was given extensive judicial and executive powers within the individual Jewish communities. Such authority was not easily enforced, however, and the grant also alludes to the potential challenges which members of the local elite posed to the jurisdiction of the *arrabi mor*.

> Furthermore, we order that [the *arrabi mor*] may, in every locale which he visits, without having to provide any specific reason, correct injustices made against these communities or their property, and to judge the *arrabis* of these communities and any powerful Jews upon whom the *arrabis* of the communities are unable to pass judgment. . . . And we give consent to him in order that he correct injustices in the places where he finds them, and that he not remove the cases from there, and if he is unable to judge them while he is in these locales, he should appoint a leader of the Jewish community from the locale where the events took place who is agreeable to both parties, to whom he should

[62] ANTT, *Chanc. de D. Fernando*, liv. I, fols. 132rv; and Pimenta Ferro, *Os Judeus*, 1st ed., no. 39. See also her discussion in *Os Judeus*, 2nd ed., 30–34.

assign a convenient time in which the case can be adjudicated without damage to either party.

Moreover we command that the elections of the *arrabis* of all the aforementioned communities come to him each year so that he may confirm by writ in our name, signed by him or by anyone he appoints, and sealed with our seal as I have mentioned. And we command that all of the appeals of civil and criminal cases that come from the *arrabis* of the aforementioned communities come before [the *arrabi mor*] or his appointee.

In the next section of Fernando's grant, the *arrabi mor* once again appears quite clearly as an officer of the royal administration whose assistants included both Christians and Jews.

And we command, moreover, that the aforementioned *arrabi mor* may employ a Christian or Jew to act as an assistant and to deliver the sentences given by [the *arrabi mor*], as pertains to his office, regarding matters in which the parties involved do not require letters sealed with our seal as we have said . . . and [the *arrabi mor]* can employ a Christian or Jewish scribe who is of good name and who is able to discharge the duties of his office and safeguard the confidentiality of the matters and writs, and who can read and write well, as pertains to the office. And we command [these scribes] to keep the ordinances that we command all the scribes of our court to keep.

The authority granted to the Portuguese *arrabi mor* was without parallel in the Iberian peninsula. However, the willingness of individual Jews to appeal directly to the king rather than to their *arrabi mor* further demonstrates the practical limits of the *arrabi mor's* power.

And we command that the aforementioned *arrabi mor* ensure that the aforementioned appeals and cases be resolved without any deceit or delay in order that the parties involved not suffer any damages, nor have reason to come before us to lodge a complaint. Moreover we command that he may summon [representatives of] the aforementioned communities whenever he deems necessary in order to resolve matters pertaining to our service and that they must respond to his command when they see his message. This he will do only after first receiving our special permission.

Fernando's letter ends with a caveat prohibiting any other civil magistrates from acting as appellate judges for cases involving Jews. The passage illustrates the degree of control enjoyed by the *arrabi mor* over the judicial procedures involving Jews, as well as his dependence on royal support for the effective enforcement of that authority.

Moreover, we command our criminal prosecutors and judges of the royal judiciary that if it happens that some of the aforementioned appeals which are made before the aforementioned communal *arrabis* come first before them instead of before the aforementioned *arrabi mor*, that they are not to receive nor judge these appeals until these have first been brought before the *arrabi mor*, that they might be judged by him or by one of his appointees.

The above information depicts the *arrabi mor* as a royal minister for Jewish affairs for the entire kingdom. However, the duties of the office went beyond handling matters involving the Jewish community, and included collecting taxes from Christian communities as well as acting as a representative of the court to other kingdoms. A letter from 1313, records Dinis' decision to send his *arrabi mor*, Judah, on a diplomatic mission to the king of Aragon. Here, the king refers to him as the *"arrabi mayor* of the Jews of our realm," emphasizing Judah's position as both a royal and a Jewish official. Other documents from the era portray the *arrabi mor* as a royal official with little or no connection to the Jewish community. In 1272, Afonso III directed a letter concerning the collection of taxes in the ports of the Algarve, to "the *arrabi* and those who would act as *almoxarifes* in his place," indicating that the post could be seen as interchangeable with that of other royal tax collectors. Even more striking is a letter from the reign of Dinis that was drawn up "by the *arrab[i] mayor* Afonso Reymondo." Here, the name would suggest that this *arrabi mor* was a Christian court official, and not a Jew at all.[63] The post paralleled that of the crown rabbis and *almoxarifes* of the other peninsular states, but enjoyed both greater continuity and more extensive authority than any other royal or local office of the era.

In a seminal essay first published in 1950, Yitzhak Baer set out a typology for the foundation and organization of the medieval Jewish community that continues to inform most studies on this subject. For Baer, Jewish communal government as embodied by the community (*kehilla*) developed out of corporate and democratic tendencies inherent in Jewish society since the

[63] ANTT, *Livro dos reis*, fol. 1–3v; Henrique David et al., "A Familia Cardona e as relações entre Portugal e Aragão durante o reinado de D. Dinis," *Revista da faculdade de Letras do Porto, História* 4 (1989), no. 4. For collecting taxes in the Algarve, see da Silva Marques, ed., *Descobrimentos Portugueses*, vol. 1, no. 16. For Afonso Reymondo, see ANTT, *Chanc. de D. Dinis, liv.* I, 3, fol. 48v, 1.a col.; and da Silva Marques, ibid., no. 33.

ancient period.[64] This image of the *kehilla* is a theoretical model based solely on legal conceptions of communal organization as interpreted by medieval rabbinic authorities.

The preceding chapter has taken a different approach to the study of the medieval Jewish polity. Rather than imagining Jews as *a priori* members of an inevitable community, I have presented the construction of the *aljama* as a slow and highly contextualized process, the product of a complex mix of internal and external forces. Throughout the latter half of the thirteenth century, the new Jewish settlements that had been established following the *reconquista* continued to be distinguished as much by the individual settler as by the organized community. The loose and often unstable organization of Jewish communities in the new territories is further characterized by the slow and uneven establishment of Jewish communal institutions on the frontier and the willingness of some Jews to live beyond the boundaries of the *aljama* and the attendant social and religious services it might provide.

The great Jewish courtiers of the age did not run the affairs of the local *aljamas*, as some scholars have suggested.[65] Rather, though they represented the highest level of authority within Jewish society, they only employed their power in an *ad hoc* manner. Local Jewish leaders may indeed have resented Jewish courtiers as non-residents who sought to interfere in the management of the local *kahal*, and as agents of Gentile (royal or seigneurial) control. Nonetheless, the weakness of the nascent communities of the frontier made them dependent on the intervention of the crown and its officials, both Jewish and non-Jewish. The rights accorded to these royal officials, and to the Portuguese *arrabi mor*, in particular, reflect both the further expansion of royal power into the Jewish community and the potential conflict between such courtiers and local Jewish officials.

This rivalry between crown rabbis and the *kahal*, though exacerbated by the growth of royal bureaucracies, formed part of a broader crisis of factionalism and dissent that represented a more fundamental challenge to Jewish communal authority. The following chapter will further explore the issue of Jewish self-government focusing on the destabilizing impact of intra-communal tensions. These internal divisions greatly undermined the effectiveness of the *kahal*, and aided in the integration of the ostensibly autonomous Jewish *aljama* into the rapidly expanding royal administrations of the Christian kingdoms.

---

[64] Baer, "The Foundations." Here, *kehilla* is synonymous with the terms *aljama* and *kahal*.

[65] Beatrice Leroy, *L'Aventure séfarade, De la péninsule ibérique à la diaspora* (Paris, 1986), 46–47.

Part II. The Jewish Community and the Frontier

CHAPTER SIX
COMMUNAL TENSIONS AND THE
QUESTION OF JEWISH AUTONOMY

Our people, who are in the estate of the Lord, are prohibited by the
Torah from showing a preference for the law of the Gentiles and their ordinances. Moreover, it is forbidden to bring litigation into their courts
even in matters where their laws are identical to Jewish law.
—R. Solomon ben Abraham ibn Adret

Uring the latter half of the thirteenth century, the
Jewish aristocracy's dominance of communal government became contested in the older and larger Jewish
centers of Toledo, Saragossa, and Barcelona. In
Toledo, pressure for social reform was precipitated by the downfall of several leading courtiers which endangered the whole community, yet royal
castigation and public denunciation of the morality of the elite did not
loosen the latter's hold on the reins of government. In the northern communities of the Crown of Aragon, popular unrest brought about more sub-
stantive social transformation as Jews from the politically disfranchised
lower classes began to challenge the rule of the traditional oligarchy. In contrast to these northern centers, the impetus to reform and reorder the Jewish polity was far less pronounced in the *aljamas* of the new territories. Here,
royal support for the greater democratization of Jewish communal councils
was sporadic, and brought about only moderate change. The violence and
social upheaval that plagued these communities was primarily the result of
tensions between powerful clans that were willing to subvert the authority
of the *kahal* in order to promote their own agendas.[1]

In the first decades of Jewish resettlement of the frontier, the greatest

---

[1] For Valencia, see Baer, *Juden*, vol. 1, no. 188; and for Mallorca, see ibid., no. 318.
Even for the Jewries of the interior, the notion of "class conflict" may be misleading. Discussing the Jewish community of thirteenth-century Barcelona, Bernard Septimus has argued that what has been viewed as an anti-aristocratic revolt was actually a struggle between various factions of the Jewish elite. See his "Piety and Power," 215.

power in communal government was wielded by the royal bailiffs and tax farmers who retained their primary associations with the old northern centers of Saragossa, Barcelona, and Toledo. By the early fourteenth century, however, the southern *aljamas* would produce their own native oligarchies, complete with feuding factions. This struggle for control of the Jewish settlements of the frontier did little to ameliorate the situation of the poorer members of the community who continued to have little voice in local government. In the Jewish communities of southern Castile and Portugal, there is no evidence that the ruling families lost any of their stature during this period, and in Mallorca the wealthy elite remained in power throughout the thirteenth and fourteenth centuries, receiving royal support for their domination of communal government in 1348 and again in 1374.[2]

Only in the kingdom of Valencia were there attempts to open the political process to include the poor, and even here, the elite ceded relatively little ground. In the community of Murviedro, change only came when Jaime II ordered his royal bailiff to intervene in the appointment of Jewish officials to assure the representation of the lower classes, and in the capital city of Valencia, the power which the members of the traditional oligarchy exercised was not loosened until 1300, and then only by royal mandate, and incompletely. In 1297, the communal leaders of the *aljama* of Valencia had petitioned Jaime II to allow them to restrict the office of *adelantado* to those Jews who were able to pay at least 30 royal pounds in taxes. Though the king initially acceded to their request, he later changed his decree in order to open up the leadership of the community to members of the lower economic classes. The problems surrounding the appointment of communal leaders and the method of tax assessment was yet another factor leading to the frequent intervention of the king and Infante into the management of the Valencian *aljama*. The situation was not easily resolved, however, and the struggle to impose election reform lasted throughout the early fourteenth century.[3]

  [2] Fita and Llabrés, "Privilegios," nos. 62, 91.
  [3] ACA, reg. 230, fol. 59. See also Mark Meyerson, "Revisiting the Wax-Press Affair in Morvedre (1326–27): Jewish Fiscal Politics in the Kingdom of Valencia," in *Jews Muslims and Christians in and around the Crown of Aragon*, ed. Harvey J. Hames (Leiden, 2004), 309–310. The battle to force the rich to pay their share of the communal tax was one that was waged by the crown and communal officials alike throughout this period. See Adret, 5:279. In an attempt to end the abuses of the wealthiest members of the Valencian *aljama* who were not shouldering their portion of the tax burden, Jaime II ordered a new system of communal taxation. ACA, reg. 197, fol. 153v; in Baer, *Juden*, vol. 1, no. 146. For the monetary requirement for office holders, see ACA, reg. 195, fol. 46, and for a similar case in Murviedro from the same year and month, see ACA, reg. 108, fol. 133v. In the end, the king had to send several more orders to the *aljama* before a council of *adelantados* was established. ACA, reg. 86, fols. 136, 141v; 157v–158; reg. 214, fol. 23; reg. 229, fol. 274.

Part II. The Jewish Community and the Frontier

As Jewish communities became reconstituted in the newly Christianized territories, they came to reflect the dynamic and often unruly atmosphere of the frontier. Nowhere were these characteristics more in evidence than in the city of Valencia, which, in the latter half of the thirteenth century, was characterized by intra-communal violence and social tensions that transcended the political disenfranchisement of the poor. On account of the legal nature of many of the sources we have for this period, there are an unusually high number of references to Jews in one form of conflict or another. It is therefore important to keep in mind that these documents present a somewhat slanted portrait of daily life of the Jews on the Iberian frontier. Nonetheless, a study of these texts can offer a glimpse at some of the dissonant elements of Sephardic communal life in the thirteenth century.

In addition to the potential for conflict between members of the three religions, there was an even greater chance of tension and violence within the Jewish community itself, for it was with their own coreligionists that Jews had the most contact. The level of tensions, distrust, and general corruption among Jews of the Iberian frontier can be gauged by a document from 1294 in which Salamon Abenzeyt is mentioned as being afraid that he will now be labeled a *malsin*, or informer, after coming forth and denouncing Jewish counterfeiters in Mallorca. It is worth pointing out that Salamon did not fear the individual reprisals of the counterfeiters, but rather the "Jews of the Jewish *aljama* of Mallorca," who would pronounce an official sentence against him for having informed the crown of the criminals' activity. The very real potential for such reprisals on the part of a Jewish communal council, along with the crime of counterfeiting itself, help spotlight the kind of internal pressures and abuses with which frontier Jews often lived.[4]

These tensions often erupted in violent clashes between Jews. In 1270, a Jew from Teruel named Jucef de Faro received an official pardon for having murdered a Muslim. While the stated reason for the pardon was that Jucef had acted in self-defense, further events demonstrate that the de Faro family was routinely involved in violent conflicts, primarily with other members of the Jewish community. Just three years after the above incident, Jaime I issued another pardon, this time to a group of Jews charged with the murder of Jucef's son. Though the accused, Jacob Avenrodrich, his sons, and his brother Abraham, were all found innocent by the king, Jucef de Faro was

---

[4] ACA, re. 252, fols. 193–194.

not willing to accept such lenience. Together with his sons Samuel and Moses, de Faro took his revenge by killing Jacob Avenrodrich's son, Samuel. It would seem, however, that de Faro's connections to the crown were not as strong as those of the Avenrodrich family, and this time he was not able to secure a royal pardon for himself and his sons. In contrast, Jacob and his son Moses continue to appear in several documents dealing with business in conjunction with the crown. At the same time that Jucef and his sons were being arrested, and perhaps as compensation for the loss of his dead brother, the king awarded Moses, another son of Jacob Avenrodrich, apartments in the tower of the small castle in Teruel.[5]

A series of documents dating from the close of the thirteenth century records a number of denunciations made between Jews in the city of Valencia; they paint a particularly colorful portrait of the contentious world of Jewish frontier communities. At the center of most of these denunciations was Jacob Abnuba (also Abnayub), one of the *aljama's* more prominent members and a communal official. In 1292, Jacob was accused of statutory rape, a form of denunciation which was not uncommon in Valencia and other communities of the period. Upon investigation of the crime, the *justicia* of Valencia was unable to prove his guilt and thus the accusations were withdrawn. Twelve years later, Abnuba once again appears in the royal register, being accused of a host of crimes including statutory rape, extortion, destroying a bench in the synagogue, and misadministration in his role as *adelantado*. This time, the case was dealt with by the king himself; he exacted a fine of 2,000 royal *solidi* before dismissing the charges.[6]

This amount, though quite large, appears to have been a standard "fine" for royal absolution from such charges. A few years after Abnuba's payment, another wealthy member of the community, Abraham Camis, paid the same amount to obtain a dismissal of several charges that had been brought against him, including adultery, assault, and attempted rape. The fine was decidedly lighter if the charge were merely assault, as is illustrated in the case of Salamon, son of Bonjueu de la Torre, who paid only 200 *solidi* to be acquitted of having attacked fellow Jew Salomon Vital of Burriana.[7]

If such cases do not actually represent a community that was lawless and morally debased, they do, at the very least, describe a community in which

---

[5] ACA, reg. 16, fol. 196v; reg. 19, fol. 47; reg. 50 fol. 176v. For Jacob and his son, Moses, see also ACA reg. 19, fol. 15v; reg. 52, fol. 23; reg. 43, fols. 6v,117v; reg. 63, fol. 34v. For the apartments at Teruel, see ACA, reg. 50, fol. 176v.

[6] ACA, reg. 19, fol. 156. See also the case of Jucef Xaprut and several other Jews from Valencia who were acquitted of a list of charges, including rape, after payment of a large fine. On Abnuba, see also ACA, reg. 199, fol. 34v; reg. 86, fol. 141v; reg. 303, fol. 204.

[7] ACA, reg. 215, fols. 268v–269. For Salamon see reg. 37, fol. 7.

Part II. The Jewish Community and the Frontier

such accusations were easily and frequently made. And in several instances, intra-communal violence does appear to have been real. In one such case, a Valencian Jew, along with his two sons and another relative, were exiled for having killed a Jewish courtier by the name of Açach Roig. That the bulk of these attacks seem to have been levied against communal leaders indicates that, in the decades following 1290, the Valencian *aljama* began to suffer from the same social unrest that had plagued northern towns, such as Saragossa, decades earlier. Nor was the turmoil in this region limited to the city of Valencia itself. When, in November of 1319, Jucef Algehen was attacked and wounded by several of his Jewish rivals in the Valencian town of Murviedro, he brought the case before the bailiff general, rather than to the Jewish courts. His decision to pursue justice outside of the *aljama* was not an attempt to circumvent Jewish law. Indeed, he asked that the bailiff pass sentence in accordance with "the rite of the Jews." Rather, Algehen sought a forum in which he might obtain a fair trial, since his assailants and their supporters were officials of the local *kahal*.[8]

Tensions and treachery were not only common between members of the same community, but among members of the same family as well. In one case, the death of the wealthy and well-regarded courtier Samuel Abenvives was the cause of great conflict among several of his relatives. The crown, which had a claim on the deceased's estate, ordered that it should be sequestered until the various claims could be settled. At this time, in violation of the royal order, Salamon and Judah Abenvives stole a chest belonging to Samuel from the house of a female relative, Na Vives. In addition to seizing the chest, the two also forged a Hebrew contract that held that they had been named executors of Samuel's will. In the end, Salamon was only brought to justice through further royal intervention, and had to pay the hefty sum of 4,000 *solidi* to the crown after ignoring threats of *herem* by the local *aljama*.[9]

Such defiance of local Jewish authority by powerful Jews was not uncommon, even when Jewish communal officials worked in conjunction with local Christian magistrates. Indeed, the crown itself often had to threaten Jews in its employ in order to assure their obedience. In 1285, Pedro III of Aragon ordered the arrest of two Jews of Játiva, Avingayet and Alaçram, who had collected taxes from the *aljama* there without forwarding the money to the crown. All of the above cases involved the offices of Christian officials, whether a local judge or *justicia*, the Infante in charge of governing the king-

[8] ACA, reg. 19, fol. 11; reg. 168, fol. 142v; Meyerson, "Jewish Fiscal Politics," pp. 306–307.
[9] ACA, reg. 206, fol. 124rv; Burns, *Notarial Culture*, no. 39, pp. 182–184.

dom of Valencia, or the king himself. These cases underscore the limited power of Jewish courts and the general fragility of Jewish communal authority, factors that often prompted the king either to intervene in communal affairs or to threaten and cajole Jews to govern themselves.[10]

CHALLENGES TO JEWISH COMMUNAL AUTONOMY

In his pioneering study *The Jews in Spain*, Abraham Neuman noted that "[Jewish] autonomy was the spiritual counterpart of the physical characteristics of the *judería*," and the view persists that royal intervention into Jewish communal affairs was limited and sporadic. However, a deeper understanding of the limits of Jewish communal authority during this period requires a closer look at the relationship between the crown, the Jewish individual, and the *kahal*. The crown's incursion into Jewish communal government often came at the request of Jewish individuals or factions who sought to evade the jurisdiction of their local council. As a result, the leaders of the *kahal* became increasingly dependent on royal authority for the effective governance of their communities.[11]

As I have already mentioned, the principal challenge to the authority of Jewish self-government came from within the community itself. While the Iberian monarchs generally succeeded in asserting their authority over the Jews in their realms to the exclusion of other lords, this arrangement was unable to prevent individual Jews from undercutting the authority of their communal councils by bringing their cases straight to the king, or to other Christian officials, when they thought it to their advantage. Already in Roman times, Jews would routinely circumvent the authority of their local officials by appealing directly to imperial judges. A similar receptiveness to Jews prepared to disregard the jurisdiction of their courts can be found among the Muslim jurists of al-Andalus Muslim who allowed for Muslim courts to handle Jewish cases if the Jews brought the case there of their own free will. In Christian kingdoms of the thirteenth century, the willingness of municipal, baronial, and, principally, royal courts to receive and adjudicate

[10] ACA, reg. 43, fol. 117v.
[11] Neuman, *The Jews of Spain*, 1:22. See also the recent comments by Carlos Carrete Parrondo, "Organización de las comunidades judías en la España cristiana," in *The Culture of Spanish Jewry*, ed. Aviva Doron (Tel Aviv, 1994), 58. On royal interference in ecclesiastical affairs, see José Angel García de Cortazar, *La Época Medieval* (Madrid, 1973), 491.

Part II. The Jewish Community and the Frontier

such cases exacerbated the situation. In 1294, Jewish officials from Valencia complained to the king that their ability to sentence Jewish criminals was being undermined by those Christians willing to protect Jewish offenders.[12] Since the ultimate source of the *kahal's* authority was the crown itself, many Jews chose to bypass their communal courts and bring their grievances to royal officials, such as the bailiff or the *alcalde*, or directly to the king. Recourse to Christian officials and courts would have been a particularly attractive option for those Jews with strong social or business ties to the crown and its local representatives. In other instances, a Jew might turn to Christian authorities as a sort of court of appeal, after failing to find satisfaction from his local Jewish officials. Portugal allowed for the crown to become involved in such appeals in the law, cited earlier, which stated that there was to be no appeal of the judgments made by the *arrabi mor* "except where the king should want to intervene." In the town of Évora, a case of an outstanding debt owed by one Jew to another was brought before the king, and on the other end of the frontier, Jacob Abnuba and Jahuda Abenvives of Valencia appealed to the king to reinvestigate a case regarding the collection of money paid to another Jew. In Murviedro, Salamon Bahia turned to Alfonso III to help force Jewish business partners to live up to their responsibilities. Cases like these should have been handled by local Jewish councils and their appeal to royal authority reflects the general inefficacy of Jewish communal government, even in relatively mundane cases.[13]

Similarly remarkable were cases in which Jews appealed to the crown, rather than their communal officials, to protect their property and inheritance rights. In one such example, Clara, the mother of Abraffim Mahir, the deceased bailiff of Játiva appealed directly to the Infante Pedro in order to receive her portion of her son's goods that had been seized by the crown. In response to her plea, Pedro III ordered his officials to release the goods to Clara. In 1286, Alfonso III of Aragon reaffirmed the grant given by his father, Pedro III, to the Jewess Astruga, widow of Jucef Ravaya, regarding her share of his former holdings. The king allowed Astruga to keep the property, tax free, and issued a general warning to all Jewish *aljamas* against im-

[12] Codex Theodosianus, 16.8.8. Such appeals to Gentile courts were forbidden by Jewish law. See The Babylonian Talmud, *Gittin*, 88b. For Jews in al-Andalus, see Matthias B. Lehmann, "Islamic Legal Consultation and the Jewish-Muslim Convivencia," *Jewish Studies Quarterly* 6 (1999): 50–53. For Jews under Hispano-Christian rule, see ACA, reg. 100, fol. 187; Baer, *Juden*, vol. 1, no. 137. See also Ishbili, *Responsa*, no. 67.

[13] PMH, *Leges*, 286–287. For Évora, see Pimenta Ferro, *Os Judeus*, 1st ed., no. 15. For Valencia, see ACA, reg. 89, fol. 60v. For Abnuba, see Régné, nos. 908, 1361, 2182, 2446, 2832. On Salamon Bahia, see ACA, reg. 80, fol. 5. Salamon also complained to the king that some Jews of Murviedro had violated privileges that had been granted by his predecessors. ACA, reg. 80, fol. 5v.

posing any ban (*nidduy*) upon her for refusal to pay taxes on it. At other times, Jews would seek royal support in reversing decisions made by their *kahal* with regard to personal property and inheritance. When the *aljama* of Valencia seized part of the estate of one of its deceased members, Alfonso III forced it to repay the amount to the Jew's heirs. In taking up the plight of the individual Jews, the crown was acting in lieu of and, in some cases, directly against the kahal whose jurisdiction in such cases was, theoretically, absolute.[14]

Property rights were not the only issue about which Jews turned to the crown when they were at odds with their own communal governments. In 1294, the Infante of Valencia revoked the *herem*, or ban, imposed by the *kahal* of Valencia on Esther bat Na Beyla, which called for her exclusion from that *judería* and its members for ten years, on the grounds that no formal complaint had been brought. The Infante then added that without a formal complaint or consent of the king or Infante, the *aljama* did not have the power to excommunicate its members.[15] Pedro's statement underscores the reality that the *kahal's* autonomy was ultimately dependent upon the crown. It is at once a demonstration of the inefficacy of Jewish government and the general campaign to extend royal authority into the local, urban sphere.

A royal document from 1290 records that Isaac Abingalell had petitioned the king to force the *adelantados* of the Valencian *kahal* to pay money that had been awarded to him by a special committee composed of arbiters of the *aljama*. Both the creation of a committee of arbiters and their apparent inability to make their decision binding illustrate the sort of disorder which prevailed in the Jewish government of Valencia, and which forced certain members of the community to seek royal intervention. The use of arbiters in the Valencian *aljama*, as well their relative impotence, was a common feature of Jewish government in the late thirteenth century. Jucef Alorqui also appealed to the king in order to receive money awarded to him in arbitration, as did Jonas Çibili. Like most appeals to the crown by Jews, these judgments were usually effectuated after the payment of a special "fine" to the royal authorities.[16]

As we have seen, Jewish communities in this period were governed by a mix of law and local custom. However, in the newly established towns of the south, there had been little time for such "local custom" to develop, and

---

[14] ACA, reg. 86, fol. 132v; reg. 63, fols. 40v–41. Once again, this royal decree appears to have been a response to a petition brought by Astruga. See also the initial grant given by Pedro III, ACA, reg. 46, fol. 107v; and reg. 74, fol. 80.

[15] ACA, reg. 89, fols. 49, 55v.

[16] ACA, reg. 81, fols. 173–174; reg. 81, fol. 175; reg. 37, fol. 7.

Part II. The Jewish Community and the Frontier

Jewish settlers coming from a variety of locales in the north of the peninsula as well as North Africa brought with them a variety of different customs and political traditions. In this context, the willingness of Jews to utilize the crown as an ad hoc court of appeals (and the latter's readiness to oblige) only exacerbated the unsteady structure of the frontier *kahal*.

Jewish disregard for the authority of the *kahal* went beyond their use of Gentile courts. Some Jews even went so far as to enlist the aid of powerful Christians to intimidate Jewish judges. In one such case, a Jew who initially agreed to accept the judgment of a Jewish court, changed his mind when he saw that the decision was going to go against him, and called upon a powerful Christian to threaten the Jewish judge involved, and to cause him to remove himself from the case. Such behavior prompted some rabbinic authorities to forbid Jews from turning to Christian courts, but such decrees were impossible to enforce.[17]

The willingness of many Jews to avail themselves of the auspices of the Christian authorities sometimes forced their communal officials to resort to legal innovations in an attempt to retain jurisdiction over the members of their communities. At times, these efforts were met with consternation and exasperation by Jewish scholars who, despite recognizing the need for developing legal customs, often disapproved of the lengths to which many communal leaders were willing to go. In one responsum, Solomon ibn Adret expressed shock and dismay that Jewish communal leaders in Perpignan wanted to adopt Christian law just to keep Jews from running to Christian courts. The above-cited case of Abraham Safiyah of Cordoba also illustrates the reality of Jewish patronage of Christian courts during the period and the lengths to which Jewish courts were willing to go in order to maintain their own jurisdiction and authority. R. Asher's explanation that the Jews of Castile judged such capital cases out of fear of the severity of Christian courts was later repeated and expanded by his son, Yehudah ben Asher, who explained that Jewish courts heard capital cases not only as a means of protecting innocent Jews from execution, but also to insure punishment for those who might be found innocent by Christian tribunals.[18]

These days we exercise criminal jurisdiction for two reasons: to save the lives of those who would be acquitted by our law and condemned to

---

[17] Adret, 1:1126. See also the ties between Prince Alfonso and members of a powerful Jewish faction in Murviedro in Meyerson, "Jewish Fiscal Politics," 311; and Moses ben Nahman, *Responsa*, no. 63.

[18] Adret, 6:254. "At any rate, to follow the customs of Gentile law seems to me to be forbidden beyond a doubt, since it is in imitation of the Gentiles, which is forbidden by the Torah: 'neither before them nor before the Gentiles.'"

death by theirs; and secondly, to bring death upon those who merit this penalty according to our standards, such as informers and similar offenders who threaten the life of the entire community, and who would not be convicted to death by the laws of the gentiles.

The Jewish judges of Castile made frequent use of this authority to insure that transgressors were severely punished, and in doing so provoked violent reaction from many Jews.[19]

It should be pointed out that Christian authorities did not always accept complete jurisdiction over the cases appealed to them by Jews. At times, they worked together with Jewish officials to help them implement their authority within the *judería*. When the Jews who possessed the monopoly on Hebrew notarial documents for the *aljama* of Valencia abused their position by overcharging clients and extorting extra payments, Jaime II ordered both the town bailiff and the Jewish community's *adelantados* to put a stop to such abuses.[20]

In other instances, the crown might assume executive powers in dealing with its Jews, but defer to Jewish communal leaders and legal experts for advice on how to best adjudicate certain issues in accordance with their law. In 1258, after it hanged the Jew al-Mubarak al-Ma'dani, the Aragonese crown proceeded to dispose of property he had possessed in the town Alcira. When his widow sued for her portion of the proceeds from his lands, the Christian authorities referred to, and ruled in accordance with, Jewish law. In a similar case regarding the status of the heirs to Isaac Cohen of Mallorca, Alfonso III agreed to act as executor of the estate, but sought to enlist officers of the Jewish community. The king appointed two Jews from the *aljama*, Maymo Abenvive and Isaac Benabram, to see if one of the heirs, Aaron, was of age, and to follow the dictates of Jewish law as to whether he was to be given his portion, or whether it was to be safeguarded on his behalf.[21]

In cases that dealt with fine points of Jewish law, the Christian monarchs of the period availed themselves of the services of Jewish legal experts, and in cases involving both Jews and Christians, the crown also made use of

---

[19] *Zikhron Yehudah*, no. 63; and also nos. 58, and 79. On the use of capital punishment against informers, see Asher ben Yehiel, *Responsa*, 17:1, 6, 8; Adret, 5:287–289. For the Jews of Castile, see *Zikhron Yehudah*, no. 75 where a judge provoked hostility from town elders after declaring that a certain member of the community should receive a severe beating; and no. 79, where a judge had his faced slashed.

[20] ACA, reg. 229, fol. 274v; and Burns, *Notarial Culture*, no. 43. For the original grant of the monopoly, see ibid., no. 41.

[21] "Et invenimus quod secundum ius et foros Iudeorum." ACA, reg. 10, fol. 66bis rv; and Burns, *Diplomatarium*, no. 131. For Mallorca, see ACA, reg. 70, fol. 172v.

Part II. The Jewish Community and the Frontier

Christian jurists.[22] Additionally, cases involving Jewish notables were often handled directly by Christian authorities due to the courtiers' connections to the crown and their ability to flout the decisions of their communal leaders. A case from 1308 between two Jewish courtiers from different kingdoms involved a host of Christian authorities but no Jewish officials. The problem began when Abraham Xorbetos, a Jewish emissary of Sancho IV of Castile to the king of Tlemcen, gave royal and personal property to a fellow Jew to safeguard. Xorbetos was then unable to retrieve these goods, and thus turned to Pedro López de Ayala, a Murcian official, for help. Ayala, in turn, took the case to the Aragonese crown. He asked Jaime II to force the *justicia* of Orihuela to produce the Jew, Abbu, and the items that had been given to him for safekeeping.[23]

The decision of individual Jews to bring their cases before Christian courts, whether in lieu of Jewish courts, or in an effort to overturn rulings by Jewish officials, had a withering effect on the legitimacy and potency of Jewish self government. This was especially true for those belonging to the wealthier clans, who often chose to incur the ban of the *kahal*, and then to have it lifted by order of the crown after payment of a fine. One Jewish courtier, Jucef Avençaprut, even succeeded in obtaining a royal grant which entitled him to an annual fee from the *aljama* of Murviedro. In the city of Valencia, it became so difficult to find eligible candidates willing to serve as officials that a written exemption from the crown was necessary in order to avoid service. When the Valencian *kahal* had to appoint *ne'emanim* to collect taxes, the wealthiest men of the community were forced to participate in a lottery in which five of them would be selected and compelled to serve. A Valencian physician, Omerio Tahuyl, was granted such an exemption due to other responsibilities to the crown. It seems that quite a number of Jews who, like Tahuyl, had connections at court, endeavored to use them in order to shirk their political and social responsibilities to their communities. In some cases, exemptions from crown taxes that had been proffered as an inducement to settlement were used as means to escape a host of other communal obligations. At Játiva, for example, the entire community was advised that royal exemptions could not be applied to obligations beyond the payment of royal taxes.[24]

[22] ACA, reg. 81, fol. 178; reg. 89, fol. 54.
[23] ACA, *Cartas Reales*, Jaime II, c. 26, no. 3322; reg. 56, fol. 77. See, also, Régné, nos. 1270, 1960. For Salomon as a scion of a courtier family, see ibid., nos. 782–783.
[24] ACA, reg. 206; fol. 124rv; pub. in Burns, *Notarial Culture*, no. 39; and ACA, reg. 66, fol. 113v. This decree was challenged by some candidates who refused to serve when chosen. Adret, 3:417. For Tahuyl, see ACA, 215, fol. 185v. For Játiva, see reg. 11, fol. 190; Burns, *Diplomatarium*, no. 327a.

The capacity of local Jewish governments to collect taxes was the primary matter of interest to the Christian kings. To this end, the crown would call for representatives from different *aljamas* to meet in order to organize the distribution of the tax burden for the Jews of a certain region. Any regional cohesion among Jewish communities was thus, during this period, more a result of Christian administrative needs than any supra-communal organization or identity on the part of the communities themselves, since relations between communal councils were informal and generally relegated to meetings regarding raising funds to pay royal taxes. In some cases, such meetings were ordered by the crown itself, as in 1284 when Pedro III of Aragon ordered Jewish representatives from Valencia, Játiva, Murviedro, and all other communities of the kingdom of Valencia to come together in order to work out the distribution of royal taxes. In an effort to establish a more reliable system of tax collection, stronger ties were sometimes established between larger *aljamas* and an array of smaller communities from the surrounding region. However, there was a great deal of resistance to even this level of cooperation, and it was necessary for the larger *aljamas* to petition the crown for an order mandating the compliance of the smaller communities. The frequency with which the crown had to order the same communities to meet in this regard further speaks to the reticence of Jews in the frontier regions, and throughout Iberia, in forming any lasting intercommunal organizations.[25]

On the Aragonese frontier, the king supported Jewish officials in imposing a ban on those members of the community who were recalcitrant in their payment of taxes. At times, however, royal intervention in the collection of Jewish taxes could also function as an obstacle to the *kahal*, and in some instances, could also result in the outright nullification of Jewish communal authority. When the *aljama* of Játiva sought to force one of its wealthier members, Vives ben Jucef Avenvives, to pay the money he owed to the community, it seized the tenures of some of his tenants. And when the latter protested to the royal court, Pedro III ruled that the *aljama* had violated the rights of the tenants who were not liable for the financial debts of their landlord. The king then instructed his bailiff to annul the *kahal's* order of seizure and announced that Vives was now willing to pay his creditors. The crown's intrusion into Jewish communal governance could also extend beyond the issue of taxes and encompass matters of Jewish law. In Mallorca,

[25] ACA, reg. 56, fol. 7v. For royal enforcement of the Valencian community's right to collect taxes from regional *aljamas*, see ACA, reg. 12, fol. 143; reg. 66, fol. 47; reg. 46, fol. 152v; reg. 57, fol. 222v.

the legality of Jewish marital contracts, or *ketubbot*, was also subject to approval by the crown.[26]

Finally, individual Jews were not alone in their appeals for royal support. Just as individual Jews would appeal to the crown in order to overturn sentences imposed by their local Jewish government, so too would communal officials turn to the king when they met resistance in their attempts to collect taxes or enforce Jewish law. In 1285, a wealthy Valencian Jew with extensive land holdings throughout the kingdom named Aaron Abinafia refused to contribute to the large tax being collected by the Valencian *aljama*. In response, Pedro III ordered that if he persisted in his intransigence, the leaders of the Jewish community would be permitted to impose sanctions against him according to Jewish law. In Mallorca, Jewish officials turned to the crown when Jewish bankers and merchants took tax money from them and then declared bankruptcy. Thus, royal authority became an integral part in the system of Jewish communal government during the thirteenth century both because of the crown's desire to exert greater control over the *aljamas* and the appeals from Jewish individuals and communal governments alike.[27]

Writing on the Crown of Aragon during the high reconquest, Donald J. Kagay has described the difficult task of public administration during this period as "violence management." For Kagay, the limited ability to enforce legislative ideals gave rise to "a system by which the principal regal, urban, and episcopal peacemakers of the Crown of Aragon would command, threaten, and cajole malefactors of every class—all in order to keep the fragile structure of public peace from being rent by the actions of private individuals."[28]

The readiness and ease with which both individual Jews and the crown undermined the autonomy and authority of Jewish government on the frontier must cause us to reevaluate the regnant model of Jewish communal organization in this and other regions. Analysis of both royal and rabbinic sources regarding Jewish communal government during this period reveals the existence of internal conflicts and tensions on a variety of levels: be-

---

[26] ACA, reg. 16, fol. 159; and ACA, reg. 67, fol. 84v. For Juceff and Bonjudas, see reg. 74, fol. 66. For Vives, see reg. 46, fol. 82v. For the *ketubbot* of Mallorca, see Fita and Llabrés, "Privilegios," no. 11, p. 27.

[27] ACA, reg. 57, fol. 222v; Fita and Llabrés, no. 36.

[28] Donald J. Kagay, "Violence Management in Twelfth-Century Catalonia and Aragon," in *Marginated Groups in Spanish and Portuguese History*, ed. William D. Phillips, Jr. and Carla Rahn Phillips (Minneapolis, 1986), 16.

tween the individual settler and the *kahal*, among wealthy clans and factions within the community, and between the local *kahal* and Jewish administrators appointed by the crown. As in the case of Abraham Safiyah of Córdoba, which was considered in the previous chapter, the violence and discord of the Valencian *aljama* illustrates the inherent weakness and inefficacy of Jewish self-government on the frontier. In contrast to the contemporary uprisings in the *aljamas* of Barcelona and Saragossa, the resistance to communal government on the frontier did not seek to invert or permanently alter the social order. Rather, the result of Jewish factionalism in cities such as Valencia was to hinder the function of Jewish self-government, causing Jewish leaders to regularly reach out to the crown for support.

CHAPTER SEVEN
MAINTENANCE OF SOCIAL BOUNDARIES
ON THE IBERIAN FRONTIER

Some intermingle with Gentiles, eat their bread, and become like them,
so that there is no difference between them except the name "Jew" alone.
—Judah ben Barzilay ha-Bargeloni

W hile the socio-juridical situation of the Iberian
frontier reflected a dedication to the equal treatment of Jewish and Christian settlers, it was also
characterized by a commitment to the preserva-
tion of the social boundaries separating these groups. Municipal charters,
royal legal codes, and Jewish communal statutes all sought to enforce the social separation of the peninsula's different religious groups through the regulation of their clothing, food, sexual intercourse, and the use of public
space. In the wake of the Fourth Lateran Council of 1215, the papacy attempted to further restrict relations between members of the different faiths
by issuing a series of ecclesiastical prohibitions against the interaction between Christians and Jews. Yet the various measures taken by both Christian
and Jewish authorities to curtail this interaction often met with resistance
from individuals in both communities, and at times were even undermined
by contradicting policies of the authorities themselves. As a result, the social
and economic ties between members of the peninsula's religious groups
were as much a hallmark of Christian Iberia in the thirteenth century as
they had been in Muslim al-Andalus centuries earlier. In order to gain a
clearer understanding of Christian-Jewish relations on the Iberian frontier
it is necessary to examine the lines along which communal boundaries were
drawn, and the degree to which these borders remained permeable
throughout this period.

The primary step taken by the Christian authorities to regulate Jewish-Gentile interaction was the designation of separate *juderías*, or Jewish quarters, in almost every town large enough to host a Jewish community. The Jewish settlements of the thirteenth-century frontier were heirs to centuries of development under Muslim and Christian rule, since the existence of a fortified urban neighborhood set aside for Jewish settlement was typical of both Muslim al-Andalus and other areas of Christian Europe. In larger towns, these neighborhoods usually developed into formal Jewish quarters, though Jews also established communities in smaller centers, including settlements in several castles. In the Iberian kingdoms, as elsewhere in Europe, the castle of the high Middle Ages was more than a rural military outpost. Built as a means of extending seigniorial authority over the local peasantry as much as for defense, castles often grew to rival small towns as administrative centers and economic entrepôts. For this reason they attracted Jewish settlers who came principally to work as merchants and to serve at baronial courts. Owing to the relatively small numbers of inhabitants in these strongholds, these settlers were well integrated into all facets of castle life. There is evidence of Jewish blacksmiths working at a castle near Lérida in the early twelfth century, as well as Jewish settlements in the Navarrese castles at Caseda and Carcastillo. A twelfth-century peace treaty between Navarre and Castile lists several strongholds as "castle of the Jews," and nearby, in the Riojan town of Haro, the Jews possessed their own castle as a donation given by Alfonso VIII of Castile. The castle, along with surrounding land bordering the Ebro, was held collectively by the "*aljama*" of the Jews." Further south, there are references to a Jewish castle in Toledo in the 1160s, and in nearby Maqueda in 1222. In the Crown of Aragon, a castle at Baneres, near Tortosa, was given outright to a group of twenty-five Jews in recognition of their service to the aristocratic Montcada family.[1]

---

[1] See the reference to Jews in one castle contributing to the cost of constructing defensive walls. *Peratay-Baba Batra*, in *Yad Ramah, Baba Batra*, chap. 1, p. 77. For Lérida, see Baer, *Juden*, vol. 1, no. 31. For Caseda and Carcastillo, see Muñoz y Romero, *Colección*, 469–471, c. 1129, insert in a document of 1336. The treaty that makes references to several "*castellum iudeorum*," dates from 1176. See Julio González, *El reino de Castilla en la época de Alfonso VIII* (Madris, 1960), vol. 2, nos. 267, 278; vol. 3, no. 962. For Toledo, see Cándido Angel González Palencia, ed., *Los Mozárabes de Toledo en los siglos XII y XIII* (Madrid, 1930), vol. 4, nos. 897, 1135 For Maqueda, see Gonzalo Viñuales Ferreiro, "Maqueda 1492. Judíos y judaizantes," *Espacio Tiempo y Forma* 11 (1998): 385, and for Baneres, see Cynthia Maya, "Jew and Muslim in Post-Conquest Tortosa," *Al-Masaq* 10 (1998): 21.

Throughout the thirteenth century, small communities of Jews could still be found living in castles in the northern reaches of the peninsula. Jews aided in the defense of castles at Ruesta and El Frago, on the border between Aragon and Navarre, and in Portugal, a document from 1258 mentions a village and castle of the Jews, in the district of Gardom.² Yet over the course of the century, larger urban Jewish quarters became the standard form of Jewish settlement in Christian Iberia. This is particularly true of the southern frontier where there is little indication of Jewish residence in castles. Here, the efforts of the Christian monarchs to exercise greater power over their new territories, and particularly over their Jews, aided the propagation of the urban Jewish quarter as the standard form of Jewish settlement in the peninsula.

THE RISE OF THE JUDERÍA

Jewish settlement on the thirteenth-century frontier paralleled the rise and popularization of the Jewish quarter throughout the Christian kingdoms. Though not a new feature to Iberia, it was during the continued expansion and urbanization of the late twelfth and thirteenth centuries that the royally chartered and controlled Jewish quarter, known most commonly as *judería* (Castilian), *judiaria* (Portuguese), or *call* (Catalan), became the paradigmatic Jewish settlement. Notwithstanding this process of regularization, the growth and dynamism of the Jewries of the frontier meant that some settlers would live outside the territorial bounds of the *judería* and, in some cases, outside the social and legal limits of the Jewish community as well.³

Jewish communities that had been established prior to this period now evolved into social spaces of greater definition and control. An example of the evolution of such settlements from the twelfth to the thirteenth century can be seen in the Portuguese castle-town of Leiria, founded by Afonso Henriques in 1135. By the 1150s, a group of Jews had established themselves outside of the fortified town along the road leading to the gate known as the

---

² For Ruesta, see ACA, reg. 198, fol. 228v. For El Frago, reg. 89, fol. 170v. For Gardom, Henrique da Gama Barros, "Judeus e Mouros em Portugal," *Revista Lusitana* 34 (1937): 181.

³ The use of collective terms such as *aljama* to describe Jewish settlements did not become widespread before the thirteenth century. In Barcelona, for example, royal documents referred to the Jews simply as *judei*. These terms denoted the physical spaced occupied by a Jewish community and should not be confused with "*aljama*," which referred to the community itself.

Porta do Sol. This early settlement is not referred to as a *judiaria*, nor is there any mention of a charter or any other royal order delimiting a particular space where Jews were to settle. Over the course of the latter half of the twelfth century Leiria's rapid expansion came to encompass the original Jewish settlement, bringing it within the town walls. By the end of the century, the Jews of Leiria inhabited an urban neighborhood cut off from further expansion by the Christian homes that now surrounded them. The settlement had developed into a more formal Jewish quarter whose corporate nature is reflected in two documents from 1306 and 1308 regarding the acquisition of its own olive grove.[4] The contours of the Jewish quarter at Leiria only became fixed during the late thirteenth century, and its eventual limits may reflect an increased concern about the relationship between members of the Jewish settlement and the predominantly Christian town. It is only with the increased probability of interaction between Christians and Jews that we first see references to this settlement as a *"judiaria."*

The Christian expansion of the thirteenth century brought with it the establishment or reestablishment of a host of new *juderías*, and in many instances the crown played a greater role in their development than in towns such as Leiria. The Christian monarchs who oversaw the *repoblación* viewed these new Jewish communities as invaluable elements to the economic and administrative stability of the new territories and set aside land for Jewish settlement in the towns of frontier. At Albarracin, in southern Aragon, Alfonso III instructed his bailiff to accept any Jews who wished to settle there, granting them privileges and settling them in their own quarter of the town near the tower of Entrambasaguas. In Portugal, the first references of the *judiaria* of Évora and to a Jewish gate there both date from the late thirteenth century. The establishment of these Jewish neighborhoods often meant the expulsion of non-Jews from that corner of the city, and in several locales Christians were asked to forfeit property in order to make way for the creation or enlargement of a *judería*. The *repartimiento* of Murcia lists several instances in which Christians were ousted from their lands due to the establishment of a Jewish quarter. This was also the case at the Castilian town of Ubeda where, after its conquest in 1236, Fernando III set aside a section of land for the establishment of a Jewish settlement. A document dating from his reign mentions a number of houses which used to be in the royal *alcázar*, and which now formed part of the new *judería*. The letter is an

---

4 ANTT, *Alcobaça*, m. 19, no. 37, c. 1293. For the early development of the community at Leiria, see Saul Gomes, "Os Judeus de Leiria Medieval como Agentes Dinamizadores da Economia Urbana," *Revista da Faculdade de Letras, Coimbra. Historia* 29 (1993): 1–9. For the *"oliual da juyaria,"* see ibid., 5.

order of compensation for houses that a certain Christian, Remir Díaz, could no longer possess since they were now in the *judería*. This decree indicates that, at least at the onset of Christian repopulation, the crown sought to prohibit Christian ownership of land in the town's Jewish quarter.[5]

The emergence of the *juderías*, both on the frontier and elsewhere in the peninsula, was, in large part, the result of royal initiatives that promoted them as the sole locale for Jewish residence. This royal policy was motivated by a number of factors including the desire to provide a protected settlement for the Jews, and to maintain the physical boundaries between various religious groups. However, the primary motive behind royal control over the areas of Jewish settlement was fiscal. While Jews had their own reasons for migrating to the cities of the frontier, the various Christian monarchs saw them as agents of administrative and economic developments. Furthermore, Jews were to act as an extension of royal authority and financial interests through the possession of crown property and the development of the royal marketplace. Greater enforcement of the limits of the Jewish quarter was therefore a result of the kings' efforts to exert greater control over what they saw as *their* Jews. The crown's proprietary interest in controlling the boundaries of Jewish settlement is reflected in a decree promulgated at the Castilian *Cortes* held at Valladolid in 1322:

> Furthermore, that all the Jews who dwell in all the parts of the kingdom should come to dwell in the royal towns which belong to the king. And that no prince nor baron nor noble nor knight nor baroness nor lady nor any other have a Jew or Jewess nor Jewish quarter, but that all Jews be of the king and dwell in his towns. And if a Jew does not want to come, the magistrates and judges or justices of the towns are to have them do it by force.[6]

An example of the fiscal motivation behind the limitation of Jewish residential space can also be seen in the development of the *judería* of Játiva. Established in the wake of city's conquest, Játiva's Jewish quarter was originally located next to the town's castle and market place. The Jewish settlement here continued to grow during the latter half of the thirteenth century, and

---

[5] ACA, reg. 81, fol. 196v. For Évora, see Pimenta Ferro Tavares, *Os Judeus*, 2nd ed., 74, For Murcia, see Torres Fontes, ed., *Repartimiento de Murcia*, 233. See also the establishment of new *juderías* in the cities of Valencia, Murcia, Seville, and Jérez, above, chap. 1. For Úbeda, see José Rodríguez Molina, *El reino de Jaén en la baja edad media: aspectos demográficos y económicos* (Granada, 1978), 283–285.

[6] *Cortes de Valladolid* of 1322, in *Cortes de los antiguos reinos*, ed. Colmeiro, 1:356; and Baer, *Juden*, vol. 2, no. 147.

by the 1290s the Jews of Játiva were found living throughout the town. The crown soon realized that Jewish expansion resulted in the loss of royal tenants, as the Jews began to forsake the protection and privileges of the *judería* in exchange for residences beyond the royal district where, perhaps, the taxes were less burdensome. In response to this loss of potential revenue, Alfonso III sent word that all members of Játiva's Jewish community were to be forced to live in their appointed neighborhood.[7]

Nevertheless, the erosion of the physical boundaries between the two communities continued at Játiva, and in 1314 Jaime II issued a series of letters in which he sought to reinforce the borders of the city's Jewish quarter. The king first called for an investigation into rumors that the Jews of Játiva were selling houses in the *judería* to Christians. He followed up with a letter the next month, in which he ordered the Jews to reside in the area known as the *algofna*, citing their rights to certain tax exemptions when they settled on crown lands. At the same time they are reminded that they are not permitted to sell or alienate property in this quarter to either Christians or Muslims. Evidently the problem was not limited to Játiva, as the king soon sent out a third letter in which he asked the bailiff general of the kingdom of Valencia to see to it that Jews throughout this frontier region stopped their practice of alienating crown land in their *juderías* to Christians. Those Jews who did not comply were to be punished by means of a ban handed down from their communal synagogue, an arrangement that shows the support such legislation received from the governing councils of local Jewish communities.[8]

The establishment of separate neighborhoods for Jews, Muslims, and Christians was intended to preserve communal boundaries and limit social interaction between the members of the three faiths. However, the goal of social separation was not one shared by many of the settlers who migrated to the frontier during the late thirteenth and early fourteenth century. Despite the advantages of living in their own quarter, such as the protection of a wall and proximity to the seat of central authority (the royal *alcázar,* or the city's cathedral), Jewish settlers still chose to reside and work in other neighborhoods. The primary motives for this diffusion appears to have been demographic and economic. The Jewish populations in these frontier communities soon outgrew their allotted districts and sought to take advantage of residential and commercial opportunities in other sections of their cities. In approximately one generation after the conquest of Seville, the restored community had spilled out of the appointed Jewish quarter, and Jews began to establish their homes and businesses in other neighborhoods throughout the city.

[7] ACA, reg. 21, fol. 45v; reg. 84, fol. 27.
[8] ACA, Cartas Reales, Jaime II, caja 39, no. 4919; reg. 211, fol. 193v; reg. 211, fol. 275.

Jews could also be found living outside their appointed districts in the towns of southern Portugal. The Jews of Lisbon and Évora sought to establish residences beyond the Jewish quarter, and in Santarem, Salamon Arrame, and his wife Maior, gave land to the great Cistercian monastery of Alcobaça in exchange for houses near, yet outside of, the *judiaria*. Individuals from both communities were also interested in taking advantage of a dynamic real estate market and other economic opportunities beyond the confines of their designated neighborhoods and thus allowed the boundary between the *judería* and the rest of town to remain extremely permeable. Land and houses in these Jewish neighborhoods were purchased by Christians from the very beginning of Christian rule, while Jews began to buy commercial and residential property throughout the rest of the city. In Valencia, Christian settlers rented shops in that city's *judería*, and a responsum of Solomon ibn Adret mentions a Jew who sold his house in Valencia's Jewish quarter to a Gentile. Finally, despite the ecclesiastical ideal of maintaining separate residential and business districts for Jews, individual churches and bishops would join with other Christian nobles and merchants in buying and operating stores in the Jewish quarter.[9]

Taken together this evidence depicts a world in which the fiscal and demographic realities of these rapidly developing frontier towns undermined the ideal of separate and controlled communal settlements. The crown, most likely at the behest of local Jewish or Christian municipal officials, would occasionally attempt to enforce the communal segregation, but to little avail. Alfonso X allowed for Christians to work for Jews, providing they did not dwell with them in the same house, and at Murcia, he proclaimed that:

No Jew in the city of Murcia shall dwell among Christians, since they have their own *judería* separated by the Orihuela gate, in the place that the *partidores* gave to them by our order.[10]

[9] González, *Repartimiento de Sevilla*, 1:311, 363; Ballesteros, *Sevilla*, 76, 185. For Évora, see Maria Angela V. da Rocha Beirante, *Évora Na Idade Média* (Lisbon, 1995), 734. For Lisbon, see ANTT, *Chanc. de D. Dinis*, Liv. I, fol. 269. For Santarem, see ANTT, *Alcobaça*, 2a incorp., m. 12, no. 273. For Valencia, see ACA, reg. 230, fol. 77; and Adret, 4:298. For ecclesiastical property within the *judería*, see the case of Cuenca, where the *cabildo* possessed stores in the *alcázar de los judíos*. Jorge Díaz Ibáñez, "Monarquía y conflictos Iglesia-concejos en la Castilla," *En la España Medieval* 17 (1994): 137–138.

[10] José Ramón Ayaso Martínez, "Tolerancia e intolerancia en los reinos cristianos de la España medieval: el caso de los judíos," *Miscelánea de estudios árabes y hebraicos* 43 (1994): 64. For the law prohibiting Christian laborers and servants to live with their Jewish masters, see *Siete Partidas*, 7.24.8.

Royal efforts to limit Jewish settlement to the town's *judería* were evidently unsuccessful, as illustrated by an open letter from 1305 by which Fernando IV sought to attract Muslim settlers back to the city of Murcia. In it, the king promised the Muslims a number of privileges and rights including that no Christian or Jew would be able to buy houses in the *morería* "as they have done until now."[11] Thus, the proliferation of Jewish shops and residences throughout the Christian and Muslim neighborhoods of a particular town paralleled royal attempts to restrict them to the confines of the Jewish quarter. Both phenomena were characteristics of Jewish settlement on the frontier during the latter half of the thirteenth century.

What is perhaps even more striking than the willingness of Jews and Gentiles to ignore limits set on commercial and residential expansion is the role played by the crown itself in this process. The same authority that had established the legal and physical boundaries meant to separate the communities was very often among those that ignored them. Within a few years of the conquest of Játiva, James I was auctioning off houses in the Jewish quarter to the highest bidder who, in some cases, was Christian. Shortly after the city of Murcia fell under Aragonese control in 1296, James II seized land from the rebellious Jew Moses Aventurel and donated it to a group of Christians. The confiscated property was located in Murcia's *judería*.[12]

Laws regarding the maintenance of communal boundaries were also frustrated by the economic and demographic structures of many frontier locales. When Játivan Muslims could not come up with the money they owed their Jewish creditors, they offered the latter houses in the *raval*, an area set aside for Muslim residence. Later, when the many local Muslims began to abandon their designated *morería*, the crown ordered the city's officials to settle the area with Jews. The situation was much the same on the Castilian frontier. Here, the case of Pedro Fernández, a settler in Seville "who was a Jew and who became a Christian," underscores the difficulty the crown had in maintaining the boundaries between these communities and the social space they shared. In 1253, the crown granted Fernández the rights to a store in the royal marketplace, or *alcacería*, a space that was traditionally rented out to Jews.[13] The grant appears to be a confirmation of rights to a store

[11] Ayaso Martinez, "Tolerancia e intolerancia," 62.
[12] The crown's contradictory policies were not limited to the Jews. See, for example, the Donald Kagay, "Royal Power," 163, regarding the complications arising from the king's decision to grant rights to the same section of town to both the local nobility and the Church.
[13] Régné, no. 39; and ACA, *Cartas Reales*, Jaime II, carp. 148, no. 970. For Játiva, see ACA reg. 260, fol. 107. For Seville, see ACS, caja 114, no. 21; and M. González Jiménez, ed., *Diplomatario andaluz*, no. 98. Mention of his ownership of the store is also found in ACS, caja 47, no. 8.

which Pedro had formerly rented as a Jew and which he would continue to operate as a Christian.

The complexities involved in segregating settlers by community were also a source of frustration for Jewish communal leaders who shared the crown's fiscal motivation to maintain a separate and manageable settlement for Jews. Charged with maintaining order in the *judería*—as well as with the collection and payment of taxes to the crown—officials of the *aljama* were most likely the first to complain to the king that Jews were settling outside the bounds of the Jewish quarter and selling land within it to Christians. Contrary to some prevailing conceptions of Jewish attitudes toward interfaith relations in medieval Spain, it should be noted that the sanctity of the Jewish community was not the principal concern of the *kahal*.[14] To be sure, the writings of Jewish moralists reflect the expected anxiety over the possible social—and sexual—interaction that might result from an increased Christian presence in an otherwise Jewish space. However, as we have already seen, the role played by rabbinic authorities and great spiritual leaders in the governance of the *aljama* was marginal at best, especially in the young communities of the frontier. Those charged with the day-to-day administration of Jewish affairs were thus far more concerned with practical matters than with piety.

Much like the crown itself, whose policies reflected an interest in efficient civil administration rather than the decisions of the Lateran Council, Jewish officials were primarily worried about the loss of potential revenues resulting from the alienation of property to those outside the Jewish community. In the letters concerning Jewish settlement written by these Jewish *adelantados* to the royal authorities, there is no pretense of distress over the preservation of religious boundaries. Rather, they reflect the *kahal's* interest in maintaining its jurisdiction and effective control over its tax base, even if members of the community extended their land holdings beyond the designated Jewish quarter. One such example can be seen in *aljama* of Tortosa, where Jewish leaders urged the town's bailiff to decree that all Jews who possessed property anywhere in the city or its *termino* pay taxes on these properties to the *aljama*. The *reconquista* and the subsequent period of coloniza-

---

[14] Recent studies by David Nirenberg, which so deftly distinguish communal ideals from individual behavior among Christians, tend to equate Jewish attitudes with broad Talmudic or Maimonidean proscriptions. See, for example, *Communities of Violence*, 134–135; and idem, "Conversion, Sex, and Segregation: Jews and Christians in Medieval Spain," *American Historical Review* 107 (2002): 1071–1072. See also Fernando Díaz Esteban, "Aspectos de la convivencia jurídica desde el punto de vista judío en la España medieval," *Actas del II congreso internacional, Encuentro de las tres culturas* (Toledo, 1985), 108. See, instead, Yom Tov Assis, "Sexual Behaviour in Mediaeval Hispano-Jewish Society," in *Jewish History*, ed. Rapoport-Albert and Zipperstein, 25–59.

tion also created a large military presence in the new territories, and Jewish officials sought exemption from the obligation to host these Christians in their homes. Among the general privileges granted to the Jews of Valencia was the right for Jews to bar Christians from lodging with them. The same privilege was extended to the Jews of Mallorca in 1281 and renewed again in 1290. The earlier document added the caveat that while Jews were not required to play host to Christians, an exception was made for members of the royal family: "We concede to the Jews of Mallorca, present and future, that they are not required to receive or be compelled to receive . . . any Christians . . . unless they are of our family." Such grants would indicate that, prior to this point, there had indeed been instances of Christians lodging with Jews. Similarly, Jewish officials also obtained royal support to prevent members of their community from staying with Christians. In the kingdom of Valencia, laws forbade Jewish travelers from lodging at a Christian house in any town where there was a *judería*. This prohibition reflects the willingness of individual Jews to cross the social boundaries which Christian and Jewish authorities sought to enforce. Moreover, it recognizes that not every town had a Jewish quarter, and that Jewish travelers were often left with no choice but to spend the night with non-Jews.[15]

The development of the Jewish quarter of the city of Mallorca may serve as an illustration of the interplay between the crown's increased efforts to exert control over the Jewish community by controlling the physical bounds of its settlements, and the corresponding attempts of individual Jews to elude such restrictions. An urban Jewish settlement or "proto" Jewish quarter had already existed in the city of Mallorca prior to the Christian rule. Following the conquest of the Balearics, Jaime I gave his royal imprimatur to the Jews' traditional settlement in the city of Mallorca as he confirmed their rights to the Almudaina and its surrounding area. However, this privilege would not long suffice as the rapid demographic and economic growth of the port city soon led its Jews to seek houses and businesses beyond their authorized district. Indeed, royal support helped usher in a wave of (mostly Catalan) Jewish merchants and artisans to the city of Mallorca in the late thirteenth century. Between 1263 and 1282, nearly a quarter of the total royal exemptions in the city were made to Jews. The crown's initial response to

---

[15] ACA, *Cartas Reales*, Jaime II, *caja* 41, no. 5052. For Valencian privileges, see ACA, reg. 19, fol. 56v–57. For Mallorca, see Fita and Llabrés, "Privilegios," no. 12; Antonio Pons, *Los Judíos del Reino de Mallorca durante los siglos XIII y XIV* (Madrid, 1960), vol. 2, no. 10. Both are taken from the *Códice Pueyo*, fol. 10. For the letter of December 21, 1290, see ACA, reg. 83, fol. 99v–100; and Régné, *pièces justificatives*, no. 22. For Jews lodging with Christians, see *Aureum Opus de Xativa*, ed. María de los Desamparados Cabanes Pecourt, and María Luisa Cabanes Català (Saragossa, 1996), no. 142.

Part II. The Jewish Community and the Frontier

this influx of Jews was merely to allow them additional room to expand their settlement, and in 1269 they were granted the right to buy houses, vineyards, and other properties "within the city and without, wherever you wish." They were allowed the right to reside in these properties, whether they owned or rented them. These rights were later confirmed in 1273 when Jews were additionally permitted to buy new houses from Christians, so long as the Jews did not cohabit with them. Interestingly, a royal edict issued the same year also put an end to another point of interfaith contact on the island, the prison. The statute claimed that while Jewish and Christian criminals in Mallorca had previously been housed together in the same prison, they would henceforth be detained in two separate buildings.[16]

In the closing decades of the century, however, royal support for the open and relatively unrestricted settlement of Jews at Mallorca slowly gave way to the establishment of a new and officially mandated Jewish quarter. In January of 1286, only months after renewing their accumulated rights and privileges, Alfonso III ordered that all Jews of the city of Mallorca were henceforth to reside in the same quarter. The decree also ordered that Christians and Jews were henceforth required to use separate butchers. In the half-century preceding this decree, Jewish butchers in Mallorca had shared the same stalls with Christians, a right which had been formally renewed as late as 1273.[17]

The officials of both the *aljama* and the municipality would be given five years to complete this relocation. A document from 1290 notes that the new site was to be located between the convents of the Minor Friars and that of the sisters of Santa Clara, but that the Jews had yet to move there. The new Jewish quarter, or *Call*, was finally established later that year in the southeast of the city, comprising the area formerly belonging to the crusading orders of the Temple and Calatrava. The royal order establishing the new quarter repeated the decree "that all the Jews of Mallorca dwell together in the same part of the city where they are to make their own *Call*." The charter also made provisions for a synagogue, a bakery, and separate Jewish butcher shops, in an attempt to unite the dispersed members of the *aljama* in one neighborhood.[18]

[16] Villanueva, *Viatge Literario*, 22: 301; Soto i Company, "*Repartiment I 'repartiments,*'" 16; Fita and Llabrés, "Privilegios," no. 8; A. Lionel Isaacs, *The Jews of Mallorca* (London, 1936), no. 18. For the prison, see Villanueva, 312.

[17] ACA, reg. 63, fol. 33. The decree was repeated later that year, ACA, reg. 66, fol. 176. For butchers, see Fita and Llabrés, "Privilegios," 26–27, no. 10.

[18] ACA, reg. 63, fol. 33; and for the confirmation of privileges in 1285, see ACA, reg. 63, fol. 23rv. For the document of 1290, see ACA, reg. 81, fol. 216. A delegation of Mallorcan Jews which appeared before the king in Barcelona later that year were told that he was unable to give the matter or their relocation his attention as he had to attend to more

The case of the Jewish community of Mallorca highlights the degree to which the goals of individual Jewish settlers often ran counter to those of the crown and, to a certain extent, the Jewish communal leaders who were responsible for collecting royal taxes. The portrait of Jewish settlement in the decades following the islands' conquest depicts a burgeoning population whose members eagerly bought properties throughout the city and beyond—with no apparent concern for the maintenance of social boundaries. As in the case of the Jewish quarter at Leiria, the evolution of the Mallorcan *Call* into the sole locale for Jewish residence was the result of external forces, rather than the preferences of Jewish settlers. Both examples represent a transition from informal settlements, whose boundaries were self-imposed and marked by a degree of fluidity, to urban Jewish quarters whose limits were fixed and controlled by the crown.

JEWISH CLOTHING

Other than the establishment of separate living quarters, the most common way of separating Jews from Christians was through the supervision of their clothing. Regulation of Jewish dress had a long and complex heritage in medieval Iberia, the roots of which can be traced back to Muslim and Roman traditions. Nonetheless, laws regarding Jewish clothing or special badges are absent from the royal charters of the various Iberian kingdoms. One of the few exceptions is the charter of the northern Aragonese town of Jaca, which stated only that Jews and Saracens were not wear the same clothing as Christians.[19] It was not until the meeting of the Fourth Lateran Council in 1215 that we see a marked shift toward the enforcement of distinguishing dress for non-Christians. In Canon 68, the Council set out the new law regarding Jewish and Muslim clothing, as well as the reasons behind it, stating:

Whereas in certain provinces of the Church the difference in their clothes sets the Jews and the Saracens apart from the Christians, in certain other lands there has arisen such confusion that no differences are noticeable. Thus it sometimes happens that by mistake Christians have intercourse with Jewish or Saracen women, and Jews or Saracens with

pressing concerns. ACA, reg. 81, fol. 219. The quote is from ACA, reg. 83, fols. 99v–100; and Régné, *pièces justificatives*, no. 22.

[19] José María Ramos y Loscertales, ed., *Fuero de Jaca* (Barcelona, 1927), art. 23.

Christian women. Therefore, lest these people, under the cover of an error, find an excuse for the grave sin of such intercourse, we decree that these people (Jews and Saracens) of either sex, and in all Christian lands, and at all times, shall easily be distinguishable from the rest of the population by the quality of their clothes.[20]

The papacy's renewed interest in the erection and maintenance of social boundaries would continue throughout the thirteenth century, gaining momentum and greater focus with regard to the distinguishing marks to be worn by Jews. A letter written by Pope Gregory IX to Thibaut I of Navarre in 1234 stands as one of the few explicit descriptions of what became known as the "Jewish badge."

Since we desire that the Jews be recognizable and distinguished from the Christians, we order you to impose upon each and every Jew of both sexes a sign, viz. one round patch of yellow cloth or linen, to be worn on the uppermost garment, stitched over the heart and another behind it, in order that they might be recognized.[21]

In both the frontier territories and the older settlements of Christian Iberia, these papal decrees were enforced with varying degrees of zeal and effectiveness. A letter written by King Pedro III of Aragon reminds his officials in the kingdom of Valencia that he has ordered the Jews of that territory to wear a rounded cloak to distinguish them from non-Jews, in the style of the Catalan communities. While various restrictions on Jewish dress existed in Valencia prior to the reign of Pedro III (see below, at Játiva), this is the first mention of the requirement of this particular garment in the new territory. In his letter, dated 11 January 1284, the king ordered that "Jews of the city and kingdom of Valencia wear rounded capes after the custom of those of Barcelona" and that "all Jews, including the poor" had until Easter to obtain their capes. However, the letter made a provision that for those locales of the kingdom of Valencia "in which there are not 10 Jewish houses, for those Jews the wearing of round capes will not be required."[22]

This letter indicates that the Jews of Valencia lived for nearly half a century under Christian rule, and even longer after the promulgation of Canon 68, before the implementation of this distinguishing garment. Even then, it appears that extra time had been given to allow poorer Jews to find a way of

[20] This translation is taken from Carpenter, *Alfonso X and the Jews*, 99–100.
[21] Grayzel, *Church and the Jews*, vol. 1, no. 78; and José Ramón Castro, *Catálogo del Archivo General de Navarra*, (Tudela, 1952), vol. 1, no. 184.
[22] ACA, reg. 46, fol. 152v.

obtaining these capes. The document also suggests that the crown was primarily concerned with larger communities in which Jews might be taken for Christians unless otherwise identified. In towns and villages that had fewer than ten Jewish households, the assumption would have been that everyone knew who the Jews were.

In addition to religious concerns that Jews might be mistaken for Christians was the particular apprehension that certain Jews could pass as members of the Christian nobility. Here, the central issue was maintaining distinctions between social ranks, rather than between confessional groups. Sumptuary laws that took aim at the opulence of the Jewish elite were another hallmark of clothing regulations during this period, as was the regularity with which these laws were flouted. In Játiva, Acxmel Avenczunana bought for his wife a royal privilege that exempted her from the city's sumptuary laws. The grant, issued by Jaime I in 1268, gave her special permission to wear clothes of whatever fabric she chose, except *presseto* (scarlet) and *nibeo* (perhaps "snow white"). Such exemptions underscore the ease by which wealthy Jews with connections at court were able to evade these laws. Royal privileges of this sort rankled the Christian nobility and wealthy townsmen and were also met with disapproval from other Jews. In 1283, the Infante Don Alfonso responded to a complaint by another Játivan Jew, Samuel, whose exemption from the kingdom's sumptuary laws had been challenged by the officers of the local Jewish community. Samuel had argued that the exemption, issued by the king, extended to his entire family and allowed for them to wear whatever garments they wanted without restrictions. The Jewish *aljama* of Játiva, however, had sought to include his relatives David Allevi, Abraham Avenavies, and Jucef Avengalell under a communal ordinance meant to reinforce Jewish observance of the kingdom's clothing statutes. In his letter to the *aljama*, Alfonso ruled in support of Samuel, a courtier who is alternately mentioned in the documentation as a faithful doctor and chief *alfaqui* attached to the royal household.[23]

Aside from the frustration stemming from the Infante's partial nullification of their decree, the *kahal* of Játiva would have had other reasons for concern in this and similar cases. Jewish courtiers such as Samuel who served the royal household did not have to live in Játiva, but his relatives did. As a result, the leaders of the Játivan community were left to confront the potential problems with local Christians who resented the fact that well-connected Jews were allowed to dress as they pleased, blurring the lines of social rank and religious community.

---

[23] ACA, reg. 15, fol. 95v. My translation of "*nibeo*" is after the suggestion offered by Regné, no. 376. See also ACA, reg. 60, fol. 25.

The issue of Jews being exempt from wearing distinguishing clothes was not easily settled, and the following year Samuel once again needed to solicit the crown to confirm his special status. The second letter regarding this case was written by Pedro III himself and was directed not at the Jews of Játiva but the Christian *justicia* and officials of the city of Valencia. Its tone is more didactic than that of Alfonso's letter, as the king offers two reasons to justify Samuel's exemption from wearing the standard Jewish cloak. First, Pedro explains that in his dual function as royal physician and scribe, Samuel is required to travel with the king or other members of the royal household. Moreover, the law regarding the need for Valencian Jews to wear a distinctive rounded cloak was derived from a custom of the city of Barcelona. Citing this fact, the king argues that since it is accepted practice that the Jewish courtiers of Barcelona do not wear this garment when attending the royal family, so too should their coreligionists in Valencia be exempt for the same reasons. In 1290, Alfonso III of Aragon reminded Valencian officials of this policy in his announcement of the exemption of two Valencian court Jews, Abrafim Abenmies and Abrafim El Jenet. In another case, a Jewish physician, Omar Abnacahuel, was exempted from having to wear the "Jewish cloak" in recompense for services rendered to James II.[24]

Thus, wealth played a significant role in muting legislation aimed at the entire Jewish community. Those Jews who had the means could generally obtain exemptions for themselves and members of their extended families; this was yet another reminder that the medieval Hispano-Jewish community was far from monolithic. Clothing regulations were among the very few aspects of Iberian legislation that threatened to restrict Jewish movement within the broader society, and Jewish courtiers and wealthy merchants such as those mentioned above had little trouble in circumventing them. In doing so, the Jewish elite sought to imitate the style, and subsequently the social status, of the Christian nobility and urban patriciate. Still others avoided distinguishing themselves from Christians for more practical reasons, as reflected in an ethical treatise of the period that openly admonished those Jews attempting to hide their religious identity from their Gentile neighbors.

When you meet Gentiles, do not disguise yourself so as to give the impression that you are not Jewish. Furthermore, when they ask you as to

---

[24] ACA, reg. 46, fol. 178v; reg. 81, fol. 10; and reg. 200, fol. 210. See, also, Régné, nos. 2869, 3005, 3075, and 3083. Although this letter, written in 1303, also cites Omar's advanced age as a reason for this privilege, he was still active and still receiving royal favors as late as 1314.

your faith, say openly "I am a Jew," rather than attempting to avoid the payment of the relevant tax.[25]

The passage makes no mention that those Jews who practiced such dissembling did so out of fear of Gentile reprisals, though this issue did, at times, come in to play. Rather, the motivation seems, once again, to have been fiscal, and the rebuke itself a reminder of just how little the average Jew was concerned about the boundaries of religious or ethnic identity.

In theory, all Jews in the Crown of Aragon were expected to wear distinguishing badges by 1300. The badge was to be red. However, if the outer garment used was red, the badge was to be white. Yet royal interest in enforcing such legislation remained tepid. The crown preferred the postponement of these regulations to their implementation by gangs of self-proclaimed enforcers. While the explicit prohibition against vigilante mobs imposing the law on their own underscores Jewish vulnerability to certain elements within Christian society, it was precisely this threat of violence that led to the continued suspension of these clothing statutes by those Jewish individuals and communities who were able to procure special exemptions from the king or local Christian authorities. A responsum from Solomon ibn Adret records that Jews were often required to contribute money to their local *kahal* for the general protection of the community, which included bribes for Christian officials in order to avoid attacks on the eve of "their festival," and to get out of wearing the "Jewish sign" on their clothes.[26]

In Castile, the crown had traditionally been disinterested in forcing its Jews to wear distinguishing clothes, especially in the period prior to the Fourth Lateran Council. Initially, the Council's pronouncements regarding Jewish dress had little impact here, and the crown's lack of enthusiasm for the enforcement of such regulations not only persisted, it was also echoed by some of the kingdom's leading bishops.

In 1218, Pope Honorius III wrote to the archbishop of Toledo with the complaint:

After careful deliberation it was established by the General Council that by their clothes Jews are to be distinguishable from Christians, and that they are to be compelled to give satisfaction to the churches for the

---

[25] Jonah ben Abraham Gerondi, *Sefer ha-Yir'ah*, 5b. See also A. T. Shrock, *Rabbi Jonah ben Abraham of Gerona: His Life and Ethical Works* (London, 1948), 163–164.

[26] ACA, reg. 116, fols. 163rv; and Adret, 5:183. The Christian festival referred to here is most likely *semana santa*, during which Christian mobs routinely attacked Jews and stoned Jewish homes and shops. See Nirenberg, *Communities of Violence*, 228–230.

Part II. The Jewish Community and the Frontier

tithes and offerings which these churches were wont to receive from the houses and other possessions of the Christians before these had come, under any title, into Jewish hands. We have learned that the Jews who dwell in your province, supported as they are by the favor of certain Christians, do not take care to observe this.[27]

Honorius' letter prompted the archbishop to reestablish a set of regulations for the Jews the following year. This concordat, which was approved by the Jews of Toledo and countersigned by the crown, detailed Jewish fiscal responsibilities to the Church. It did not, however, make any mention of Jewish dress. Instead, the archbishop, together with the support of King Ferdinand III, petitioned the pope to relent on this issue in consideration of the fact that the Jews of Castile had only recently fled the harsh, discriminatory measures of the Almohads, and reacted strongly to the idea of being forced to wear distinguishing clothing. The pope agreed to suspend the imposition of the Council's decree, if only for the time being.

To the archbishop of Toledo:
On behalf of our dearest son in Christ, Ferdinand, the illustrious king of Castile, as well as on behalf of yourself, we have been informed that the Jews who reside in the Kingdom of Castile are so seriously wrought up over that which was decided with regard to them in the general Council in the matter of wearing a sign, that some of them choose rather to flee the Moors than to be burdened with such a sign. Others conspire because of this, and make secret arrangements. As a result, the King, whose income in large measure derives from these very Jews, can hardly raise his expenses, and serious misfortune may befall the Kingdom. Wherefore we have been humbly petitioned both on behalf of this King as well as yourself, that our permission be given you to set aside the execution of this edict, since you cannot proceed to its enforcement without great trouble.

The following year, Honorius acceded to a similar request made by Aragon's Jaime I, who also cited the potential economic hardship caused by Jews who fled his realm in defiance of the new clothing regulations. Jaime had argued that the spirit of the Council's statutes had long been observed

[27] This translation is from Grayzel, *Church and the Jews*, vol. 1, no. 36. Royal control of the Spanish and Portuguese Church during this period was extensive. See Peter Linehan, *The Spanish Church and the Papacy*, 215–217, and J. M. Nieto Soria, "Los judíos como conflicto jurisdiccional entre monarqauía e iglesia en la Castilla de fines del siglo XIII: su causistica," in *Actas del II congreso internacional, Encuentro de las tres culturas* (Toledo, 1985), 251.

in Aragon, and that "the difference in the clothes of either sex has from ancient times set apart and distinguished and still distinguishes relations with Christian women or Christians with Jewish women." The problem, the king maintained, was that there were some Christian authorities who had begun to use the recent edict of the Lateran Council as a pretext to force Jews "to wear a new sign not so much in order that such crimes should be avoided, as because they thus have the chance to extort money."[28]

All three of Honorius' letters mention that the enforcement of these regulations had caused grave economic consequences, citing the decision of many Jews to abandon the Christian kingdoms rather than wear the distinctive clothing. Such claims were most likely a convenient excuse given to the papacy, since there does not seem to be any evidence that the great merchant families left Christian Iberia at this time. Those who lobbied the papacy to enforce the clothing regulations resorted to similar exaggerations and fabrications, as can be seen in Pope Gregory IX's response to the complaints of some Andalusian bishops.

> Know that at the instance of our dear sons the clerics of the districts and dioceses of Córdoba and Baeza, we have learned that whenever, as often happens, the Christians of these districts and dioceses have to leave their homes and property and remain away for a long time occupied in fighting and pursuing the Saracens, the Jews as often run about the districts and cities of these provinces and dioceses, bearing no visible sign, and, in order to deceive the Christians even more, claiming that they are themselves Christians. They thus kidnap Christian boys, and steal whatever else they can, and sell them to the Saracens.[29]

Here, the fears of potential social and sexual mixing which characterize the bulk of papal legislation regarding minority dress are replaced by the claim that Jews are kidnapping Christian boys. This is one of the earliest such examples of this calumny to be found in the Iberian kingdoms and is directly tied to the chaos and uncertainty of life on the frontier during the initial stages of conquest. Gregory's letter dates from 1239, which would indicate that the complaints from Córdoba and Baeza were made in the immediate wake of their conquest in 1236.

In Portugal, as in the other peninsular states, there existed a great deal of

---

[28] For the archbishop's agreement with the Jews of Toledo see Grayzel, *Church and the Jews*, 1:147 n. 3. For Honorius' letter to Toledo, see ibid., no. 38, and for Aragon, ibid., no. 44. Honorius, who appears to have been greatly influenced by the observations of a certain friar Gundeslav, rescinded his suspension of the Council's regulations in 1221. Ibid., no. 51.

[29] BCC, ms. 125, fol. 3r; and S. Grayzel, *Church and the Jews*, no. 99.

tension between the papacy and the crown over the imposition of distinguishing dress for Jews. In the winter of 1265–66, a group of Portuguese bishops headed by the archbishop of Braga complained to Pope Clement IV that Afonso III had taken to giving an inordinate number of rights to the Jews. Among these were the fact that Jews and Muslims belonging to the crown were not made to wear distinguishing clothing. The use of a particular Jewish badge was not enforced in Portugal until the middle of the fourteenth century, and even then, there were exceptions made for those Jews in the employ of the state.[30]

It was only with the reign of Alfonso X of Castile that we are able to see a gradual shift toward the enforcement of the decrees of the Fourth Lateran Council. Laws restricting Jewish dress are absent in the *Fuero Real*, but the influence of Canon 68 can be seen in the *Siete Partidas:*

Many transgressions and outrages take place between Christian men and Jewish woman and Christian women and Jewish men because they live and dwell together in the towns and go about dressed one like the other. And to put an end to the errors and the evils which might come about for this reason, we order that all those Jews and Jewesses who live in our realm shall wear a certain sign upon their heads, and that they do this so that people can easily tell who is a Jew or a Jewess.[31]

However, Alfonso's support for the Council's clothing regulations was less a result of the Church's desire to separate members of the different faiths than it was the continuation of long-standing royal concerns over excessive demonstrations of wealth. Any restrictions regarding Jewish clothing imposed by the Castilian crown must therefore be seen as part of a greater attempt at the enforcement of modest dress and, through it, the preservation of social order. Due in large part to economic difficulties suffered during his reign, Alfonso enacted laws restricting luxurious dress and other forms of ostentation by Christians and Jews alike.[32] It was as part of this attempt to control the use of luxury items that the king instituted the first

[30] Grayzel, *Church and the Jews*, vol. 2, no. 23. For Portugal, see Amador de los Ríos, *Historia Social*, 2:196–198.
[31] *Las Siete Partidas*, 7.24.11. For an example of this distinguishing headgear, see *Las Cantigas de Santa María*, no. 34.
[32] Baer, *Juden*, vol. 2, nos. 65, 72, a 78 for the *Cortes* of Seville, Valladolid, and Jérez. See also Baer's comments in "Todros ben Yehudahh ha-Levi and His Times," *Zion* 2 (1936): 24 [Hebrew]; and María Martínez, "Idumentaria y sociedad medeivales (ss. XIIXV)," *En la España Medieval* 26 (2003): 35–59.

broad laws regarding Jewish clothing at the *Cortes* of Valladolid in 1258. The prohibitions for Jewish clothing included expensive fabrics and furs, as well as the use of certain colors, such as crimson. Jews were also forbidden to use luxury items that might afford them undue stature, such as saddles with gold or silver fringes. These laws were reiterated in 1268 at the *Cortes* held at the frontier town of Jérez:

No Jew may wear white fur, nor sandals or shoes low-cut in any way, nor a saddle that is gilt or silvered, nor a bridle that is gilt or silvered, nor spurs that are gilt or silvered, nor dark leggings, nor any reddish hued cloth if it not be dark brown or any shade thereof I should order. Jewish women may wear colored cloths with white furs having a border of otter, but may not wear scarlet or orange or martin fur, or ermine fur, nor golden cords, nor gold work, nor ribbons, nor golden veils, nor wooden clogs, nor golden shoes nor sleeve linings with gold or silk.[33]

The fact that Alfonso was also imposing similar legislation on Christians and that he reserved the right to grant exemptions to anyone he chose indicates that these were not anti-Jewish measures *per se*. Indeed, Alfonso entrusted one of his Jewish administrators, Çag de la Maleha, with the task of enforcing this law, and empowered him to grant exemptions as he saw fit. The enactment of these sumptuary laws was part of a broader policy to limit the growing power of the great magnates of Castile and to establish closer ties with the towns, and was accompanied by royal tax exemptions for the urban non-noble knights. Such laws, while noteworthy in that they reflect the beginning of a desire to separate groups, are not evidence of the success of such a program. Rather, thirteenth-century clothing regulations were merely the opening salvos in what would prove to be a long and drawn-out battle to enforce social difference throughout Iberia, a struggle that would last well into the early modern period. In the end, most monarchs of the period either ignored the papacy's campaign regarding the Jewish badge or undermined its strength by enforcing the laws for the masses and granting exemptions to the wealthy.[34]

[33] Claudio Sánchez Albornoz, *Spain: A Historical Enigma* (Madrid, 1975) 2:817–818. This passage is taken from the English version, translated by Colette Joly Dees and David Sven Reher.

[34] For royal policy in Castile, see Teófilo Ruiz, "Festivités, colours et symbols du pouvoir en Castille au XVe siècle," *Annales E.S.C.* 3 (1991): 521–546.

As can be seen in the legislation regarding Jewish dress, one of the greatest fears of both Christians and Jews regarding their social interaction was the potential for sexual relations between members of the different faiths. Intercourse between Jews and Christians had been prohibited since Antiquity, and laws forbidding the practice can be found throughout the royal charters of medieval Iberia. For cases in which Jewish men were convicted of having intercourse with Christian women the *fueros* ordered that both were to be put to death—often by being burned alive.[35] Yet the fervor with which theses charters sought to punish sexual misconduct was not limited to the preservation of boundaries between religious communities. In the code of Cuenca, a death sentence was also assigned to both parties in cases in which a servant was caught with the wife of his lord. The severity of such statutes was thus part of a general concern over the maintenance of a complex social hierarchy and not aimed at signaling Jewish alterity. Indeed, the sections of municipal *fueros* regarding sexual intercourse with Jews are generally free of calumny or prejudice. While seeking to maintain sexual boundaries between the two communities, they are careful not to make Jews easy targets for false accusations. This careful attitude can be seen in the charter given to the Portuguese outpost of Castello-Bom sometime in the late twelfth or early thirteenth century. It states that three witnesses are needed for such an accusation to be believed, one of which must be a Jew.

> Magistrates who apprehend a Jew with a Christian woman are to settle the case with two Christians and one Jew [as witnesses] or two Jews and one Christian.[36]

This cautious approach toward sexual transgressions is typical of the protective attitude toward the Jews found in nearly all of the municipal charters

[35] Prohibition of mixed marriages can be found in both Roman imperial and early ecclesiastical legislation. See the Theodosian Code (3.7.2, 16.8.6); the Justinian Code (1.14.16, 1.9.6); the canons of the Council of Elvira (canons 16, 78); Chalcedon (canon 14), Clermont (canon 6); Orleans III (canon 13); and Toledo III (canon 14). For the *fueros*, see Cuenca, chap. 11, rub. 48, and chap. 38, rub. 2; Cáceres, rub. 386; Huete, rub. 227; Catello-Bom, *PMH, Leges*, 760; Castello-Melhor, ibid., 910; Sepúlveda, rub. 71; Tudela, rub. 77. For laws concerning Muslim men and Christian women, see *Las Siete Partidas*, 7.24.9.
[36] *PMH, Leges*, 760.

of the twelfth and thirteenth centuries. It is only in Alfonso X's *Siete Partidas* that we can detect an echo of the religious fervor that began to permeate the peninsula in the latter half of the thirteenth century.

Jews who lie with Christian women are guilty of great insolence and presumption. As such, we order that henceforth all Jews guilty of having committed such an act shall die. Since Christians who commit adultery with married women deserve death, how much more so do Jews who lie with Christian women, for these are spiritually espoused to Our Lord Jesus Christ by virtue of the faith and baptism they received in His name. And the Christian woman who commits such a transgression should not remain unpunished. We decree, therefore, that if she be a virgin, married woman, widow, or profligate whore, she shall receive the same punishment as the Christian woman who lies with a Muslim, as we indicated in the last law of the title dealing with Muslims.[37]

Despite the righteous indignation reflected here, the Iberian kings of the thirteenth and early fourteenth centuries showed little interest in putting such legislation into effect. Instead, they preferred to use the threat of such punishment as a means of exacting money from Jews accused of sexual misconduct. Jews found it best to "purchase" such royal pardons regardless of whether or not sufficient proof of their guilt had been demonstrated. In Valencia, Jahuda Aladef was accused of a variety of crimes including procuring Jewish prostitutes for Christians. Though Jaime II was informed of Aladef's innocence, the king nonetheless was able to extract a fine of 2,000 royal sous in exchange for an official pardon. While relations between Jewish men and Christian women remained a capital offense throughout this period, those Jews who could afford to pay a heavy fine were easily able to defend themselves against accusations of such sexual improprieties.[38]

The possibility for inter-religious relations certainly did exist, especially in the newly conquered territories where Christians made up a minority and where their population was mostly male. When officials in the Andalusian town of Niebla realized that their *fuero* did not contain the usual clause pro-

---

[37] *Las Siete Partidas*, 7.24.9; and D. Carpenter, *Alfonso X and the Jews*, 35, from whence this translation is taken. The law concerning Christian women who have intercourse with Muslim men is found in *Siete Partidas*, 7.25.10. Though the punishments differ slightly for virgins, married women, and whores, the penalties generally include stoning and loss of property for the first offense, and death for the second.

[38] ACA, reg. 202, fol. 204. See also the case of the Jew found guilty of seducing a Christian convert at his brother's farmhouse. ACA, reg. 61, fol. 101v; cited in Régné, no. 1045.

hibiting sex between members of different religious groups, they appealed to Fernando IV for an amendment. In response to their concern, Fernando granted them the right to govern by the appropriate clauses from the *fuero* given to Jérez de la Frontera, itself a copy of the *fuero* of Seville. Municipal councils in frontier towns were equally concerned with preventing any social-sexual interaction at public bathhouses; and municipal legislation provided for members of the three different religions to visit the baths on separate days. The usual day set aside for Jews was Friday, and often Sunday as well, an accommodation that clearly took into consideration the Jewish Sabbath.[39] However, the general policy of social and religious segregation at frontier bathhouses was not absolute. In 1280, a letter from Pedro III of Aragon reiterated the right held by local Jews and Muslims to use the baths situated just outside of Tortosa, but did not mention that bathers of different faiths should be assigned separate days. In other instances, municipal charters sought to separate Christian and non-Christian bathers, but were less concerned about separating Jews and Muslims. The *fuero* of Teruel states:

> The bathers are to go to the public baths on Tuesdays and Thursdays and Saturdays, according to the *fuero*. Moreover, women are to go to the baths on Mondays and Wednesdays. Moreover, Jewish and Muslim men are to go on Fridays and not on any other day for any reason.[40]

As this passage indicates, Jewish and Muslim bathers were to be segregated from Christians, but not from each other. It must be noted here that Christian authorities were primarily concerned with the sexual conduct of minority men and that there existed a double standard in Christian society concerning sexual relations with minorities. Whereas Christian men could be expected to take Muslim concubines without risking social repudiation, the mere idea of intercourse between Christian women and Muslim or Jewish men raised an uproar. The accusations of such relationships often caused the accused to flee the city and were thus used as means of blackmailing wealthier members of these minorities. In contrast, Jewish and Muslim women who had intercourse with Christian men, liaisons that were far more prevalent, did not provoke the same unease in Christian society. In the *furs*

---

[39] Baer, *Juden*, vol. 2, no. 109; A. Benavides, *Memorias del rey D. Fernando IV*, no. 155, pp. 210–211. See the *fueros* of Cuenca, chap. 2, rub. 32; Baeza, rub. 132; Úbeda, tit. 9, law 2; and *Las Siete Partidas*, 7.24.8. See also James F. Powers, "Frontier municipal baths and social interactiosn in thirteenth-century Spain," *American Historical Review* 84 (1979): 649–667.

[40] Max Gorosch, ed., *El Fuero de Teruel* (Stockholm, 1950), 225.

of Valencia, the punishment for a Christian man found guilty of sexual relations with a Muslim woman was only flogging, not death. The same code is similarly lenient with regard to the punishment of illicit unions that produced offspring, stating only that "A Christian who shall impregnate a Jewish maidservant must pay the court twelve sous of the current money."[41]

It is thus noteworthy that fear of religious and social "pollution," which has been cited as a reason for Christian concern over the maintenance of communal boundaries during this period, cannot be seen as stemming from sexual contact alone. Rather, it developed out of a more complex understanding of the relationship between the body and religion that touches on medieval concepts of honor, power, sex, and religion. Writing about contemporary Christian attitudes toward Muslim women, John Boswell noted that "Those members of society with no power, i.e., Muslims and women, were penalized for unions which were permissible for members with power, i.e., Christians and men." For Christians, the act of seduction of a Jewish or Muslim woman served to reinforce their domination of these faiths. The Jewish custom of taking Muslim concubines was not one learned from the Christian conquerors, but rather one that had been retained since the days of Muslim rule. Indeed the continued practice of extolling the beauty and sensuality of Muslim women by Jewish poets marks a link with their Andalusi past and may represent a continued preference of Arabic culture to that or their new Latin-Christian overlords. However, that such liaisons now took place within a new historical context is also significant. Old practice or not, the taking of Muslim concubines in the wake of Christian conquest must be viewed as an assertion of power and social standing by which Jews assumed the posture of the dominant culture.[42]

The generally permissive attitude of Christian society toward intercourse between Christian men and women of other faiths is underscored by the absence of any civil penalties for such acts in the *fueros* of this period. In Castile, Sancho IV warned his male subjects not to commit sin "neither with a Jewess nor a Moorish woman, since they are women of another Law and other faith." Such theologically motivated admonitions against relations with non-Christian women were rare, and appear more as a royal effort to

---

[41] Dualde Serrano, ed., *Fori antiqui Valentiae*, 155. The *fuero* of Tudela also made provisions for Jews to pay for children born out of wedlock. Tudela, rub. 139.

[42] John Boswell, *Muslim Communities under the Crown of Aragon in the Fourteenth Century* (New Haven, 1977), 344. On the continued popularity of Arabic style among the Jewish elite in Christian Spain, see Yom Tov Assis, "The Judeo-Arabic Tradition in Christian Spain," in *The Jews of Medieval Islam*, ed. Daniel Frank (New York, 1995), 111–124. For Jewish relations with their servants under Islam in general, see Mordechai A. Friedman, *Jewish Polygyny in the Middle Ages* (Jerusalem, 1986), 291–339 [Hebrew].

Part II. The Jewish Community and the Frontier

appease the Church than a true reflection of social ideals.[43] Indeed, contemporary Christian literature often portrayed both Muslim and Jewish women as highly eroticized objects of desire. Alfonso X's *Cantigas de Santa María* include the popular Castilian folktale of Marisaltos, a beautiful Jewess who is thrown from a cliff by the men of her own community when she is "found in error and caught." The reference to Marisaltos' beauty and the intimation of her availability to Christian men portray her as sexually alluring to Christians. Significantly, it is her own coreligionists who attempt to kill her for her transgressions, while the Virgin Mary intercedes to save her from death and eventually brings about her conversion. Throughout the *Cantigas*, and in medieval Iberian literature in general, Jewish women are depicted in a positive and often eroticized manner, in contrast to Jewish men who are generally portrayed as ugly and vile.[44]

Contemporary Jewish attitudes toward the subject of sexual boundaries reflect a similar dichotomy between theoretical prohibition and popular acceptance. The sexual permissiveness that had characterized the culture of the Jewish elite in Muslim al-Andalus continued under Christian rule and stood in stark contrast to the condemnations of sexual misconduct issued by various rabbinic authorities of the period. In his visit to the Iberian kingdoms in 1236, the French rabbi Moses de Coucy was shocked by the tolerance of sexual relations between Jews and Gentiles. After returning home he noted:

You have thus learned that he who has sexual intercourse with a Gentile woman is considered as if he were married to idolatry . . . I have dwelt at length on this matter in my sermons delivered to the "exile of Jerusalem that is in Spain."[45]

Other Jewish moralists and reformers argued that unrestrained social contact with Christians, and particularly in the context of life at court, in-

---

[43] Agapito Rey, ed., *Castigos e documentos para bien vivir ordenados por el rey don Sancho IV,* in *Indiana University Humanities Series,* 24 (1952), 117.

[44] Walter Mettman, ed., *Cantigas de Santa Maria/Alfonso X, o Sabio,* (Coimbra, 1959–1972). See *Cantiga,* no. 197. Her crime of intercourse with a Christian is made explicit in the contemporary chronicle of Rodrigo de Cerrato. See Louise Mirrer, "The Jew's Body in Medieval Literary Portraits and Miniatures: Examples from the *Cantigas de Santa Maria* and the *Cantar de mio Cid," Shofar* 12 (1994): 27. On protrayal's of Jewish men and women in medieval Spanish literature, see Vikki Hatton and Angus Mackay, "Anti-Semitism in the *Cantigas de Santa María," Bulletin of Hispanic Studies* 60 (1983): 189–199; and Edna Aizenberg, *"Una Judía Muy Fermosa:* The Jewess as Sex Object in Medieval Spanish Literature and Lore," *La Corónica* 12 (1984): 190–191.

[45] R. Moses de Coucy, *Sefer Mitsvot ha-Gadol* (The Major Book of Commandments) (Jerusalem, 1988); see Negative Commandment 112, no. 3, near the end.

vited sin. The great Catalan rabbinic authority Moses ben Nahman wrote to his son in Castile to warn him against the temptations of courtly life there. Similarly, Menahem ben Aaron ibn Zerah's fourteenth-century treatise *Zedah la-Derekh (Provisions for the Journey)* was written as a manual for proper behavior for Jews attending the royal court. In it, he laments,

I have seen those who walk in the court of our master the king, who shield and protect His nation according to their stature and place. However, because of the unsettled time and because of their desire for luxuries and other unnecessary items, they have declined in their observance of the commandments, particularly those who travel, their servants and those who sit before the king. They abandon prayer and blessings; they ignore the laws of permitted and prohibited food, Shabbat and holidays, laws concerning women and laws of wines, even completely abandoning those laws.[46]

Jewish leaders were also apprehensive about increased social interaction with Muslims, particularly the practice of taking Muslim women as concubines. The success of the *reconquista* in the first half of the thirteenth century produced a large population of Muslim slaves, including many female slaves who were owned by both Jews and Christians. For Jewish men, relations with Muslim women were far safer than intercourse with Christian women, which would invite harsh reprisals from the men of the dominant community. Those who took Muslim maidservants as concubines risked only the rebuke of moralists within their own community, a fate which many were prepared to accept. A responsum of Solomon ibn Adret cites Jewish widowers who lived openly with their Muslim concubines.[47]

Rabbinic authorities repeatedly inveighed against Jews having intercourse with slave girls, and with Gentile women in general. As a leading figure of moral reform among the Jews of Toledo, Jonah Gerondi held such interfaith relations as perhaps the greatest of all offenses:

One who cohabits with a maidservant is like those culpable of a capital crime. As our sages said: "One who cohabits with a Gentile woman should be struck by a fervent believer [. . .]." And thus, in a sense, this sin is more significant than all others culpable for a court-imposed death sentence. For those others are only sentenced to death after wit-

[46] Menahem ben Zerah, *Zedah Laderekh* (Warsaw, 1889), 4a.
[47] Adret, 1:26.

nesses, warning, and judgment of the Sanhedrin. But this sinner is to be killed by whoever comes upon him.[48]

Rabbi Jonah's efforts received support from his cousin, Nahmanides, who wrote to him, "Warn them, in your community, against concubinage, for if they learn that there is no prohibition, the door will be opened to lewdness." The practice of taking Muslim concubines was so prevalent among Jews of the period that its condemnation can even be found in as esoteric a work as the mystical treatise *Sefer ha-Zohar* (*The Book of Splendor*), where such relations are portrayed as a violation of Jewish sanctity. Yet, while such prohibitions demonstrate the repugnance that Jewish intellectuals felt toward the sexual relations with Gentiles, they also reflect a certain social reality. Wealthy Jews emulated their Christian counterparts in taking Muslim concubines, as Christian authorities were far less interested in the boundary between Jews and Muslims than that separating either of these from Christians.[49] A poem written by the Toledan Jew, Todros ben Judah Halevi Abulafia, testifies to the popularity of this practice, as well as the Jew's preference for Muslim over Christian women.

Yea, one should love an Arab girl
Even if she is not beautiful or pure.

But stay far away from a Spanish girl
Even if she's as radiant as the sun.

A Spanish girl has got no charm, even
If she puts on silk or wears the finest brocade.

Her clothes are filled with crap and crud,
Her hems are blotted with her uncleanness.

Her Harlotry is not taken to heart; she is
So ignorant of intercourse she knows nothing.

But every Arab girl has charm and beauty
Which capture the heart and alleviate frustration.

She looks as lovely as if dressed in golden embroidery,
Nevertheless she is naked.

[48] Jonah ben Abraham Gerondi, *Sha'arei Teshuva;* Gate 3, no. 131; translation from *The Gates of Repentance*, ed. Yaakov Feldman (Northvale, 1999), 207.
[49] Nahmanides' comments are recorded in Adret, 7: 284. See also Baer, *History*, 1:436; *Zohar*, 2:3b, 7a, 87b; and *Zikhron Yehudah*, no. 91.

And at the right moment she pleases;
She knows all about fornication and is adept at lechery.[50]

While such relations might lead to marriage and conversion of the concubine, the latter was hardly a prerequisite for those who took Muslim women to bed. The popular will to transgress social-sexual boundaries is further underscored by the readiness with which many Jewish men patronized Gentile prostitutes. Judah ben Asher argued that Jewish communities should not expel Jewish prostitutes, for fear that Jewish men would then turn to Christian or Muslim whores, and "mix the holy seed with Gentile women." Another responsum mentions a cantor who had to be removed from his office after entering into a variety of illicit relationships, including some with Gentile prostitutes and a boy. At Játiva, fraternization between Christians, Muslims, and Jews was relatively common, and by 1283 the situation had reached a point that Alfonso III of Aragon was moved to call for an investigation into the sexual relations between the three communities there.[51]

Sexual permissiveness in general, and relations with non-Jews in particular, were often cited by Jewish reformers as the cause for communal instability and anti-Jewish attacks by Christians. This was the case in Toledo during the 1280s when a royal backlash against Jewish courtiers was interpreted as retribution for illicit Jewish behavior. Jewish communal leaders responded with a renewed attempt to ban sexual intercourse with Gentiles. Their reforms came in response to, or in conjunction with, a sermon delivered by one of Castile's leading rabbinic authorities, Todros ben Joseph Abulafia, who admonished,

There is also the matter of the servant women, a stumbling block for the Jews. They wear embroidery, and licentiousness ensues . . . As a result of our sins, many children have been born to female servants of Jewish fathers.

Regarding the Muslim women with whom Jews are accustomed to behave licentiously, this too is forbidden . . . Jews, who are a holy people, must not profane their seed in the womb of a Gentile woman, thereby gathering offspring for idolatry.

---

[50] Todros ben Judah Halevi Abulafia, *Gan Hameshalim ve-hahidoth*, ed. David Yellin (Jerusalem, 1932–36), no. 721. The translation is taken from Ross Brann, *The Compunctious Poet* (Baltimore, 1991), 145.

[51] *Zikhron Yehudah*, nos. 17, 91. For the cantor, see Joel Müller, ed., *Teshuvot Geonei Mizrah u-Ma'arav* (Berlin, 1966 [1888]), no. 171. For Játiva, see ACA, reg. 61, fol. 101v. Tacit recognition of the common practice of interfaith sex can also be seen in legal discussions regarding the offspring between Jewish men and Muslim servants. Adret, 1:1183.

Part II. The Jewish Community and the Frontier

The frequency with which Jewish men ignored the social-sexual boundaries that were meant to separate them and Gentile woman was such that reformers like Abulafia encouraged the entire community toward vigilance of the behavior of their fellow Jews. Abulafia exhorted all Jews to inform on such behavior, warning that passive acceptance would be seen as complicity.

> Whoever knows that another Jew is having sexual relations with a Muslim or Christian woman must inform the judges. . . . Furthermore, if the head of a household in which a Muslim woman is living becomes aware of such evil behavior on behalf of the young men or any others, he is obligated to have the guilty person imprisoned; otherwise the specified punishment [*herem*] will apply to him.[52]

Whether or not such sexual transgressions contributed to the downfall of Jewish courtiers, there can be little doubt that such activity did, in fact, take place. The poetry of Abulafia's nephew, Todros ben Judah, whose own life encompassed both sexual permissiveness and chastity, underscores the relative inefficacy of Jewish prohibitions against sex with non-Jews. In one poem, he writes of his affair with a Muslim woman who was also the concubine of another Jew. Frustrated with their relative powerlessness against Jews who pursued relations with Gentile women, rabbinic authorities called for others to attack transgressors who they caught in such activity.[53]

Like their Christian counterparts, Jewish authorities were even more concerned with the virtue of the women in their community. When a Jewish widow in Castile was discovered to have taken a Christian paramour, the great rabbinic scholar Asher ben Yehiel and the powerful courtier Yehudah ibn Waqar joined forces to punish her severely. Her nose was to be cut off as a means of disfiguring her and dissuading her Christian lover from pursuing the relationship and was a warning to others against such transgressions. Such drastic measures notwithstanding, moralists from all three faiths had great difficulty in preserving the sexual boundaries between the their communities during the thirteenth and early fourteenth centuries. Lamenting

---

[52] Abulafia's sermon can be found in the responsa collection of Judah ben Asher, *Zikheron Yehudah*, 43a–45b. See also Marc Saperstein, "The Preaching of Repentance and the Reforms in Toledo of 1281," in *Models of Holiness in Medieval Sermons*, ed. Beverly Mayne Kienzle (Louvain-la-Neuve, 1996), 166. The finely embroidered clothes of Muslim women were seen as part of their distinctive allure. See, for example, the poem by Abulafia's nephew, Todros Abulafia, in Yellin ed., *Gan ha-meshalim we-hahidoth*, vol. 2, pt. 1, no. 721.

[53] *Gan Hameshalim ve-hahidoth*, pt. 2, vol. 2, nos. 602, 433. For rabbinic calls to violence, see *Zikhron Yehudah*, no. 63; and Jonah Gerondi, *Sha'arei Teshuva*, Gate 3, no. 131.

the plight of Jewish women of his day, Adret wrote, "Today, unruly persons are on the increase and there is no one to reproach his fellow man . . . The daughters of Israel are chaste, but the generation corrupts them."[54]

The problem of sexual relations between Jews and Gentiles resonated differently within each religious community, and the concerns of Christian ecclesiastical and governmental officials over inter-faith sex were not always the same as those held by their Jewish (or Muslim) counterparts. For the former, sex was closely tied to power, and relations between Christian men and minority women were a means of asserting Christianity's dominant position within Iberia's heterodox society. Conversely, Christian authorities demonstrated far greater concern over the potential intercourse between Christian women and minority men. Writing about Spain in the fourteenth century, David Nirenberg has noted that "prostitutes became the focal point for anxiety about sexual frontiers, the site at which dishonor threatened the Christian community." Yet if, as Nirenberg observes, interfaith intercourse did not generally "form an important focus of public concern or anchor a rhetoric or anxiety about sexual boundaries between religious communities," Jewish leaders did evince "public concern" about interfaith sex *per se*.[55]

In January of 1282, Pedro III of Aragon wrote to Salomon Vidal, his bailiff for the Valencian towns of Burriana and Villareal, instructing him that "for each and every one of the Saracens who go to settle in that place Villa Real," he should build "a covered house and corral surrounded by a wall" on the outskirts of the town.[56] This brief passage offers us a glimpse at the sort of social interaction typical of medieval Iberia which is often summed up by the term "*convivencia*," a Christian king ordering his Jewish bailiff to encourage Muslim immigration by constructing separate housing for Muslim settlers.[57] The image created here is one of close interaction between the peninsula's three religious communities, engendered by a royal initiative that sought a pragmatic solution to administrative, economic, and demographic problems. However, the reference to the creation of separate and protected residences for would-be Muslim immigrants also highlights

[54] Asher ben Yehiel, *Responsa*, 18:13; and Adret, 1:1209.

[55] Nirenberg, "Conversion, Sex, and Segregation," 1075. Nirenberg also elaborates on this theme in *Communities of Violence*, chap. 5.

[56] ACA, reg. 52, fol. 19v.

[57] The term *convivencia* has been used to describe the tripartite society of medieval Spain and Portugal ever since it was introduced by Américo Castro in his classic study *España en su historia*, 200–209. More recently, the historiographical impact of the term has been discussed by Thomas Glick in *Islamic and Christian Spain in the Early Middle Ages* (Princeton, 1979), 6–13.

the degree to which these same monarchs sought to control the parameters of this interaction.

The latter half of the thirteenth century can be seen as a period of transition for Iberian Jewry with respect to its interaction with Gentile society. While the crown set aside land in the new territories for Jewish settlement, Jews were not initially limited to these neighborhoods. Indeed, there are several examples of royal permissiveness regarding Jewish settlement outside the Jewish quarter and Christian ownership of property within it. The extension of royal power into the towns and cities of the frontier had been a force that had helped to promote and protect Jewish settlement there from the beginning of Christian rule, and had continued to defend the rights of individual Jews even at the expense of Jewish communal organization and effectiveness. It was not until the end of the thirteenth century that the assertion of royal authority and control so instrumental in establishing the initial Jewish presence in southern Iberia, and which had safeguarded Jewish social and economic interests for decades, began to circumscribe the dynamism and mobility of Jewish life in this region.

As the territories conquered during the first half of the century gave way to a more settled frontier, royal and ecclesiastical authorities became increasingly focused on the separation of religious communities. Since 1215, the papacy had pushed for greater separation of Jews and Christians on social and religious grounds, principally to avoid "mistaken" sexual interaction between members of the different faiths. However, the gradual move toward greater enforcement of the *judería* as the sole area for Jewish settlement and the regulation of Jewish clothing and sexual relations were the result of political and economic interests of the crown, not ecclesiastical pressure.[58] Furthermore, while leaders of the Jewish communities generally supported efforts to strengthen social boundaries, individual Jews continued to resist any policies that would restrict their social and economic movement within the larger society.

---

[58] This is a point that contrasts sharply with Baer's vague (though influential) argument for the influence of ecclesiastical policies regarding the Jews. *History*, 1:116.

CONCLUSION

H
istorians of medieval Spain and Portugal have traditionally understood the Jewish experience in the *reconquista* and *repoblación* to be marginal at best; a
view that stems from the practice of analyzing their
relative contributions to these phenomena. It is thus left to the historian of
medieval Jewry to reclaim them from the margins of the general history of
their host societies, and to allow them to be the protagonists of their own
narrative. When we abandon the search for the Jewish role in non-Jewish
history, and instead begin to study the impact of shared historical processes
on the Jews, the enterprise proves far more profitable. By looking at the nature of Jewish life in southern Iberia during the high Middle Ages, we dis-
cover a rich and varied society that was greatly affected by both the creation
of a broad frontier and its eventual colonization.

Writing on thirteenth-century Valencia, Robert Burns has observed that
the frontier created there by Jaime I ("the Conqueror"), "was not merely a
border but a region of warfare and peril to the realms, a permanent state
perduring long after James' death."[1] My presentation of Jewish life throughout southern Iberia has suggested otherwise. Far from being a region
marked by persistent danger and instability, the borderland between Christian and Muslim dominated territory established in the thirteenth century a

---

[1] Robert I. Burns, "The Significance of the Frontier in the Middle Ages," in *Medieval Frontier Societies* (Oxford, 1989), 322. This portrait of warfare and peril is also challenged by the recent work of Mark Meyerson on the Jews of Murviedro (Morvedre). See his *Jews in an Iberian Frontier Kingdom* (Leiden, 2004) and *Jewish Renaissance in Fifteenth-Century Spain* (Princeton, 2004).

land of opportunities, a region characterized by a dynamic, fluid, if often volatile society that attracted an array of settlers from throughout the peninsula and beyond. For many of the wealthy Jewish courtiers of the interior, the frontier offered the chance to extend their already considerable economic holdings and political influence. For those Jews who migrated to the frontier as settlers, the available land, exemptions from royal taxes, and a host of other economic possibilities available in these new territories outweighed the social and religious benefits of life within the borders of the Jewish quarter and, in some instances, the Jewish community as well. For a half-century following the Christian campaigns, the growth and dynamism of the Iberian frontier gave rise to Jewish settlements that were marked by a high degree of openness and the mobility of their residents. The greatest "peril" facing the Jewries of the frontier was the independence and factionalism of their own members.

Christian expansion of the late twelfth and early thirteenth century brought with it a new age of Jewish settlement in the territories of Mallorca, Valencia, Murcia, Andalusia, and southern Portugal. After centuries of decline under Muslim rule, the Jewish communities of these regions began to flourish once again as new *juderías* were formally chartered and their contours reestablished. For Jewish historians, the transition of Hispano-Jewish society from Muslim to Christian rule has traditionally been contrasted with the early development of Jewish communities in northern Europe. Whereas the latter evolved slowly from small settlements of merchants who had come to the region seeking economic opportunities, medieval Sephardic communities have been seen as fully matured communities that merely reestablished as Christian forces reclaimed the peninsula.[2] However, closer analysis of the Jewish experience in southern Iberia during the thirteenth century suggests that there may be greater affinities between Sephardic and Ashkenazic settlement patterns than previously imagined. Individual Jews, not communities, dominated the early period of settlement on the Iberian frontier, and even as communities began to take shape, the region continued to be characterized by areas of low Jewish population and slow institutional development. While the land partitions of the mid thirteenth century reflect the persistence of a native Jewish population in some areas of the frontier, the return of Jewish life to the region under Christian rule cannot be characterized as the reestablishment of preexisting communities. Jews already living in the region at the time of its conquest lost lands to both Christian

[2] This paradigm is typified by the charter given to the Jews of Tudela by Alfonso I of Aragon in 1115, Baer, *Juden*, vol. 1, no. 570; and in English translation in Chazan, *Church, State, and Jew*, 69–70.

and Jewish settlers alike, and in many instances Christian rule represented a significant expansion of the urban and rural property owned by Jewish individuals and communities.

As the *reconquista* gave way to the long process of resettlement, the chaos and instability caused by war and the mass-migrations of whole populations was replaced by a colonized frontier that was steadily incorporated into the political, cultural, and socioeconomic life of the various peninsular states. For these new Jewish settlements, this meant communal organization and standardization based on models that developed from centuries under Muslim and Christian rule. Throughout the peninsula and the Balearics, Jewish settlements, which had been given new life with the arrival of Christian rule, soon began to resemble the older Jewish communities of the interior in their social structure and communal institutions. The driving forces behind this process of standardization were the various Iberian monarchies who also began to increase their claim to sovereignty over the Jews and their authority and influence in Jewish communal affairs. This intensification of royal control over the Jews and their property was part of a broader campaign to expand monarchical power at the expense of the other estates.

The families of municipal *fueros* that Iberian kings of the thirteenth century granted to towns and cities throughout the new territories continued the tradition of judicial equality toward Jewish settlers that had characterized the frontier for centuries. In spite of growing ecclesiastical demands to isolate the Jewish community and restrict their contacts with Christians, Iberian monarchs continued to protect Jewish settlers on the frontier and to maintain conditions in which their civic status, economic opportunities, and social mobility approximated that of their Christian counterparts.

In the Jewish *aljamas* of the frontier, the dominant political paradigm would continue to be the council of communal representatives that ruled in conjunction with the guidance and support of rabbinic authorities. But beginning in the thirteenth century, Jewish communal officials faced a new obstacle to the imposition of their authority. During the latter half of the century, the crown's increased theoretical claims of sovereignty over the Jews found concrete expression in the creation of new administrative posts that brought the fiscal and judicial management of the *aljamas* into a closer bond with rapidly developing royal bureaucracies. Royally appointed *alcaldes* began to oversee cases between Jews and Christians, and crown rabbis were granted jurisdiction over individual communities and whole kingdoms, challenging the power and autonomy of the local *kahal*. In addition to heightening tensions between the municipalities and their Jewish residents, this incursion of royal power into the municipal sphere also had a debilitating effect on the already fragile authority of Jewish communal government.[3] The political and judicial autonomy of the Jewish community was further undermined by Jewish individuals and communal councils alike, both of whom increasingly sought to involve the crown and its ministers in the processes of local government.

As the thirteenth century drew to a close, royal intervention into the affairs of their communities and royal enforcement of the physical and social boundaries of the *judería* began to signal the end of the open society of the frontier. Still, the eventual dissipation of the favorable social and economic conditions that had characterized the society of the new territories was more a process than an event. As Iberian kings and Jewish leaders both sought to control the limits of Jewish settlement in order to increase revenue and limit social interaction with non-Jews, they encountered opposition from Jewish settlers who continued to be drawn to the cities of the frontier by economic opportunities. Throughout the latter half of the thirteenth century, individual Jews and Christians bought, sold, and exchanged houses and shops which inevitably led to the expansion of Jewish homes and business far beyond the bounds of their designated quarters. Even as municipal and ecclesiastical pressure combined with royal initiatives to create an increasingly restrictive atmosphere within the Jewish settlements of southern Iberia, there persisted within these *juderías* the active pursuit of the sort of dynamic and unfettered society that had come to symbolize the frontier for over fifty years.

[3] A point which should be taken into consideration by those who would search the era prior to the tragic events of 1391 for the origins of the demise of Iberian Jewry.

GLOSSARY

adelantado   A communal leader or councilman.

alcacería   An urban district owned by the crowns and set aside for Jewish shops and residences.

alcázar   A fortified structure that typically acted as the seat of royally authority in a given town.

alfaquí   A judicial position under Muslim rule, the post expanded into that of a civil servant with broad responsibilities in Christian Iberia.

alfaquim   A royal courtier and general advisor, often a scribe and translator of Arabic.

alfoz   The lands surrounding and belonging to a given municipality.

aljama   The Castilian or Aragonese term for a Jewish community (see also *kahal*).

Almohad   The dynasty of Muslim Berbers who came to power in North Africa and Iberia, and whose harsh policies toward Christians and Jews forced many to emigrate.

Almoravid   The dynasty of Muslim Berbers who preceded the Almohads, ruling in southern Iberia from 1086–1147.

almoxarife   The royal official in charge of tax collection.

alquería   A small rural village or area.

alvazil   A royal magistrate.

arançada   A unit of land measurement equal to about 3,866 square meters.

berurim (sing. baror)   Jewish communal officials (see also *mukademim*).

beth din   A formally ordained Jewish tribunal.

caballeros villanos   Urban, non-noble knights of Castile.

cabildo   A cathedral chapter.

caloña   A fine paid for killing someone. While the caloña for Christians was usually paid to the victim's family, in the case of Jews the fine was paid to the crown.

call   A Catalan term for the Jewish quarter or the community that resided therein.

concejo (Portuguese concelho)   The governing council of a municipality.

cortes (Catalan corts)   Parliamentary body or session.

convivencia   The term often used to describe the coexistence of different religious groups in medieval Iberia.

cuadrilla   A unit of land made up of smaller parcels or of villages.

dhimma (pl. dhimmi)   Protected minorities, generally Jews and Christians, living under Islam.

diezmo   The tithe on land many agricultural products owed to the church.

fanecata, fanega   A unit of land (about 1.6 acres) required to grow a *fanega* of seed.

fuero (Portuguese foro)   A municipal or royal charter regulating laws and privileges.

guidaticum   A writ of safe conduct given to ensure the protection of settlers and their property.

hakhamim   Lit. "sages" or "wisemen," the Hebrew term used to refer to scholars of Jewish law.

halakha   Jewish law.

heredad   A variable unit of land measurement.

herem   Decree of excommunication from a Jewish community.

hermandad   League or association of towns organized for defense or the promotion of mutual interests.

jovate   A unit of land measurement equal to 11.36 hectares.

judería (Portuguese judiaria, Catalan call)   The Jewish quarter of a town.

kahal   A Hebrew term for a Jewish community or its governing council (see also **kehilla**).

kehilla (pl. kehillot)   A Jewish community or an individual congregation (see also **kahal**).

maravedí   A Castilian coin or, more commonly, a unit of monetary measurement.

minhag   Jewish legal custom.

Moor   Medieval term for a Muslim.

mukedam (pl. mukademim)   A Jewish communal official (see also **baror**).

nidduy   A lesser ban issued by the Jewish community against one of its members.

pecheros   Members of the urban working classes in Castile.

piyyutim   Jewish liturgical poems.

reconquista   The term given to the general process of Christian conquest of Muslim territory in medieval Iberia.

repartimiento   The process of land partition or the official register of the division.

repoblación   Resettlement or colonization of a conquered region

sou (Latin solidus, Aragonese sueldo)   Catalan monetary denomination roughly equal to 1/20 of a pound.

tabelion   A keeper of accounts, or financial representative.

tahulla   A unit of agricultural land (about 1.12 hectares).

termino   The area of land governed by a given municipality.

vecino   A citizen of a town.

yugada   Unit of land that could be worked by a team of oxen in one day (about 32 hectares).

zekenim (Castilian viejos)   Hebrew term for Jewish "elders," often used to denote communal officials.

BIBLIOGRAPHY

Primary Sources

Abulafia, Meir ha-Levi. *Responsa, Or Tzaddikim.* Warsaw, 1902.
——. *Yad Ramah, Baba Batra.* Warsaw, 1887.
Abulafia, Todros ben Judah ha-Levi. *Gan Hameshalim ve-hahidoth.* 2 pts. in 3 vols. Edited by David Yellin. Jerusalem, 1932–1936.
Alfonso X, el Sabio, king of Castilla and León. *Opúsculos Legales del rey don Alfonso el Sabio.* 2 vols. Madrid, 1836.
——. *Las Siete Partidas del rey don Alfonso el Sabio.* 3 vols. Madrid, 1807.
——. *Primera crónica general.* Vol. 2. Edited by Ramón Menéndez Pidal. Madrid, 1955.
——. *Cantigas de Santa María.* Edited by Walter Mettmann. Coimbra, 1959–1972.
——. *Fuero Real, edición y analisis crítico.* Edited by Gonzalo Martínez Díez. Ávila, 1988.
——. *Espéculo, Texto jurídico atribuido al Rey de Castilla Don Alfonso X, el Sabio.* Edited by Robert MacDonald. Madison, 1990.
Algora Hernando, Jesús Ignacio, and Felicísimo Arranz Sacristán, eds. *El Fuero de Calatayud.* Zaragoza, 1982.
Asher ben Yehiel. *Sheelot u-Teshuvot (Responsa).* Venice, 1607.
——. *Hidushe Baba Bathra.* Vilna, 1880–1886.
Baer, Fritz, ed. *Die Juden im christlichen Spanien.* 2 vols. Berlin, 1936.
Ballesteros, Mercedes Gaibrois de, ed. *Historia del reinado de Sancho IV de Castilla.* 3 vols. Madrid, 1928.
Bar Ilan Responsa Project, CD ROM version 8.0. Ramat Gan, Israel, 2000.
Benavides, Antonio, ed. *Memorias del rey D. Fernando IV de Castilla, Vol. II, Colección Diplomática.* Madrid, 1860.
Bofarull y Mascaró, Próspero de, ed., *Repartimientos de los reinos de Mallorca, Valencia y Cerdeña.* Barcelona, 1856. [Facsimile edition in *Colección de documentos inéditos.* Vol. 11. Barcelona, 1975.]
Burns, Robert I. *Diplomatarium Regni Valentiae, 1257–1263.* 3 vols. Princeton, 1991–.
——. *Jews in the Notarial Culture: Latinate Wills in Mediterranean Spain, 1250–1350.* Berkeley, 1996.
Cabanes Pecourt, María de los Desamparados, and Antonio Huici Miranda, eds. *Los Documentos de Jaime I de Aragón.* 5 vols. Valencia, 1976–.

Cabanes Pecourt, María de los Desamparados, and Ramón Ferrer Navarro, eds. *Libre del Repartiment del Regne de Valencia.* Saragossa, 1979.

Cabanes Pecourt, María de los Desamparados, and María Luisa Cabanes Català, eds. *Aureum Opus de Xátiva.* Saragossa, 1996.

Cabanes Pecourt, María de los Desamparados, Asunción Blasco Martínez, Pilar Pueyo Colomina, eds. *Vidal Mayor: edición, introducción y notas al manuscrito.* Saragossa, 1997.

Canellas López, Angel, ed. *Colección diplomática del concejo de Zaragoza.* Vol. 1. Saragossa, 1972.

Castro, Américo, and Federico de Onís, eds. *Los fueros Leóneses de Zamora Salamanca, Ledesma, y Alba de Tormes.* Madrid, 1916.

Chazan, Robert, ed. *Church, State, and Jew in the Middle Ages.* West Orange, N.J.., 1980.

Cinta Mañé, María, comp., and Yom Tov Assis, ed. *The Jews in the Crown of Aragon: Regesta of the Cartas Reales in the Archivo de la Corona de Aragon.* Part 1:1066–1327. Jerusalem, 1993.

Cohen, Gerson, ed. *A Critical Edition with a Translation and Notes of the Book of Tradition (Sefer ha-Qabbalah), by Abraham ibn Daud.* Philadelphia, 1967.

Colón, Germà, and Arcadi García, eds. *Furs de Valencia.* 4 vols. Barcelona, 1970–.

Colmeiro, Manuel, ed. *Cortes de los antiguos reinos de León y de Castilla.* Madrid, 1861.

Corriea da Serra, José Francisco, ed. *Collecção de livros inéditos de historia Portugueza.* Vol. 5. Lisbon, 1824.

Dualde Serrano, Manuel, ed. *Fori antiqui Valentiae.* Madrid, 1967.

Dufourcq, Charles. "Nouveaux Documents sur la Politique Africaine de la Courounne D'Aragon." *Analecta Taraconensia* 16 (1953): 1–32.

Elbogen, Ismar. "Hebraische Quellen zur Frühgeschichte der Juden in Deutschland." *Zeitschrift für die Geschichte der Juden in Deutschland* 1 (1929): 34–43.

Epstein, Isadore. *The "Responsa" of Rabbi Solomon ben Adreth of Barcelona 1235–1310 as a Source of the History of Spain.* London, 1923. Reprinted in *Studies in the communal life of the Jews of Spain: as reflected in the Responsa of Rabbi Solomon b. Adreth and R. Simon b. Zemach Duran.* New York, 1968.

Estal, Juan Manuel de, ed. *El Reino de Murcia bajo la soberanía de Aragón.* 3 vols. Alicante, 1985.

———. *Alicante, de villa a ciudad (1252–1490).* Alicante, 1990.

Fita, Fidel. "La judería de Segovia: Documentos inéditos." *Boletín de la Real Academia de la Historia* 9 (1886): 344–389.

Fita, Fidel, and Gabriel Llabrés y Quintana. "Privilegios de los hebreos mallorquines en el códice Pueyo." *Boletín de la Real Academia de la Historia* 36 (1900): 15–35, 122–148, 185–209, 273–306, 369–402, and 458–494.

Friedberg, Emil, ed. *Corpus Iuris Canonici.* 2 vols. Leipzig, 1881.

Fuente, Vicente de La. *Historia Eclesiástica de España.* 6 vols. Madrid, 1873–1875.

Gargallo Moya, Antonio, ed. *Los Fueros de Aragon [según el ms. del Archivo Municipal de Miravete de la Sierra (Teruel)].* Saragossa, 1992.

Gedalia ben Joseph ibn Yahia. *Sefer Shalselet ha-Kabbalah.* 1587. Jerusalem, 1962.

González, Julio, ed. *El Repartimiento de Sevilla.* 2 vols. Madrid, 1951.

———. *El Reino de Castilla en la época de Alfonso VIII.* 3 vols. Madrid, 1960.

———. *Reinado y diplomas de Fernando III.* 3 vols. Córdoba, 1986.

González Jiménez, Manuel, ed. *Diplomatario andaluz de Alfonso X.* Seville, 1991.

González Jiménez, Manuel, and Antonio González Gómez, eds. *El Libro del Repartimiento de Jérez de la Frontera, estudio y edición.* Cádiz, 1980.

González Palencia, Cándido Angel, ed. *Los Mozárabes de Toledo en los siglos XII y XIII.* 4 vols. Madrid, 1930.

Gorosch, Max, ed. *El Fuero de Teruel.* Stockholm, 1950.

Grayzel, Solomon, ed. *The Church and the Jews in the XIII Century.* Vol. 1. Philadelphia, 1933.

Bibliography

———. *The Church and the Jews in the XIII Century*. Vol. 2. New York, 1984.

Halkin, Abraham S., ed. *Sefer ha-'iyunim veha-diyunim: 'al ha-shirah ha-'ivrit*. Jerusalem, 1975.

Herculano, Alexander, and José da Silva. Mendes Leal, eds. *Portugaliae monumenta histórica a saeculo octavo post Christum usque ad quintumdecimum. Leges et Consuetudines*. 2 vols. Lisbon, 1888.

Isaac ben Jacob Alfasi. *Sheelot u-Teshuvot, (Responsa)*. Leghorn, 1781.

Isaacs, Abraham Lionel. *The Jews of Majorca*. London, 1936.

Jonah ben Abraham Gerondi. *Sha'arei Teshuva*. Jerusalem, 1967.

———. *Sefer ha-Yir'ah*. Bene Berak, Israel, 1969.

Juan Manuel, Infante of Castile. *Libro de los estados*. Edited by Robert Brian Tate and Ian R. Macpherson. Oxford, 1974.

Judah ben Asher. *Zikhron Yehuda, Sheelot u-Teshuvot*. Edited by J. Rosenberg and D. Cassel. Jerusalem, 1967.

Kagay, Donald J., trans. and ed. *The Usatges of Barcelona: The Fundamental Law of Catalonia*. Philadelphia, 1994.

Lacruz Berdejo, José Luis. "Fueros de Aragon hasta 1265." *Anuario de Derecho Aragonés* 2 (1945): 23–361.

León Tello, Pilar. *Judíos de Toledo*. 2 vols. Madrid, 1979.

Linder, Amnon, ed. *The Jews in Roman Imperial Legislation*. Detroit, 1987.

Livro I de misticos de Reis. Livro II dos reis D. Dinis, D. Alfonso IV, D. Pedro I. In *Documentos para a historia da cidade de Lisboa*. Lisbon, 1947.

Lumbreras Valiente, Pedro, ed. *Los fueros municipales de Cáceres*. Cáceres, 1974.

López Dapena, Asunción. *Cuentas y Gastos (1292–1294) del Rey Sancho IV el Bravo*. Córdoba, 1984.

Maldonado y Fernández del Torco, José, ed. *El fuero de Coria*, Madrid, 1949.

Mans Puigarnau, Jaime M., ed. *Decretales de Gregorio IX: versión medieval española*. Vol. 1. Barcelona, 1939.

Marques, João Martins da Silva, ed. *Descobrimentos Portugueses*. Vol. 1 (1147–1460). Lisbon, 1944.

———. *Descobrimentos Portugueses: Suplemento ao vol. I, (1057–1460)*. Lisbon, 1944.

Masià i de Ros, Angels. *Jaume II: Aragó, Granada i Marroc*. Barcelona, 1989.

Menahem ben Aharon ibn Zerah. *Zedah la-Derekh*. Warsaw, 1880.

Miret y Sans, Joaquim, ed. *Itinerari de Jaume I*. Barcelona, 1918.

Mora, Pau, and Lorenzo Andrinal, eds. *Diplomatari del monestir de Santa Maria de la Real de Mallorca*. Palma, 1982.

Moses ben Jacob de Coucy. *Sefer Mitsvot ha-Gadol*. Jerusalem, 1988.

Müller, Joel, ed. *Teshuvot Geonei Mizrah u-Ma'arav*. 1888. Berlin, 1966.

Muñoz y Romero, Tomás, ed. *Colección de fueros municipales y cartas pueblas de las [sic] reinos de Castilla, León, Corona de Aragon y Navarra*. Madrid, 1847.

Nieto Cumplido, Manuel, ed. *Corpus Mediaevale Cordubense*. 2 vols. Córdoba, 1979–1980.

Oliver y Esteller, Benvenido. *Lliber de les Costums Generals escirtas de la ciutat de Tortosa*. Madrid, 1881.

Ordenaç oes Afonsinas, Livro II. 2nd ed. 1792. Lisbon, 1998.

Peset Reig, Mariano and Juan Gutiérrez Cuadrado, eds. *El fuero de Ubeda*. Valencia, 1979.

Pons, Antonio. *Los judíos de Mallorca durante los siglos XIII y XIV*. 2 vols. Palma de Mallorca, 1984.

Powers, James F., trans. and ed. *The Code of Cuenca: Municipal Law on the Twelfth-Century Castilian Frontier*. Philadelphia, 2000.

Ramírez Vaquero, Eloísa, ed. *El Fuero de Plasencia: estudio histórico y edición crítica del texto*. 2 vols. Mérida, 1987.

Ramón Castro, José. *Catálogo del Archivo General de Navarra*. vol. 1. Tudela, 1952.

Ramos y Loscertales, José María, ed. *El Fuero de Jaca*. Barcelona, 1927.

Régné, Jean, comp. *History of the Jews in Aragon, Regesta and Documents 1213–1327.* Edited by Yom Tov Assis. Jerusalem, 1978.

Reuben ben Nissim Gerondi. *Sheelot u-Teshuvot, (Responsa).* Edited by Leon A. Feldman. Jerusalem. 1984.

Rey, Agapito, ed. *Castigos e documentos para bien vivir ordenados por el rey don Sancho IV.* Indiana University Humanities Series 24 (1952).

Rivera Romero, Victoriano, ed. *La carta de fuero concedida á la ciudad de Córdoba por el rey D. Fernando III.* Córdoba 1881.

Rodríguez de Lama, Ildelfonso, ed. *Colección diplomática medieval de la Rioja.* Vol. 2. Logroño, 1989.

Rosell, Caetano, ed. *Crónicas de los reyes de Castilla.* Vol. 1. 1878. Madrid, 1953.

Roudil, Jean, ed. *El Fuero de Baeza.* The Hague, 1962.

Sáez, Emilio, ed. *Los fueros de Sepúlveda.* Segovia, 1953.

Sánchez, Galo, ed. *Fueros Castellanos de Soria y Alcalá de Henares.* Madrid, 1919.

———. *Libro de los fueros de Castiella.* Barcelona, 1924.

———. *El Fuero de Madrid.* Madrid, 1963.

Scott, Samuel Parsons, trans. and ed. *The Visigothic Code (Forum Judicum).* Boston, 1910.

Simonsohn, Shlomo, ed. *The Apostolic See and the Jews: Documents: 492–1404.* Toronto, 1988.

Soldevila, Ferran, ed. *Jaume I, Crónica o Llibre dels Feits.* Barcelona, 1982.

Solomon ben Abraham ibn Adret. *Sheelot u-Teshuvot, (Responsa).* Vol. 1 (Bologna, 1539); vols. 2, 3 (Leghorn, 1657, 1778); vol. 4 (Vilna, 1881); vol. 5 (Leghorn, 1825); vols. 6, 7 (Warsaw, 1868); vol. 8, Adret's responsa attributed to Nahmanides (Warsaw, 1883).

Soto i Company, Ricard, ed. *Còdex català del Llibre del Repartiment de Mallorca.* Barcelona, 1984.

———. "Repartiment I 'repartiments': L'ordenació d'un espai de colonització feudal a la Mallorca del segle XIII." In *De Al-Andalus a la sociedad feudal: los repartimientos bajomedievales,* 1–51. Barcelona, 1990.

Tilander, Gunnar, ed. *Los Fueros de Aragón.* Lund, 1937.

Torres Fontes, Juan, ed. *El Repartimiento de Murcia.* Madrid, 1960.

———. *Colección de Documentos para la historia del reino de Murcia.* Vol. 2, *Documentos del siglo XIII.* Murcia, 1969.

———. *Fueros y privilegios de Alfonso X el Sabio al Reino de Murcia.* Murcia, 1973.

———. *Documentos de Alfonso XI.* Murcia, 1997.

———. *Repartimiento de la huerta y campo de Murcia en el siglo XIII.* Murcia, 1971.

———. *Repartimiento de Lorca, estudio y edición.* Murcia, 1977.

———. *Repartimiento de Orihuela.* Murcia, 1988.

Valls y Taberner, Fernando. *Los privilegios de Alfonso X el Sabio a la ciudad de Murcia.* Barcelona, 1923.

Ventura, Leóntina, and Ana Santiago Faria, eds. *Livro Santo de Santa Cruz.* Coimbra, 1990.

Villanueva, Jaime, ed. *Viatge Literario a las Iglesias de España.* Vol. 22. Madrid, 1852.

Yom Tov ben Abraham Ishbili. *Sheelot u-Teshuvot, (Responsa).* Edited by Yoseph Kapah. Jerusalem, 1959.

Yom Tov ben Joseph ibn Falaquera. *The Book of the Seeker (Sefer Ha-Mebaqqesh).* Edited and translated M. Herschel Levine. New York, 1976.

SECONDARY SOURCES

Abulafia, David. "From Privilege to Persecution: Crown Church and Synagogue in the City of Majorca, 1229–1343." In *Church and City, 1000–1500: Essays in Honour of Christo-*

pher Brooke, edited by David Abulafia, Michael Franklin, and Miri Rubin, 111–126. Cambridge, 1992.

Aizenberg, Edna. "*Una Judía Muy Fermosa:* The Jewess as Sex Object in Medieval Spanish Literature and Lore." *La Corónica* 12 (1984): 187–194.

Albeck, Shalom. "The Principles of Government in the Jewish Communities of Spain until the 13th century." *Zion* 25 (1960): 85–121 [Hebrew].

——. " 'Dina de malkhuta dina' bi-kehilot sefarad." In *Abraham Weiss Jubilee Volume*, 109–125. New York, 1964.

Almeida, Fortunato de. *História da Igreja em Portugal.* 4 vols. Coimbra, 1910–1922.

Alomar Esteve, Garbriel. *Urbanismo regional en la Edad Media: Las "Ordinacions" de Jaime II (1300) en el reino de Mallorca.* Barcelona, 1976.

Amador de los Ríos, José. *Historia social, política y religiosa de los Judíos de España y Portugal.* 3 vols. Madrid, 1875–1876.

Arquivo de Beja: Boletim da Camara Municipal. Vol. 1. Beja, 1944.

Assis, Yom Tov. "Sexual Behaviour in Mediaeval Hispano-Jewish Society." In *Jewish History: Essays in Honour of Chimen Abramsky*, edited by Ada Rapoport-Albert and Steven J. Zipperstein, 25–59. London, 1988.

——. "Synagogues in Medieval Spain." *Jewish Art* 18 (1992): 6–29.

——. "The Judeo-Arabic Tradition in Christian Spain." In *The Jews of Medieval Islam*, edited by Daniel Frank, 111–124. New York, 1995.

——. "Diplomàtics jueus de la Corona catalanoaragonesa en terres musulmanes (1213–1327)." *Tamid* 1 (1997): 7–40.

——. *Jewish Economy in the Medieval Crown of Aragon, 1213–1327.* Leiden, 1997.

——. *The Golden Age of Aragonese Jewry: 1213–1327.* London, 1997.

Ayaso Martínez, José Ramón. "Tolerancia e intolerancia en los reinos cristianos de la España medieval: el caso de los judíos." *Miscelánea de estudios árabes y hebraicos* 43 (1994): 49–81.

Baer, Yitzhak. "Todros ben Yehudah ha-Levi and His Times." *Zion* 2 (1936): 19–55 [Hebrew].

——. "The Foundations and Beginnings of the Jewish Community Structure in the Middle Ages." *Zion* 15 (1950): 1–41 [Hebrew]. Reprinted in English as "The Origins of Jewish Communal Organization in the Middle Ages." In *Binah: Studies in Jewish History, Thought, and Culture*, edited by Joseph Dan, 59–82. New York, 1989.

——. *A History of the Jews in Christian Spain.* 2 vols. Translated by L. Schoffman et al. Philadelphia, 1961.

Ballesteros, Antonio. *Sevilla en el siglo XIII.* Madrid, 1913.

Barbosa, Pedro Gomes. "Alguns grupos marginais nos documentos de Danta Maria de Alcobaça (séc. XII e XIII)." In Documentos, lugares e homens: estudos de história medieval, 105–131. Lisbon, 1991.

Baron, Salo. *The Jewish Community.* 3 vols. Philadelphia, 1942.

——. *A Social and Religious History of the Jews.* 2nd ed. Vols. 5, 10, 11. New York, 1965, 1967.

Barros, Henrique da Gama. "Judeus e Mouros em Portugal." *Revista Lusitana* 34–35 (1937): 165–265, 161–238.

Beirante, Maria Angela V. da Rocha. *Evora na Idade Média.* Lisbon, 1995.

Bensch, Stephen. "From Prizes of War to Domestic Merchandise: The Changing face of Slavery in Catalonia and Aragon, 1000–1300." *Viator* 25 (1994): 63–93.

Berend, Nora. *At the Gates of Christendom: Jews, Muslims and 'Pagans' in Medieval Hungary, c. 1000–c. 1300.* Cambridge, 2001.

Bisson, Thomas, ed. *Fiscal Accounts of Catalonia under the Early Count-Kings.* 2 vols. London, 1984.

——. " 'Statebuilding' in the Medieval Crown of Aragón." In *Actas del XV Congreso de historia de la corona de Aragon*, 141–158. Jaca, 1993.

Blidstein, Gerald J., "A Note on the Function of 'The Law of the Kingdom Is Law' in the Medieval Jewish Community." *Journal of Jewish Sociology* 15 (1973): 213–319.

Bofarull y Sans, Francisco de, ed. "Jaime I y los Judíos." In *Actas del I Congrès d'Historia de la Corona d'Aragó*, 819–943. Barcelona, 1909.

Boswell, John, *Muslim Communities under the Crown of Aragon in the Fourteenth Century*. New Haven, 1977.

Branco, Maria João V. "The Kings Counsellors' two Faces." In *The Medieval World*, edited by Janet Nelson and Peter Linehan, 518–533. London, 2001.

Brann, Ross. *The Compunctious Poet: Cultural Ambiguity and Hebrew Poetry in Muslim Spain*. Baltimore, 1991.

Brodman, James W. *Ransoming Captives in Crusader Spain: the Order of Merced on the Christian-Islamic Frontier.* Philadelphia, 1986.

Burns, Robert I. "Journey from Islam: Incipient Cultural Transition in the Conquered Kingdom of Valencia (1240–1280)." *Speculum* 35 (1960): 337–356.

———. "A Mediaeval Income Tax: The Tithe in the Thirteenth-Century Kingdom of Valencia." *Speculum* 41 (1966): 438–452.

———. "Jaume I and the Jews of the Kingdom of Valencia." In *X Congreso de Historia de la Corona de Aragón*, 2:245–322. Saragossa, 1976.

———. *Muslims, Christians and Jews in the Crusader Kingdom of Valencia*. Cambridge, 1984.

———. "The Significance of the Frontier in the Middle Ages." In *Medieval Frontier Societies*, edited by Robert Bartlett and Angus MacKay, 307–330. Oxford, 1989.

———. "The *Guidaticum*, Safe-Conduct in Medieval Arago-Catalonia: A Mini-Institution for Muslims, Christians, and Jews." *Medieval Encounters* 1 (1995): 51–113.

Carlé, María del Carmen. *Del concejo medieval castellano-Leonés*. Buenos Aires, 1968.

Carpenter, Dwayne. "Jewish-Christian Social Relations in Alphonsine Spain: A Commentary on Book VII, Title XXIV, Law 8 of the *Siete Partidas*." In *Florilegium Hispanicum, Medieval and Golden Age Studies presented to Dorothy Clotelle Clarke*, edited by John S. Geary. Madison, 1983.

———. *Alfonso X and the Jews: An Edition of and Commentary on Siete Partidas 7. 24 "De los judíos."* Berkeley, 1986.

———. "Organización de las comunidades judías en la España cristiana." In *The Culture of Spanish Jewry–Proceedings of the First International Congress*, edited by Aviva Doron, 57–64. Tel Aviv, 1994.

Castro, Américo. *The Spaniards: An Introduction to Their History*. Translated by Willard F. King and Selma Margaretten. Berkeley, 1971.

Chamberlain, Robert S. "The Concept of the *Señor Natural* as Revealed by Castilian Law and Administrative Documents." *Hispanic American Historical Review* 19 (1930): 130–137.

Christys, Ann. "Crossing the Frontier in 9th-Century Hispania." In *Medieval Frontiers: Concepts and Practices*, edited by David Abulafia and Nora Berend, 35–53. Cambridge, 2002.

Coelho, Maria Helena da Cruz, and Armando Luís de Carvalho Homen, eds. *Portugal em Definição de Fronteiras (1096–1325): do Condado Portucalense à Crise do Século XIV.* Lisbon, 1995.

Constable, Olivia Remie. "Muslim Spain and Mediterranean Slavery." In *Christendom and its Discontents: Exclusion, persecution and rebellion, 1000–1500*, edited by Scott Waugh and Peter Diehl, 264–284. Cambridge, 1996.

Craddock, Jerry. "La cronológica de las obras legislativas de Alfonso X el Sabio." *Anuario Histórico del Derecho Español* 51 (1981): 364–418.

Cruces Blancos, Esther. "Datos sobre compraventas de tierras en Córdoba tras los primeros años de presencia Castellana (1242–90)." In *Andalucía entre Oriente y Occidente (1236–1492)*, edited by Emilio Cabrera, 209–226. Córdoba, 1988.

David, Henrique, Amandio Barro, and João Antunes. "A Familia Cardona e as relações entre Portugal e Aragão durante o reinado de D. Dinis." *Revista da Faculdade de Letras do Porto, História* 4 (1989): 273–279.

Bibliography

Díaz Ibáñez, Jorge. "Monarquía y conflictos Iglesia-concejos en la Castilla bajomedeival. El Caso del obispado de Cuenca (1280–1406)." *En la España Medieval* 17 (1994): 133–156.

Elazar, Daniel J. "The Kehillah: From Its Beginnings to the End of the Modern Epoch." In *Comparative Jewish Politics: Public Life in Israel and the Diaspora*, edited by Sam N. Lehman-Wilzig and Bernard Susser, 23–63. Bar-Ilan, Israel, 1981.

Fita, Fidel. "Jérez de la Frontera, su judería en 1266." *Boletín de la Real Academia de la Historia* 10 (1887).

Fletcher, Richard. *Moorish Spain*. New York, 1992.

Fonseca, Luís Adão da. "Portugal na Península Ibérica. Horizontes marítimos, articulação política e relações diplomáticas (sec. XII-XVI)." In *Las Españas Medievales*, edited by in Julio Valdeón Baruque, 82–93. Valladolid, 1999.

Friedman, Mordechai Akiva. *Jewish Polygyny in the Middle Ages*. Jerusalem, 1986 [Hebrew].

García de Cortazar, José Angel. *La Época Medieval*. Madrid, 1973.

García y García, Antonio. *Estudos sobre la canonística portuguesa medieval*. Madrid, 1976.

García Soriano, Justo. "La Reconquista de Orihuela, Su leyenda y su historia." *Boletín de la Real Academia de la Historia* 104 (1934): 199–218.

Glick, Thomas. *Islamic and Christian Spain in the early Middle Ages*. Princeton, 1979.

———. *Irrigation and Hydraulic Technology, Medieval Spain and its Legacy*. London, 1996.

———. "Reading the *Repartimientos*: Modeling Settlement in the Wake of Conquest." In *Christians, Muslims, and Jews in Medieval and Early Modern Spain*, edited by Mark Meyerson and Edward English, 20–39. Notre Dame, 2000.

Goitein, Shlomo Dov. *A Mediterranean Society: the Jewish communities of the Arab world as portrayed in the documents of the Cairo Geniza*. 6 vols. Berkeley, 1967.

Gomes, Saul Antonio. "Os Judeus de Leiria Medieval como Agentes Dinamizadores da Economia Urbana." *Revista da Faculdade de Letras, Coimbra. Historia* 29 (1993): 1–29.

González Jiménez, Manuel. "Frontier and Settlement in the Kingdom of Castile." In *Medieval Frontier Societies*, edited by Robert Bartlett and Angus Mackay, 49–74. Oxford, 1989.

———. "Repartimientos andaluces del siglo XIII, perspectiva de conjunto y problemas." In *De Al-Andalus a la sociedad feudal: Los repartimientos bajomedievales*, 95–117. Barcelona, 1990.

———. "¿Re-conquista? Un estado de la cuestión." In *Tópicos y realidades de la Edad Media*, edited by Eloy Benito Ruano, 155–178. Madrid 2000.

González Mínguez, César. *Fernando IV de Castilla (1295–1312): la guerra civil y el predominio de la nobleza*. Vitoria, 1976.

Grossman, Avraham. *The Early Sages of Ashkenaz*. Jerusalem, 1981 [Hebrew].

———. "Legislation and Responsa Literature." In *The Sephardi Legacy*, vol. 1, edited by Haim Beinart, 188–219. Jerusalem, 1992.

Halkin, Abraham S. "History of the Forced Conversion under the Alhmohads." In *The Joshua Starr Memorial Volume*, 101–110. New York, 1953 [Hebrew].

Hatton, Vikki, and Angus Mackay. "Anti-Semitism in the *Cantigas de Santa Maria*." *Bulletin of Hispanic Studies* 60 (1983): 189–199.

Hinojosa Montalvo, José. "Bosquejo histórico de los judíos en tierras alicantinas durante la baja edad media." In *Actes Ir. Col.loqui d'Història dels Jueus a la Corona d'Aragó*, 207–220. Lleida, 1989.

Iglesias Ferreiros, Aquilino. "Derecho municipal, derecho señorial, derecho regio." *Historia. Instituciones. Documentos* 4 (1977): 115–197.

Jordan, William C. "Problems of the Meat Market of Béziers 1240–1247: a question of anti-Semitism." *Revue des Études Juives* 135 (1976): 31–49.

Kagay, Donald J., "Violence Management in Twelfth-Century Catalonia and Aragon." In *Marginated Groups in Spanish and Portuguese History*, edited by William D. Phillips Jr. and Carla Rahn Phillips. Minneapolis, 1986.

———. "Structures of Baronial Dissent and Revolt Under James I (1213–76)." *Mediaevistik* 1 (1988): 61–85.

———. "Royal Power in the Urban Setting: James I and the Towns of the Crown of Aragon." *Mediaevistik* 8 (1995): 161–170.

Klein, Elka. "Protecting the Widow and the Orphan: A Case Study from 13th-Century Barcelona." *Mosaic* 14–17 (1993–1995): 65–81.

Ladero Quesada, Miguel Angel. "Andalucía en sus origenes medievales (de las Navas de Tolosa a la conquista de Granada)." In *Andalucía Medieval: nuevos estudios*, edited by C. Torres Delgado et al., 39–71. Córdoba, 1979.

Langmuir, Gavin. *Toward a Definition of Antisemitism*. Berkeley, 1990.

Laredo, Abraham Isaac. "Las 'Sheelot u-Teshubot' como fuente para la historia de los judíos españoles." *Sefarad* 5 (1945): 441–456.

Lehmann, Matthias B. "Islamic Legal Consultation and the Jewish-Muslim 'Convivencia.'" *Jewish Studies Quarterly* 6 (1999): 25–54.

León Tello, Pilar. "Disposiciones sobre judíos en los fueros de Castilla y León." *Sefarad* 46 (1986): 279–293.

Leroy, Beatrice. *L'Aventure séfarade, De la péninsule ibérique à la diaspora*. Paris, 1986.

Lewis, Archibald. "The Closing of the Medieval Frontier." *Speculum* 33 (1958): 475–481.

Linehan, Peter. "The 'Gravamina' of the Castilian Church in 1262–3." *English Historical Review* 85 (1970): 730–754.

———. *The Spanish Church and the Papacy in the Thirteenth Century*. Cambridge, 1971.

———. "The Spanish Church Revisited: The Episcopal *Gravamina* of 1279." In *Authority and Power: Studies on Medieval Law and Government Presented to Walter Ullman on His 70th Birthday*, edited by idem and Brian Tierney, 127–147. Cambridge, 1980.

———. *History and Historians of Medieval Spain*. Oxford, 1993.

———. "At the Spanish Frontier." In *The Medieval World*, edited by Peter Linehan and Janet Nelson, 37–59. London, 2002.

Llop Jordana, Irene. "Jewish Moneylenders from Vic according to the *Liber Judeorum* 1341–1354." *Hispania Judaica Bulletin* 2 (1999): 75–87.

Lomax, Derek. *The Reconquest of Spain*. London, 1978.

Lourie, Elena. "Anatomy of Ambivalence: Muslims under the Crown of Aragon in the Late Thirteenth Century." In chap. 7 of *Crusade and Colonisation*, 1–77, Brookfield, Vermont, 1990.

MacKay, Angus. *Spain in the Middle Ages: From Frontier to Empire, 1000–1500*. New York, 1977.

Manzano Moreno, Eduardo. "Christian-Muslim Frontier in al-Andalus: Idea and Reality." In *The Arab Influence in Medieval Europe*, edited by Dionisius A. Agius and Richard Hitchcock, 83–99. Reading, 1994.

Martínez, María. "Idumentaria y sociedad medeivales (ss. XIII–XV)." *En la España Medieval* 26 (2003): 35–59.

Maya, Cynthia. "Jew and Muslim in Post-Conquest Tortosa." *Al-Masaq* 10 (1998): 15–25.

Melechen, Nina. "Loans, Land, and Jewish-Christian Relations in the Archdiocese of Toledo." In *Iberia and the Mediterranean World of the Middle Ages*, edited by Larry Simon, 185–215. Leiden, 1995.

Menéndez Pidal, Ramon. *The Spaniards in Their History*. Translated by Walter Starkie. New York, 1950.

Meyerson, Mark. "Revisiting The Wax-Press Affair in Morvedre (1326–27): Jewish Fiscal Politics in the Kingdom of Valencia." In *Jews Muslims and Christians in and around the Crown of Aragon*, edited by Harvey J. Hames. Leiden, 2004.

———. *Jews in an Iberian Frontier Kingdom Society Economy and Politics in Morvedre. 1248–1391*. Leiden, 2004.

———. *Jewish Renaissance in Fifteenth-Century Spain*. Princeton, 2004.

Mirrer, Louise. "The Jew's Body in Medieval Literary Portraits and Miniatures: Examples from the *Cantigas de Santa Maria* and the *Cantar de mio Cid.*" *Shofar* 12 (1994): 17–30.

Montes, Isabel Romero Camacho. "Finaucieros judíos en la primera época de la repoblación del reino de Sevilla." *Anuario de estudios medievales* 29 (1999): 365–407.

Moreno Koch, Yolanda. "The Taqqanot of Valladolid of 1432." *American Sephardi* 9 (1978): 58–145.

Moya Ulldemolins, Joaquim M. "El Diezmo eclesiastico en el obispado de Córdoba." *Axerquia* 13 (1985): 73–103.

Neuman, Abraham. *The Jews in Spain.* 2 vols. Philadelphia, 1942.

Nieto Soria, José Manuel. "La conflictividad en torno al diezmo en los comienzos de la crisis bajomedieval Castellana, 1230–1315." *Anuario de estudios medievales* 14 (1984): 211–236.

———. "Los judíos como conflicto jurisdiccional entre monarqauía e iglesia en la Castilla de fines del siglo XIII: su causistica." In *Actas del II congreso internacional, Encuentro de las tres culturas,* 243–252. Toledo, 1985.

Nirenberg, David. *Communities of Violence: Persecution of Minorities in the Middle Ages.* Princeton, 1996.

———. "Conversion, Sex, and Segregation: Jews and Christians in Medieval Spain." *American Historical Review* 107 (2002): 1065–1093.

O'Callaghan, Joseph. *The Cortes of Castile-León: 1188–1350.* Philadelphia, 1989.

———. *The Learned King: The Reign of Alfonso X of Castile.* Philadelphia, 1993.

———. "Kings and Lords in Conflict in Late Thirteenth-Century Castile and Aragon." In *Iberia and the Mediterranean World of the Middle Ages,* edited by Paul E. Chevedden, Donald J. Kagay, and Paul G. Padilla, 2:117–135. Leiden, 1996.

———. *Reconquest and Crusade in Medieval Spain.* Philadelphia, 2002.

Pastor de Togneri, Reyna. *Del Islam al Cristianismo: en las fronteras de dos formaciones económicos-sociales: Toledo, siglos XI–XIII.* Barcelona, 1975.

Pescador, Carmela. "La Caballería popular en León y Castilla." *Cuadernos de historia de España* 33–34 (1961): 101–238; 35–36 (1962): 56–201; 37–38 (1963): 88–198; and 39–40 (1964): 169–260.

Pick, Lucy K. *Conflict and Coexistence: Archbishop Rodrigo and the Muslims and Jews of Medieval Spain.* Ann Arbor, 2004.

Powers, James F. "Frontier municipal baths and social interactions in thirteenth-century Spain." *American Historical Review* 84 (1979): 649–667.

Pradalié, Gérard. *Lisboa da Reconquista ao fim do século XIII.* Lisbon, 1975.

Rivlin, Joseph. *Bills and Contracts from Lucena, (1020–1025 CE).* Ramat-Gan, Israel, 1994 [Hebrew].

Rodríguez Molina, José. *El reino de Jaén en la baja edad media: aspectos demográficos y económicos.* Granada, 1978.

Romano, David. *Judíos al servicio de Pedro el Grande de Aragón (1276–1285).* Barcelona, 1983.

Roth, Norman. "Two Jewish Courtiers of Alfonso X Called Zag (Isaac)." *Sefarad* 43 (1983): 75–85.

———. "The Civic Status of the Jew in Medieval Spain." In *Iberia and the Mediterranean World of the Middle Ages,* edited by Paul E. Chevedden, Donald J. Kagay, and P. G. Padilla, 2:139–161. Leiden, 1996.

Ruiz, Teofilo. "Expansion et changement: La conquete de Séville et la société castillane (1248–1350)." *Annales Economies Sociétés et Civilisations* 34 (1979): 548–565.

———. "Festivités, colours et symbols du pouvoir en Castille au XVe siècle." *Annales E. S. C.* 3 (1991): 521–546.

———. *Crisis and Continuity, Land and Town in Late Medieval Castile.* Philadelphia, 1994.

———. *From Heaven to Earth: The Reordering of Castilian Society, 1150–1350.* Princeton, 2004.

Ruiz Gómez, Francisco. "Juderías y aljamas en el mundo rural en la Castilla medieval." In

Xudeus e Conversos na Historia, edited by Carlos Barros, 2:111–151. Santiago de Compostela, 1994.

Sánchez Albornoz, Claudio. *Spain: A Historical Enigma*. 2 vols. Translated by Colette Joly Dees and David Sven Reher. Madrid, 1975.

Saperstein, Mark. "The Preaching of Repentance and the Reforms in Toledo of 1281." In *Models of Holiness in Medieval Sermons*, edited by Beverly Mayne Kienzle, 157–174. Louvain-la-Neuve, 1996.

Scheindlin, Raymond P. *Wine, Women, and Death: Medieval Hebrew Poems and the Good Life*. New York, 1986.

Septimus, Bernard. "Piety and Power in Thirteenth-Century Catalonia." In *Studies in Medieval Jewish History and Literature*, edited by Isadore Twersky, 197–230. Cambridge, Mass, 1979.

——. *Hispano-Jewish Culture in Transition: The Career and Controversies of the Ramah*. Cambridge, Mass., 1982.

Shatzmiller, Joseph. "Rabbi Isaac of Manosque and and His Son Rabi Peretz: The Rabbinate and its Professionalization in the Fourteenth Century." In *Jewish History, Essays in Honour of Chimen Abramsky*, edited by Ada Rapoport-Albert and Steven Zipperstein, 61–83. London, 1988.

Shideler, John. *A Medieval Noble Family: The Montcadas, 1000–1230*. Berkeley, 1983.

Shneidman, Jerome Lee. "Jews as Royal Bailiffs in Thirteenth-Century Aragon." *Historia Judaica* 19 (1957): 55–66.

——. "Protection of Aragonese Jewry in the Thirteenth Century." *Historia Judaica*. 1 (1962): 49–58.

——. *The Rise of the Aragonese-Catalan Empire, 1200–1350*. 2 vols. New York, 1970.

Shrock, Abe Tobie. *Rabbi Jonah ben Abraham of Gerona: His Life and Ethical Works*. London, 1948.

Simon, Larry J. "Muslim-Jewish relations in Crusader Majorca in the Thirteenth Century: An Inquiry Based on Patrimony Register 342." In *Christians, Muslims, and Jews in Medieval and Early Modern Spain*, edited by Mark Meyerson and Edward English, 125–140. Notre Dame, 2000.

Soloveitchik, Haym. "Pawnbroking: A Study in *Ribbit* and of the Halakah in Exile." *Proceedings of the American Academy for Jewish Research* 38–39 (1970–1971): 203–268 [Hebrew].

——. *The Use of Responsa as a Historical Source*. Jerusalem, 1990 [Hebrew].

Suárez Bilbao, Fernando. *El fuero judiego en la España cristiana: Las Fuentes jurídicas, siglos V–XV*. Madrid, 2000.

Tavares, Maria José Pimenta Ferro. *Os Judeus em Portugal no século XIV*. 1970. 2nd ed. Lisbon, 2000.

Toch, Michael. "Jewish Migration to, within and from Medieval Germany." In *Le Migrazioni in Europa secc. XIII–XVIII*, edited by Simonetta Cavaciocchi, 639–652. Florence, 1993.

Vanlandingham, Marta. *Transforming the State: King Court and Political Culture in the Realms of Aragon (1213–1387)*. Leiden, 2002.

Vassberg, David. *Land and Society in Golden Age Castile*. Cambridge, 1984.

Viñuales Ferreiro, Gonzalo. "Maqueda 1492. Judíos y judaizantes." *Espacio Tiempo y Forma* 11 (1998): 383–404.

Weinryb, Bernard Dov. "Responsa as a Source for History (Methodological Problems)." In *Essays presented to Chief Rabbi Israel Brodie on the Occasion of His Seventieth Birthday*, edited by H. J. Zimmels et al., 399–417. London, 1967.

Bibliography

INDEX

Aben Menir, Judah, 126
Abenvives, Jahuda, 137
Abenvives, Vives ben Jucef, 142
Abinaffia, Aharon, 38, 143
Abnuba, Jacob, 134, 137
Abulafia, Meir Halevi, 95, 113–114
Abulafia, Todros ben Joseph, 172–173
Abulafia, Todros ben Judah Halevi, 171–173
Adarra, Judah de, 69
Afonso Henriques, king of Portugal, 85, 87, 147
Afonso II, king of Portugal, 56, 91
Afonso III, king of Portugal, 91, 163
    appoints Arrabi Mor, 124–125, 129
    legislative activity, 76–77
al-Andalus, 12, 16, 27, 36, 53, 67, 111, 115
al-Bargeloni, Judah, 106
al-Mansur, Andalusi king, 111
Alazar, Jahuda, 96
Albarracin, 148
Albeck, Shalom, 106
Alcaçabi, Juçaf, 24
Alcaldes, 85–88, 125, 137
Alconstantini family, 19–20, 114
    Bahiel, 18
    Moses, 69
    Salamon, 18, 68–69, 84, 118–119
Alfaquims (royal scribes), 16–18, 31, 83
Alfasi, Isaac, 106
Alfonso II, king of Aragon, 81
Alfonso III, king of Aragon, 44, 51, 66, 81–82, 87, 99, 119, 125–126, 137
Alfonso VI, king of Castile, 67, 89
Alfonso VII, king of Castile, 12, 43, 80

Alfonso VIII, king of Castile, 46–48, 77
Alfonso X, king of Castile, 45, 48–50, 68, 71, 84–85, 94, 106,
    and legislative activity, 76, 101
    and sumptuary laws, 163–164
Alfonso XI, king of Castile, 28, 49–50, 53–54, 90
Algarve region (Portugal), 51, 61
Alicante, 31, 41, 64
Aljamas, 105–106
    See also Jewish community
Almohad, 11–12, 161
    See also al-Andalus
Almoravid, 11–12
    See also al-Andalus
Almoxarifes, 18, 33, 43, 68, 93–94, 118, 124–125, 129
Ampurias, count of, 81
Andalusia, 32–33, 68, 71, 79, 99
    See also al-Andalus and individual cities
Asher ben Yehiel, 64, 95, 103, 113, 173
    and Abraham Safiyah case, 119–123
Astruch, A., 69
Astruch, David and Vidal, 69
Avenbruch, Salamon, 118–119
Avendino, Jacob, 21
Avenrodrich family, 133–134
Aventurel, Moses, 153

Baer, Yitzhak, 34, 129–130
Baeza, 80, 162
Bakery, 61, 99
Barcelona, 14, 79, 82, 103
Barchilon, Abraham, 68

Barchilon, Juçef, 20
Baron, Salo, 51–52
Bastioneros, 89
Baths, 99–100, 167
Beja, 88, 95, 125
Beth din, 109–110
Blidstein, Gerald, 105
Braga, 163
Burgos, 48, 79
Burriana, 37–38, 41, 102, 174
Butchers, 92, 102–103, 110

Cabaçay, Juçef, 117
Caballeros villanos, 38
Çag Alconqui, 18
Çag de la Maleha, 45, 68, 84, 164
Calatayud, 82, 118
Call
  See Juderías
Caloña, 80
Cantigas de Santa María, Las, 169
Capital punishment, 139–140
Cartagena, 90
Castel Rodrigo, 92
Cavalleria, Judah de la, 19, 40, 68–69, 118–119
Cemeteries, 25, 98, 101–102
Cervera, 102
Christians
  Christian courts, 67, 91, 135–137, 139, 141
  learning Hebrew from Jews, 70
  litigation with Jews, 96
  nobles, 18–19, 30, 62, 81–84
  notaries, 69–70
  subservience to Jews?, 93–94, 151
  violence/mobs, protection from, 102
  See also Sexual relations
Church, 82, 91
  See also Landownership: and tithes
Cid, The, 16, 55
Clement IV, 51, 163
Clothing, regulations, 107, 156–164
Cocentaina, 103
Coimbra, 33, 88
Concejos, 79, 85–88
Convivencia, 174
Córdoba, 38, 40, 48–49, 62, 64, 67, 95–96,
  99, 101, 114–115
  See also Safiyah, Abraham
Coria, 77
Cortes, 79, 86, 90, 95, 164
Coucy, Moses de, 169
Court Jews, 17–22
  See also Almoxarifes; Rabbis

Decretales, 100
Denia, 65

Dinis, king of Portugal, 51, 88, 129
  and Jewish lending, 58–59, 76, 78
  and sovereignty over Jews, 81, 125
Diezmos (tithes)
  See Landownership
Don Çuleyma, 61, 68
Don Mayr, 68
Doña Pascuala, 67
Don Todeoç, "El Rab," 117
Don (Dom) Yehudah, 126–129

Ecija, 33
Elche, 18, 32, 83–84, 102, 103
Eleazar family, 114
Ella, 103
Espéculo de las Leyes, 118
Évora, 137, 148

Fernando I, king of Portugal, 126–129
Fernando III, king of Castile, 23, 27, 76, 85,
  101, 148, 161
Fernando IV, king of Castile, 28, 167
Ferruziel, Joseph, 67
Fonseca, Luís Adão da, 74
Frontier, concept of, 3, 74
Fueros, 77–81
  Fuero Juzgo, 77, 91
  Fuero Real, 85, 101
  of Cuenca, 56, 86–87, 89–90
  of Ledesma, 67, 82
  of Salamanca, 67, 82, 92
  of Teruel, 56, 80, 167
  of Tortosa, 14, 90
  of Valencia, 28–29, 32, 41 65–66, 79–81,
  86, 96

Gerona, 82
Gerondi, Jonah, 170–171
Granada, 63–64, 68
Gregory IX, 48, 93, 157, 162
Gregory X, 51, 66
Guedelha, Arrabi mor of Portugal, 90–91
Guidaticum, 30–31

Haym, Rabbi of Toledo, 115–118
Heqdesh (Jewish communal fund), 103
Hermandades, 79
Hombres buenos, 86
Honorius III, 47, 160–162

Ibiza, 107
Ibn Adret, Solomon ben Abraham, 83, 95,
  106–113, 116, 151, 160, 174
Ibn Daud, Abraham, 12, 26, 115
Ibn Ezra, Moses, 15–16
Ibn Falaquera, Shem Tov ben Joseph, 111–112

Ibn Jau, Jacob, the Nasi, 111, 115
Ibn Shoshan, Moses, 83
Ibn Waqar, Isaac, 83
Ibn Waqar, Yehudah, 120–122, 173
Ibn Yahia, Aaron, 69
Ibn Yahia, Gedalia and Joseph, 99
Innocent III, 46–47
Innocent IV, 48, 101

Jaca, 156
Jaén, 48
Jaime I, king of Aragon, 94, 158, 161–162
    appoints Jewish officials, 116, 118–119
    and Jewish lending, 58
    and legislation activity, 76, 78–79
    and slave trade, 66
Jaime II, king of Aragon, 56, 59, 84, 89, 101,
    112, 119, 140, 150
Játiva, 32, 70, 102, 141–142, 149–150, 152,
    158–159, 172
Jérez de la Frontera, 23–24, 89, 99, 103, 117
Jewish community
    autonomy of, 70, 105–107, 131–132, 136–
        143
    in castles, 146–147
    clans in, 24, 69, 112, 114, 118–119, 141
    Jewish law, 109–111
    in northern Europe, 13, 70, 89, 177
    officials, 105–108, 111–112
    segregation from Christians, 159–160
    structure of, 104–112
    See also Aljamas; Christians; Juderías;
        Rabbis
Jewish quarter
    See Juderías
Jewish status, 76–81, 90
Juan Manuel, prince of Castile, 83, 120–121
Juderías, 25, 147–156

Kagay, Donald J., 85, 143
Kahal
    See Aljamas; Jewish community
Kingship, 76–77

Landownership, 33, 66–67, 117, 151–152
    and inheritance, 43–44
    and Jewish landlords, 39, 142–143
    royal authority over, 42–45
    rural, 39–41
    and tithes, 45–53
    urban, 37–39
    and women, 40
    See also Juderías; Repartimientos
Las Navas de Tolosa, battle of, 2
Lateran Council, Fourth, 46–47, 93, 145,
    156–157

Leiria, 40, 124, 147–148
Lérida, 116, 146
Leyes del Estilo, 117–118
Liber Judiciorum, 77
Lisbon, 33–34, 40, 42, 80, 87–88, 93, 99,
    102, 124
Lorca, 93

Mallorca, 25, 64–65, 79, 87, 99, 101–102, 107,
    112, 140, 142–143, 154–156
Malsinim, (informers), 133, 140
Maqueda, 83
Menorca, 18, 107
Military Orders, 43, 56–57, 63, 83
Mills, 60–61
Minhag (Jewish legal custom), 107–108,
    138–139
Miranda del Ebro, 89
Molina, 82
Molina, Maria de, queen of Castile, 84
Moneylending, 56–60
Monopolies, 61, 69–70, 140
    See also Jewish community: clans in
Montalban, 84
Montenegro, 59–60
Morella, 31–32
Murcia (city), 56, 69, 86, 93, 152
    (region), 79, 84, 90
Murviedro, 51, 96, 102, 132, 134, 141
Muslims, 83, 89, 103–104, 117, 125
    courts of, 136
    killed by Jews, 45, 133
    rebellion of, 21, 23, 62–63
    settlers, 41, 152, 174–175
    trade with, 62–65
    See also al-Andalus; North Africa; Sexual
        relations; Slaves

Naci Azday, 116
Nageri, Samuel, 101
Nahman, Moses ben, 95, 113, 118, 170–171
Navarre, 146
Negro, Salomon, 42–43
Neuman, Abraham, 136
Niebla, 29, 33, 59, 87, 166–167
Nirenberg, David, 174
North Africa, 11, 30, 68
    Sigilmasa, 30, 115
    Trebalos, 30–31
    See also Muslims

Obidos, 39–40
Orihuela, 21, 59, 117, 141

Paterna Harah, 20
Pedro III, prince and king of Aragon, 51, 66,

Index

Pedro III *(continued)*
    76, 79–80, 82, 94, 96, 102, 119, 143,
        157–159, 174
Peñiscola, 60
Physicians, 67, 70, 83, 115, 141, 159
Portella, Ishmael de la, 119
Portella, Muça, 69

Rabbis
    appointed by king, 107, 113–130
    Arrabi mor, Portugal, 124–130, 137
    legal scholars, 109, 113–123, 140–141
    Rab de la corte, Castile, 119
    and synagogues, 99
    See also Jewish community
Ramon Berenguer IV, count of Barcelona,
    14
Reconquista, 1–2, 11–14, 27–29
Repartimientos (land partitions), 18, 20–26,
    101, 117
    See also Landownership
Responsa literature, 4–5
Roman law, 78–79, 93, 100
Royal protection, 94–96
Ruiz, Teofilo, 76–77

Sabadel, Jacob, 117
Safiyah, Abraham, 119–123, 139
Sancho I, king of Portugal, 87–88, 99
Sancho II, king of Portugal, 77
Sancho IV, king of Castile, 45, 50, 68,
        85–86, 141
Santarem, 40, 88, 125, 151
Saragossa, 19, 79, 103, 107–108, 118–119
Seville, 26–27, 32, 49–50, 68–69, 71, 90,
        99–101, 114, 117, 150, 152–153
Sexual relations, 162, 165–174
Sicily, 65
Siete Partidas, Las, 39, 94–95, 101, 163,
        166–167
Sigilmasa
    See North Africa

Silves, 51
Slaves, 65–66
Synagogues, 100–101, 155

Tarragona, Council of, 66
Tax collection, 57, 69, 107, 117, 135, 142–
        143
Teruel, 101, 134
    See also Fueros
Tithes
    See Landownership
Toledo, 26, 47, 64, 68, 103, 115, 160–162
Tortosa, 65, 83, 102–103, 153, 170–173
    See also Fueros
Trebalos
    See North Africa

Usatges de Barcelona, 78

Valencia (city)
    communal institutions of, 99, 101–103
    communal strife in, 70, 132–136
    Gentiles in Jewish quarter, 151
    Jewish vizir over, 16
    pre-conquest community of, 22–23
    See also Fueros
Valencia, Kingdom of
    Jewish courtiers in, 68–70
    Jewish settlers in, 21–22
    jurisdiction over Jews in, 87
    and segregation of Jews, 157–158
Valladolid, 48, 149
Vidal Mayor, 78
Vidal, Salomon, 38, 41, 174
Visigoths, 1, 77–78, 91

Xixon, Astug Jacob, 60

Yehudah ben Asher, 113, 117, 139–140, 172

Zamora, Council of, 56
Zedah la-Derekh, 170

VOLUMES IN THE SERIES
Conjunctions of Religion and Power in the Medieval Past
Edited by Barbara H. Rosenwein

Medieval Cruelty
Changing Perceptions, Late Antiquity to the Early Modern Period
by Daniel Baraz

Shifting Landmarks
Property, Proof, and Dispute in Catalonia around the Year 1000
by Jeffrey A. Bowman

Shaping a Monastic Identity
Liturgy and History at the Imperial Abbey of Farfa, 1000–1125
by Susan Boynton

Unjust Seizure
Conflict, Interest, and Authority in an Early Medieval Society
by Warren Brown

Discerning Spirits
Divine and Demonic Possession in the Middle Ages
by Nancy Caciola

Ermengard of Narbonne and the World of the Troubadours
by Fredric L. Cheyette

Speaking of Slavery
Color, Ethnicity, and Human Bondage in Italy
by Steven A. Epstein

Surviving Poverty in Medieval Paris
Gender, Ideology, and the Daily Lives of the Poor
by Sharon Farmer

Struggle for Empire
Kingship and Conflict under Louis the German, 817–876
by Eric J. Goldberg

Rancor and Reconciliation in Medieval England
by Paul R. Hyams

Order and Exclusion
Cluny and Christendom Face Heresy, Judaism, and Islam (1000–1150)
by Dominique Iogna-Prat

The Bishop's Palace
Architecture and Authority in Medieval Italy
by Maureen C. Miller

The Sephardic Frontier
The Reconquista and the Jewish Community in Medieval Iberia
by Jonathan Ray

The Consumption of Justice
Emotions, Publicity, and Legal Culture in Marseille, 1264–1423
by Daniel Lord Smail

Weaving Sacred Stories
French Choir Tapestries and the Performance of Clerical Identity
by Laura Weigert